W9-ACE-264

WOMEN IN ISLAM
Tradition and Transition
in the Middle East

WOMEN
IN ISLAM

Tradition and Transition

in the Middle East

NAILA MINAI

Seaview Books
NEW YORK

A Note on Transliteration

Conventions vary on transliterating non-roman languages into English and other roman languages. For ease of reading, proper names and titles are presented here without Arabic accents. *Al-* ("the") has been used throughout the text, but *el-* is used in the Notes and Bibliography where sources have published under that form, as an aid to further research.

Permission to reprint portions of the following works is gratefully acknowledged:

Abbott, Nabia. *Aishah, the Beloved of Mohammed.* Chicago: University of Chicago Press, 1942. (All quotes attributed to Aysha)
————. *Two Queens of Baghdad: Mother and Wife of Harun al Rashid.* Chicago: University of Chicago Press, 1946. (Quotes of Caliph al-Hadi and Khayzuran)
Boullata, Kamal, ed. *Women of the Fertile Crescent: Modern Poetry by Arab Women.* Washington, D.C.: Three Continents Press, 1978. ("Tattoo Writing" by Fawziyya Abu Khalid, and "Dearest Love—III" by Salma al Jayyusi)
Fernea, Elizabeth Warnock, and Basima Qattan Bezirgan, eds. *Middle Eastern Muslim Women Speak.* Austin: University of Texas Press, 1977. ("Oh, My Sister," "The Hidden Dream," and "The Sin")
Mikhail, Mona N. *Images of Arab Women: Fact and Fiction.* Washington, D.C.: Three Continents Press, 1979. (Part of Rusafi's poem)

Library of Congress Cataloging in Publication Data

Minai, Naila.
    Women in Islam.

    Bibliography: p.
    Includes index.
    1. Women, Muslim. 2. Women in Islam. I. Title.
HQ1170.M55   305.4'8   80–52405
ISBN 0–87223–666–8   AACR2

Seaview Books/A division of PEI Books, Inc.

For my *mother* and *father*

Contents

Acknowledgments

I extend my deep gratitude to:

my family for their infinite patience;

Francine Krisel for encouraging me to develop an idea into this book and for offering invaluable advice on the manuscript as well as on many other aspects of the writer's trade;

Nafisa for helping with the research;

Patricia O'Reilly for opening her private library to me;

Maxine Wood for sharing her experiences as a writer;

my agents, Joyce Frommer, Sheri Safran, and Diana Price, for their unfailing support;

my copy editor, Gilda Abramowitz, and editorial assistants Cameron Barry and Connie Ennis for contributing their talents with sensitivity;

and my editor, Anne Kostick, for expertly inspiring and guiding me through all the stages which made this book possible.

Many others enriched the book by generously sharing their knowledge and resources on various aspects of the Middle East. Moumtaz Joukhadar offered illuminating advice on the Quran and Arabic literature; Marva Nabili, on the literature and media of Iran; Dr. Richard Lemay and Dr. Boydena Wilson, on the Arab caliphate. My heartfelt thanks go to all of them as well as to Anthony Ferreira for his help with research on the caliphate. I also thank sociologist Dr. Farida Allaghi for her advice on women's education and work in the Arab world.

In gathering information on Fatma Aliyé, the first Ottoman woman journalist, I acknowledge with deep appreciation the generous assistance given by Ismet Topus, Aliyé Sarhan, Professor Melahat Togar, Professor Dr. Suheyl Unver, Taha Toros, Seniha and Nesrin Morali, Mina Gokkan, and Vasfi

Riza Zobu. I am grateful to Professor Talat Halman, Vasfi
Riza Zobu, Vedat Nedim Tor, and Mahsoud Bey for sharing
their knowledge of the Ottoman period. For information on
the early days of the Turkish Republic I am greatly indebted
to Dr. Gulcin Kandemir, Mualla Peker, and Ali Sulutas.

I also thank the Oriental Division of the New York Public
Library and the following for their help: Lois, Zulaiha, Aisha,
Tom, Djamilla, Abeda, Saliha, Tamim, Bonnie, Daphne,
Farida, Nellie, Nairu, Nagwa, Razia, Amina, Amal, Huda,
Sema, Samia, Yousef, Muhammad, Mansur, Mahmut, Dan-
ielle, Turkan, Réhane, George, Gulsum, N.H., Mies, Shakir,
and many others not named here.

Although the book owes much to all of these people, I
alone am responsible for its contents.

—N.M.

Introduction

Women are all one nation.
—Turkish proverb

This book is about the Muslim women of the Middle East and North Africa. It tells of women who helped build the Islamic religion and civilization and of odalisques who symbolized the Islamic feminine mystique. It is about saints, scholars, and revolutionaries as well as more "ordinary" women raising their children and working in villages and cities, or in the desert encampments of their nomadic tribes. They may be Arabs, Turks, Iranians, Kurds, or Berbers, each with their different languages and customs. Many have known the veil and polygamy at some point in their history. All of them and many others constitute the richly varied woman's world of the Middle East.

Rapid Westernization and industrialization in the twentieth century have added another dimension to this kaleidoscope by accentuating cultural gaps between the American- or European-educated rich and the semiliterate homebound slum resident in the same city, and between one generation and another in the same family. Today's American family may include a "homemaker" of the fifties, a flower child, and a three-piece-suited business executive. But consider what separates the generations in a Middle Eastern family. My Turkish-Tatar grandmother was tutored at home, married a polygamous man, and has never discarded her head veil, even when traveling abroad, although she was too liberal to hide her face.

My mother never wore the veil, studied in schools close to home, and settled down as a housewife in a monogamous marriage. I left my family as a teenager to study in the United States and Europe, where I hitchhiked from country to country during vacations. Later on, as a journalist I traveled more widely, eventually making a solo trip across the Sahara. It never occurred to me not to exercise a profession throughout my life. But the generation gaps in our family are nothing compared to what some others are experiencing. One example is Fatima Mernissi, a globe-trotting multilingual Moroccan author and professor, who was brought up by an illiterate mother. The Muslim woman, then, must be viewed not only through her faith but also through local cultural traditions and her socioeconomic background.

Through such diversity runs a strong thread of unity in the Middle East, thanks to many shared experiences over the centuries. Roman, Arab, and Ottoman empires facilitated cultural cross-pollination in the area right into the twentieth century. All have come under Western rule or sphere of influence in recent history. Now oil wealth has sharpened the homogenizing forces by encouraging workers to migrate from one area to another within the Muslim world itself. Above all, Islam itself has continued to serve as the most potent unifying force, since it governs not only spiritual life but secular matters. Although Islam did split into sects—the Sunni majority and the Shiite minority, each with its subdivisions—their main quarrel was political rather than theological, and has generally affected women's status only in minor details. The religious law concerning women is interpreted with varying degrees of strictness from one country to another. Many countries have recently enacted supplementary legislation on women to cover their individual needs, but few have made drastic departures from the essentials of Islamic law. Some aspects of modernization have also set a homogenizing trend, especially among the well-educated. A professor from, say, Morocco, is likely to have more in common with her Turkish or Lebanese counterpart than with her Moroccan maid or laundress. Underneath the veil her Saudi sister, who can teach only in women's colleges, may have much in common with her, too. Most importantly, television and radio—now easily accessible to the masses—can disseminate new ideas and role models to the illiterate and semiliterate people who make up the majority of the population in almost every Middle Eastern country. It is within this frame of historical and cultural unity that I weave my story of various Middle Eastern women.

This book is not meant to be an exhaustive study of Middle Eastern women, but rather a personal view by a Muslim woman who has spent her life commuting between the East and the West. I have written of women I have known and of those about whom I have heard or read, placing their stories in the larger pattern of the Middle Eastern mosaic to enhance the meaning of both.

I have described their worlds from two perspectives—historical and individual. Like everyone else, Middle Eastern women are shaped by their religious and cultural heritage, which is explored in Part I. The types of women who have been immortalized as heroines also form an important part of the collective feminine psyche. The Islamic world is more acutely aware of its heritage and its heroines today than ever before in recent history, for it is trying to reconcile its roots to the modern world of Western technology.

As pawns and partners in their peoples' attempts to reconcile their heritage to the modern world, and in the modernization process itself, Middle Eastern women exert a profound influence on their society today. They do not have to be famous heroines to make their mark. Thus, one of the major characters in the contemporary Middle Eastern novel is the secluded and submissive mother who keeps her educated sons unhappily chained to anachronistic traditions because of her psychic myopia. Another favorite is a woman of any age who liberates her men by liberating herself. Man is what his mother, wife, and daughter are. Part II is about these Middle

Eastern women, who afford a valuable glimpse into a society in transition and turmoil.

Since Islamic laws and local traditions rule a woman largely according to her age and marital status, each chapter considers a different stage of a woman's life. Except in a very few isolated areas, the patriarchal code of ethics prevails, reinforced by Islam. The woman's ultimate role is to provide legitimate heirs to her husband, hence the emphasis on controlling her activities during her reproductive years and allowing her relatively greater freedom in childhood and old age. In this light, the passage from one age to the next can bring dramatic changes in a woman's life. Details vary enormously, but this life story of an "average" Middle Eastern woman is a useful reference point around which variations and exceptions can be discussed. I have described a few members of each age group as they live today, and compared them to women in other socioeconomic groups or countries in order to capture the texture of their lives and illuminate at the same time the salient features of the larger canvas of Middle Eastern womanhood.

All of the women presented here are real, though I have given some of them fictitious names and changed minor details of their biographies. The women whose real names are given (with their permission, unless their views have been previously published) are public figures representing many points of view also harbored by their lesser-known sisters, who have for so long been considered by the world voiceless and mindless prisoners of the harem.

Part III concludes with a chapter on Islamic revivalism, not only because it represents another facet of the Middle Eastern woman but also because it has inspired significant soul-searching among the more moderate Muslims who have until now taken relentless industrialization and Westernization as their inevitable future. In a feverish rush to catch up with the Western world, they had embraced its thorns as well as its roses. And they had thrown out the good aspects of their own heritage along with the bad. In Western terms, the question represents a search for ways to preserve life on a more human scale in the face of massive industrialization and urbanization. The results should be of interest to the West, too.

In writing about women in Islam I have focused on the Middle East (including North Africa) because it is the cradle of Islamic religion and civilization, which spread its influence far beyond its geographical boundaries through trade and conquest, often by relay. The Arabian Muslims conquered the Middle East and North Africa in the seventh and eighth centuries A.D. Converted to Islam, the Berbers and Arabs of North Africa crossed to Europe in the early eighth century to establish a Moorish civilization whose glories were epitomized in the Alhambra. Christian resistance limited the spread of Islam in Europe, but the influence of the Arab empire had a more lasting effect on Persia, which in turn passed on Islam to India, China, and the Siberian steppes via the Silk Route. The Indians carried the Prophet Muhammad's message to Southeast Asia in the thirteenth and fourteenth centuries, from where it journeyed as far as the Philippines. On the southern flank of the Middle East area Islam filtered down to sub-Saharan Africa along caravan routes and has continued to gain new converts at a phenomenal rate to this day. Despite the Soviet government's hostility to religions, Muslims, most of whom are of Turkic-Tatar stock, have survived as an ethnic and religious entity, constituting about 9 percent of the population of the U.S.S.R. in 1975. Since they have the highest birthrate in the country, they are expected to outnumber the Russians in the near future. There are also sizable numbers of Muslims in the United States. This makes one in every six or seven persons of this world a Muslim. The majority of Muslims —about 400 million—are concentrated in the Middle East, and the almost 300 million who live in other areas look to the Middle East as their spiritual center and often adopt its traditions, if only in fragmentary fashion. This trend may be stepped up among Islamic revivalists who wish to identify with the source of Islam.

Beyond political considerations prompted by its oil and its

relationship to Muslims outside its boundaries, the Middle East holds a special interest for Western women. They and their Middle Eastern sisters have much to share with each other in their struggle for emancipation. Both have a dismal record of political participation. Only a privileged minority are in high-paying top professions, while the rest are shunted into low-paying dead-end jobs or live under the Damocletian sword of polygamy, whether simultaneous or consecutive. The sexual liberation movement of the West has often proved just as tyrannical as the sexual restrictions of the East. Women from both worlds age socially long before their biological time has come. They have yet to metamorphose in their respective societies from sexual objects to women. Because their experiences have not always been identical but rather like the opposite sides of the same coin, women of both cultures may benefit from comparing notes. It is mainly in the hope of encouraging such communication that I tell my side of the story as a Muslim woman of the Middle East.

PART I

1

ꊠꊠꊠꊠꊠꊠꊠꊠꊠꊠ

Women in Early Islam

Woman is made hard and crooked like a rib.
—Arabian proverb popular
in the seventh century A.D.

Women are the twin halves of men.
—The Prophet Muhammad

Khadija, an attractive forty-year-old Arabian widow, ran a flourishing caravan business in Mecca in the seventh century A.D., and was courted by the most eligible men of her society. But she had eyes only for an intelligent and hardworking twenty-five-year-old in her employ named Muhammad.[1] "What does she see in a penniless ex-shepherd?" her scandalized aristocratic family whispered among themselves. Accustomed to having her way, however, Khadija proposed to Muhammad and married him. Until her death some twenty-five years later, her marriage was much more than the conventional Cinderella story in reverse, for Khadija not only bore six children while co-managing her business with her husband, but also advised and financed him in his struggle to found Islam, which grew to be one of the major religions of the world.

It was a religion that concerned itself heavily with women's rights, in a surprisingly contemporary manner. A woman was to be educated and allowed to earn and manage her income. She was to be recognized as legal heir to her father's property along with her brother. Her rights in marriage were also clearly spelled out: she was entitled to sexual satisfaction as well as economic support. Nor was divorce to consist any longer of merely throwing the wife out of the house without paying her financial compensation.

This feminist bill of rights filled an urgent need. Meccans in the seventh century were in transition from a tribal to an urban way of life. As their town grew into a cosmopolitan center of trade, kinship solidarity had deteriorated, but municipal laws had not yet been fully established to protect the citizens. Women were particularly vulnerable, their rights closely linked with the tribal way of life their people had known before renouncing nomadism to settle in Mecca around A.D. 400. In nomadic communities of the desert a woman was not equal to a man. During famine a female could be killed at birth to increase her brother's food supply. However, if she managed to reach adulthood she had a better status in the desert than in the city, largely because her labors were indispensable to her clan's survival in the harsh environment. While the men protected the encampment and engaged in trade, she looked after the herds and produced the items to be traded—meat, wool, yogurt, and cheese, all of which bought weapons and grains as well as other essentials. As a breadwinner the tribal woman enjoyed considerable political clout. Even if she did not always participate in council meetings, she made her views known. Only a fool refused to heed his womenfolk and risked antagonizing a good half of his tribe, with whom he had to live in the close confines of the camp and caravan.

If tribal discord was uncomfortable in the best of circumstances, it was catastrophic during the battles that broke out frequently among the clans over pasture and watering rights or to avenge heroes slain by the enemy. With the battlefront so close to home, a woman was needed as a nurse, cheerleader, and even soldier. She was sometimes captured and ransomed or sold into slavery. If her tribesmen could not pay her captors the required number of camels in ransom, they valiantly stormed the enemy's camp to rescue her. These were men brought up on recitations of epic poems about brave warriors who rescued fair damsels in distress. Poets and poetesses of the tribe kept chivalry alive, constantly singing praises of heroism among their people and condemning cowardliness and disloyalty. No one who wanted a respectable place in his tribe could afford to ignore the ubiquitous "Greek chorus," for life without honor was worse than death to a nomad, who could not survive as an outcast in the desert.

Marriage customs varied from tribe to tribe,[2] but the most popular were those that tended to maintain the woman's independence, if only incidentally, by having her remain within her family circle after marriage. If the husband was a close relative, the couple set up a conjugal tent near both of their parents. A husband who was not kin merely visited her at her home. In some clans women could be married to several visiting husbands at the same time. When the wife bore a child, she simply summoned her husbands and announced which of them she believed to be the child's father. Her decision was law. Actually, it did not matter greatly who the biological father was, since children of such unions belonged to the matrilineal family and were supported by communal property administered by her brothers of maternal uncles.

Life in the desert was so hard and precarious that some of the most impoverished tribes renounced nomadism to submit to a less independent existence in towns. Muhammad's ancestors, a segment of the Kinanah tribe, were among them. They settled down at the crossroads of important caravan routes in the place which is now Mecca, and prospered as middlemen under the new name of Quraysh. Their great wealth and power undoubtedly helped their deities extend their spiritual influence far beyond Mecca's boundaries and make Kaaba, their sanctuary, the most important shrine in central Arabia. As keepers of the shrine the leading Quraysh families grew immeasurably rich, but the wealth was not equitably distributed. As survival no longer depended on communal sharing and on women's contributing equally to the family budget, Meccans became more interested in lucrative business connections than in kinship ties. Glaring socioeconomic differences —unknown among nomads—emerged. Women lost their rights and their security.

If brothers went their separate ways, their sister who continued to live with them after marriage lost her home unless one of them took her and her children under his protection. A woman could not automatically count on her brothers to assume this duty, for with the rise of individualism the patrilineal form of marriage, which had coexisted with other marital arrangements in seventh-century Mecca, was gaining popularity. A self-made man tended to prefer leaving his property to his own sons, which sharpened his interest in ensuring that his wife bore only his children. The best way to guarantee this was to have her live under close supervision in his house. The woman thus lost her personal freedom, but the security she gained from the marital arrangement was precarious at best in the absence of protective state laws. Not only did she have to live at her in-laws' mercy, she could be thrown out of the house on her husband's whim. Khadija escaped such a fate because she was independently wealthy and belonged to one of the most powerful families of the Quraysh—a fact that must have helped her significantly to multiply her fortune.

It was against such a backdrop of urban problems that Islam was born.[3] Even though Muhammad lived happily and comfortably with his rich wife, he continued to identify with the poor and the dispossessed of Mecca, pondering the conditions that spawned them. He himself had been orphaned in early childhood and passed on from one relative to another. Since his guardians were from the poor and neglected branch of the Quraysh, Muhammad earned his keep as a shepherd from a very early age. But he was luckier than other orphans, for he at least had a place in loving homes and eventually got a good job with Khadija's caravan, which allowed him to travel widely in the Middle East.

These journeys had a direct bearing on his spiritual growth and gave focus to his social concerns by exposing him to Christian monks and well-educated Jewish merchants. They intrigued him, for they seemed to have put into practice a monotheistic faith which a few Meccans of the educated circles were beginning to discuss. How did the Christian God inspire such diverse nationalities to worship Him alone? How did the Judaic God manage to unite widely dispersed Semitic groups under one set of laws which provided for the protection of women and children even in large cities? The astral deities that Muhammad's people inherited from their nomadic ancestors demanded offerings but gave nothing in return. After discussions with people of various faiths, Muhammad sought the ultimate solution to his community's problems in the solitude of a cave on Mount Hiraa overlooking Mecca, where he often retreated in his spare moments, with Khadija or by himself.

While meditating alone one day in the cave, Muhammad heard a voice which he believed to be the angel Gabriel's. "Proclaim in the name of thy Lord and Cherisher who created, created man out of a clot of congealed blood" (Quran, surah [chapter] xcvi, verses 1–2),[4] it said, pointing out that there was only one God and that man must serve Him alone. When Muhammad recovered from his ecstasy, he ran back, shaken, and described his experience to his wife. Having shared his spiritual struggles, Khadija understood that her husband had received a call to serve the one God whom the Christians and the Jews also worshipped. Bewildered and confused, Muhammad went on with his daily work in the city and occasional meditations on Mount Hiraa. Again the voice commanded him to tell his people about the one omnipotent

God, who would welcome believers into heaven and cast wicked people into hell. With Khadija's repeated encouragement, Muhammad finally accepted his prophetic call and devoted the rest of his life to preaching God's word as the new religion of Islam (which means *submission* [*to the will of God*]). Converts to it were called Muslims (*those who submit*). They were not to be called Muhammadans, because they did not worship Muhammad, who was merely a human messenger for the one God. Though invisible and immortal, this God was named Allah after the Zeus of the old Meccan pantheon.

Numerous revelations that Muhammad received from Allah throughout his life were compiled shortly after his death into the Muslim bible, named the Quran, which formed the basis for the Shariah, or Islamic law. A supplement to it was provided by the Hadith, or Muhammad's words, which were recorded over many years as his survivors and their descendants remembered them. Despite the exotic Arabic words in which it is couched, Islam's message is similar in its essentials to the one promulgated by Judaism and Christianity, and can be summed up by the Ten Commandments. *Allah*, after all, is but the Arabic name for the God worshipped by both Jews and Christians. But the rituals differed. Muhammad required his followers to obey the commandments through the practice of five specific rituals, called the pillars of Islam. A Muslim must (1) profess faith in one God; (2) pray to Him; (3) give alms to the poor; (4) fast during Ramadan, the month in the lunar calendar during which Muhammad received his first revelation; and (5) go on a pilgrimage to Mecca at least once in his lifetime (if he can afford to do so) to pay respects to the birthplace of Islam and reinforce the spirit of fellowship with Muslims from all over the world. Although these laws preached fairness and charity among all mankind, God— through Muhammad—preferred to establish specific guidelines to protect the interests of women.

Once he had united enough people under Allah to make a

viable community, Muhammad devoted an impressive number
of his sermons to women's rights. In doing so, however, he did
not attempt to fight the irreversible tide of urbanization. Nor
did he condemn the trend toward patrimonial families, although they often abused women. Too shrewd a politician to
antagonize Mecca's powerful patriarchs, he introduced a bill
of rights for women which would not only ensure their protection under patriarchy but also reinforce the system itself so
that it would stand as a mini-tribe against the rest of the world.

He did this mainly by providing for women's economic
rights in marriage in such a way that they had a financial stake
in the system which constantly threatened to erode their independence. Upon marriage a man had to pay his bride a dowry,
which was to be her nest egg against divorce or widowhood.
While married to him, she could manage the dowry and all
other personal income in any way that she pleased, exclusively
for her own benefit, and will them to her children and husband
upon her death. In her lifetime she did not have to spend her
money on herself, or her children for that matter, since only
the man was responsible for supporting his family. If the
woman stayed married to her husband until his death, she also
inherited part of his property. While her share was less than
her children's, she was assured of being supported by her sons
in widowhood. By the same line of reasoning, her inheritance
from her father was half that of her brother's: her husband
supported her, whereas her brother had to support his wife.
The daughter's right to inherit tended to divide the patriarch's
wealth, but the problem was customarily solved by having her
marry a paternal first cousin. Failing that, the inheritance became a part of yet another Muslim family in the same tribe of
Islam, united through faith rather than kinship. In either case,
a Muslim woman with neither a paid occupation nor an inheritance enjoyed a modicum of financial independence, at the
price of her submission to a patriarchal form of marriage.

But she was to be allowed to choose her own spouse, according to the Hadith: "None, not even the father or the sov-

ereign, can lawfully contract in marriage an adult woman of sound mind without her permission, whether she be a virgin or not." This freedom was to be assured by a law that required the dowry to be paid to the bride herself. Since the parents were not to pocket it, as they often did before Islam, they were presumably above being "bought." But the brides' freedom remained largely theoretical, since most of them were barely ten years old when engaged to be married for the first time. Aysha, whom Muhammad married after Khadija's death, was only about six or seven years old when she was betrothed and about ten when she moved into her husband's house with her toys. Muhammad was not playing legal tricks on women, however. He did revoke the parents' choice of mate when their daughters complained to him about it.[5] Although parents were to be honored and obeyed, he made it clear that the grown-up daughter was to be respected as an individual—so much so that the marriage contract could be tailored to her specific needs: the bride could impose conditions on her contract. A cooperative wife, he pointed out, was the best foundation for a stable marriage.

Though Muhammad repeatedly preached compassion and love as the most important bonds of marriage, he also gave men financial enticements to keep the family together. The husband was allowed to pay only a part of the dowry upon marriage, with the balance payable upon divorce. If the dowry was large enough, the arrangement deterred the husband from throwing out his wife without substantial cause. In fact, under Islam he could no longer just throw her out. He had to pay her not only the balance of the dowry but also "maintainance on a reasonable scale" (Quran ii:241). He was also to support her through the ensuing *idda*, the three months of chastity which the Shariah asked her to observe in order to determine whether she was carrying his child. If pregnant, she was to be helped until she delivered and had nursed the infant to the point where he could be cared for by the husband's family. All of her children remained under the paternal roof. In a patriarchal society where men were not eager to support others' children or to provide employment for women, the child custody law assured children a decent home and enabled the divorcée to remarry more easily, but even an independently wealthy woman was forbidden to walk out of her husband's home with her children.

Any sexual behavior that would weaken the patriarchal system was strongly discouraged or made illegal. If the custom of taking a visiting husband was frowned upon, her taking more than one at a time was condemned as adultery, which was punishable by whipping. Although men were also forbidden to sow wild oats, they could marry up to four wives and have as many concubines as they could afford. This law may have been partly a concession by Muhammad to the widely accepted custom among wealthy urban men, but he also saw it as a way to attach surplus women to the men's households for their own protection as well as to maintain social order. Due to frequent intertribal warfare and attacks on the merchants' caravans, women always outnumbered men. The conflict became increasingly serious as Muhammad's following grew large enough to threaten the purse and the prestige of the families who amassed fortunes from pilgrims to the Kaaba. So vicious were the attacks that in A.D. 622,[6] after Khadija died, Muhammad moved his budding Muslim community to Medina, an agricultural community without important shrines that would be threatened by Allah. Moreover, the perpetually quarreling clans of Medina welcomed Muhammad because of his reputation as a just man and a skillful arbitrator.

Muhammad succeeded brilliantly in settling the clans' differences and won a prominent place in Medina. This made Meccans even more determined to destroy him before he built up an alliance against them. Violent battles between the Muslims and the Meccans followed. Alliances and betrayals by various tribal factions during each battle engendered more battles, which decimated the Muslim community. The number of widows mounted to such catastrophic proportions after the

battle fought at Uhud, near Medina, that God sent a message
officially condoning polygamy: "Marry women of your
choice, two, or three, or four." But He added, "If you fear that
you cannot treat them equitably, marry only one" (iv,3). A
polygamous husband was required to distribute not only material goods but also sexual attention equally among his wives,
for sexual satisfaction, according to Muhammad, was every
woman's conjugal right. Besides, a sexually unsatisfied wife
was believed to be a threat to her family's stability, as she was
likely to seek satisfaction elsewhere.

Unmarried men and women also posed a threat to Muhammad's scheme of social order, which may be one reason
why he frowned upon monasticism. Sexual instincts were natural, he reasoned, and therefore would eventually seek fulfillment in adultery* unless channeled into legitimate marriage.
Wives and husbands were thus necessary for each other's spiritual salvation. "The curse of God be upon those women who
remain unwed and say they will never marry," he said, "and a
man who does not marry is none of mine."

Though the Quran abolished the ancient custom of stoning adulteresses to death and called instead for public whipping—a hundred lashes administered to male and female
offenders alike—Muhammad knew that the sexual double
standard would single out women as targets of slander. After
a bitter personal experience, he hastened to build safety features into his antiadultery and antifornication laws.

One day Aysha was left behind inadvertently by Muhammad's caravan when she stepped away to look for a necklace
that she had lost. She was brought back to the caravan the
following morning by a man many years younger than her
middle-aged husband, which set tongues wagging. Even Ali,
Muhammad's trusted cousin and son-in-law, cast doubt on her
reputation. The Prophet's faith in his wife was severely
shaken. Aysha was finally saved when her husband fell into a
trance, which indicated that he was receiving a message from

* Here *adultery* refers to premarital as well as extramarital sex.

God. Relief spread over his face. God had vouched for her innocence. The "affair of the slander," as it came to be known, was closed.[7] Four witnesses were henceforth required to condemn women of adultery, as against only two for business transactions and murder cases. Moreover, false witnesses were to be whipped publicly.

Other than false witnesses, violators of women's rights were not punished on this earth. The law would catch up with them in the next world, where they would be cast into the fire (an idea borrowed from the Christians). The good, on the other hand, would reside forever in a heavenly oasis with cool springs in shady palm groves where their every whim would be served by lovely dark-eyed houris. Like the Christian preachers who promised believers a heaven with pearly gates and haloed creatures floating about on white clouds, Muhammad merely presented images that would spell bliss to the common man. Though he did not specify who was going to serve the deserving women, probably for fear of offending their husbands, Muhammad guaranteed a place for them in paradise. Women had the same religious duties as men, and their souls were absolutely equal in God's eyes, with not even the responsibility for original sin weighing upon them. Islam rejects the idea of original sin altogether, claiming that every child is born pure. Nor does the Quran single out Eve as the cause of man's fall (though folklore in various parts of the Middle East does condemn her). According to the Quran, Allah tells both Adam and Eve not to eat the apple. "Then did Satan make them slip from the Garden" (ii,36). Allah scolds them both equally, but promises mercy and guidance when they repent.

Muhammad's decision to rely on each man's conscience to fulfill his Islamic obligation toward women reflected a realistic approach to legislation. He seems to have recognized how far he could carry his reforms without losing his constituents' support. In a city where woman had neither economic nor political weight, men would take only so much earthly punishment for disregarding her rights. By the same token, they would not entirely give up their old prerogative of divorcing their wives for any cause without answering to a third party, or pay them more than comfortably affordable compensation. Muhammad therefore struck a compromise in his laws, but repeatedly emphasized the spirit of kindness and respect for women which was implied in them. When deprived of their true spirit, the laws were open to abuse, but were still better than no protection at all. For example, a man could legally divorce any number of wives without good cause if he met his financial obligations. But the amount of both the dowry and the alimony was determined purely by his conscience, and no court of law could enforce payment. Even if a man honestly did the best he could, the financial compensation that he paid supported the divorcée only for a short while unless he was extremely rich. This left at a disadvantage the older woman with diminished chances for remarriage. Muhammad therefore made a special virtue of marrying older women, and stressed that God disliked divorce enormously. "A Muslim must not hate his wife," he said repeatedly, "and if he be displeased with one bad quality in her, let him be pleased with another which is good."[8] As a fellow husband, he tactfully sympathized with the local saying "Woman is made hard and crooked like a rib," but added, "If ye wish to straighten it, ye will break it."

Mothers, however, were above snide remarks. "Heaven lieth at the feet of mothers," said Muhammad, summing up God's repeated commands to love and respect mothers, and by extension all older women. Helping needy women was as great a virtue as fasting all day and praying all night.

"I have done a great crime. Is there any act by which I may repent?" a man asked Muhammad one day.

"Have you a mother?" the Prophet said.

"No," the man replied.

"Have you an aunt?"

"Yes."

"Do good to her, and your crime will be pardoned."

Daughters, often unwanted and killed at birth, were also treated with special tenderness by Muhammad, whose four surviving children were all girls. Female infanticide was outlawed. Education was to be open to girls as well as boys. The girl's interests were to be considered when marrying her off. "Marriage is a servitude," he pointed out, "therefore, let each one of you examine in what hands he places his daughter." In a society where women could not live unattached to a family, paternal duty did not end with the daughter's marriage. "Shall I point out to you the best of virtues?" Muhammad said. "It is your doing good to your daughter when she is returned to you having been divorced by her husband." Since daughters did not constitute old-age security for their parents, Muhammad could only promise their guardians special rewards in the next world. "Whoever hath a daughter and doth not bury her alive or scold her or prefer his male children to her, may God bring him into paradise," he said.

Women fared rather well under Muhammad's social reforms. Secure within the still-tribelike community of Islam, they not only took advantage of the rights granted them but fought to keep them. Although the Prophet had repeatedly stressed that learning was a "duty incumbent on every Muslim, male and female," women found themselves tied to housework and falling behind men in Muhammad's classes on religion. They petitioned Muhammad to set up a class for them at a mutually convenient time, and he obliged. At one of their meetings women objected that God's words were always addressed to men. Although in Arabic the masculine is used when referring to both men and women, Muhammad came back some time later with a revelation containing the "he or she" jargon that American feminists adopted thirteen centuries later: "The men who resign themselves to God and the women who resign themselves, and the believing men and the believing women, and the devout men and the devout women, and the men of truth and the women of truth, and the patient men and the patient women, and the humble men and the humble women . . . for them hath God prepared forgiveness and a rich recompense" (xxxiii,35).

A few of the learned women also acted as imams[9] (the equivalent of ministers in Islam, which does not have an ordained clergy). As he chose the most learned and respected man in a group to lead the prayers when he was absent, Muhammad appointed the most learned woman to lead when only women congregated for prayer. On the other hand, Umm Waraqah, one of the best students of the Quran, was asked to be imam for both the men and women of her large household. She did not set a precedent for later generations, however, since Muhammad never specified the conditions under which women could be imams. Today, women may lead only women. Those who are well versed in the Quran and the Hadith serve as imams and teachers mainly in sexually segregated societies.

Under Islam, poetesses rediscovered their role as historians, journalists, propagandists, social critics, and cheerleaders of their community. They celebrated the ideals which united their Islamic tribe, moved men to defend them against enemies, and sang of their victories. They eulogized those fallen in battle and elevated them to martyrdom, inspiring the living to avenge the dead and plaguing the conscience of those who transgressed the accepted code of ethics. The undisputed poet laureate in Muhammad's time was a woman named Al-Khansa.[10] She started her career as a typically promising young poetess, reciting at births, weddings, and funerals. She soon proved to be a prodigy who delighted in showing off her virtuosic skill in improvising verses, and regularly walked away with the highest prizes at the most prestigious poetry contest, held annually at the fair of Ukaz near Mecca. When she lost her brother in battle, everyone said that she became fully possessed by those spirits (jinn) who commune only with the best poets, for her grief unlocked verses that epitomized her people's suffering in their constant fight for survival. Al-Khansa eventually followed her sons to battle, reciting verses to arouse women and men to fight on for Islam.

Although most women fighters were poetesses and nurses who took up arms in self-defense or to avenge their loved ones' death, some volunteered as soldiers. The list of women warriors was in fact rather long, given the small size of the early Islamic community. Typical among them was Umm Umarah, one of Muhammad's earliest converts. She fought alongside her husband and sons in many battles, retiring only after she lost a hand. Like any old soldier, she was proud to show off her battle scars.

Perhaps the most endearing of the women veterans was Safiya, Muhammad's seventy-year-old aunt, who stood guard when the Muslim community in Medina was under siege. She noticed an enemy prowling around the weak point of the fortification. Unable to warn the men in time, she clubbed down the intruder herself.

The old chronicles and poems celebrating the daring exploits of these Amazons may not stand the scrutiny of today's historians in every detail, but they point out that the ideal woman in the mass media of early Islam was neither a housewife nor a sex object, but man's colleague. She would have been quite at home with Judith, Queen Esther, and Joan of Arc.

Such spirited women did not always take well to polygamy, and they defied it openly when they could fall back on indulgent paternal families. Muhammad's great-granddaughter Amina took full advantage of her right to impose conditions in her marriage contract. Her husband was not to take another wife or concubine, or prevent her from spending *his* money, or keep her from running her own life as she saw fit. Breach of contract was to be cause for divorce. Despite his laws allowing polygamy, the Prophet seems to have considered monogamy the ideal state for women, for he protested vehemently when he heard that Ali, the husband of his favorite daughter, Fatima, intended to take a second wife. "She is part of me, and what harms her harms me," he insisted.

Yet Muhammad himself married about a dozen women

after Khadija's death, having God justify the excess number as the privilege of a prophet. By then, however, he was not only the preacher of a new religion but also the secular chief of an important Muslim community. While he married some women because they were old or widowed and others because he was personally attracted to them, he also married to strengthen political alliances, as did David and Solomon of the Old Testament. He set up his wives in a typical Medinan house made of unfired brick, giving each an apartment opening onto a common courtyard. He made a sincere effort to treat every wife equally, devoting a night to each in turn. Although he never established with any of them as deep a spiritual rapport as he had enjoyed with Khadija, he gave each wife freedom to develop her own talents, and shared with each what she could best give. Saudah, the middle-aged widow of an early Muslim convert, earned a good income with her skill in fine leatherwork. Zaynab, the widow of Muhammad's cousin who was killed at war, was devoted to charitable works and was revered as "Mother of the Poor." Umm Salama, the widow of another Muslim martyr, was an astute political adviser to Muhammad and acted as imam for women. Aysha, who was only about ten years old at the time of her marriage, had been so well tutored by her husband in religious matters that he told his followers to consult her in his absence.[11] A model husband to all of his wives, he helped with household chores and mended his own clothes. No wonder he smugly told his followers one day: "Whosoever has two wives and prefers one over the other will appear on Judgment Day with one side of his body crooked."

It did not take him long to eat his words. Admitting himself to be all too human, he soon became more attached to the bright and witty Aysha, who also happened to be the daughter of his closest friend, Abu Bakr. "She is the only woman in whose company I receive my revelations," Muhammad explained when his wives complained that he spent most of his time in her apartment. With new wives arriving one after another, even Aysha did not feel totally secure in her favored position. She recalled many years later the anguish that she felt when a new wife was added to the harem: "When the Messenger of Allah married Umm Salama, I was exceedingly sad, having heard much of her beauty. I was gracious to her, desiring to see her for myself. And by Allah, I saw that she was twice as beautiful and graceful as she was reputed to be."

The lovely Umm Salama turned out to be a formidable rival indeed, heaping abuse on Aysha at every opportunity and setting up other co-wives against her. Aysha proved to be an equal match, however, and the harem soon split into political camps which closely mirrored the men's factions then vying for power in the Islamic community. Aysha and other daughters of Muhammad's closest friends, who hoped to widen their influence as their chief's right-hand men, were allied against Umm Salama and other representatives of the old Meccan aristocracy, which considered itself the natural leaders of the community. Although Muhammad was accessible to everyone, being related to him opened up so many avenues of power and prestige among Muslims that each of his fathers-in-law trembled lest his daughter's misbehavior result in her divorce and an end to his privileges. Every quarrel in the harem was watched as anxiously as the Dow-Jones average. When the wives plagued Muhammad for clothes that he could not afford, some of the fathers discreetly offered to fill the need out of their own pockets. Equally proud of their high status as the chief's wives, the women refused the gift.

Wishing aloud for the peaceful days that he had enjoyed with Khadija, Muhammad escaped into meditation. It is at this point that God began to send him messages that have been widely interpreted as antifeminist: "Men are the protectors and maintainers of women because God has given the one more strength than the other, and because they support them from their means. As to those women on whose part ye fear disloyalty and ill conduct, admonish them [first], [next] refuse to share their beds, [and last] beat them" (iv,34). Liberal scholars have pondered this, for the text in Arabic is full of subtleties open to more liberal interpretation. Some see in this passage permission to punish her only lightly, as a warning, while the most liberal ones claim that the husband may punish his wife only after her guilt has been determined by a court of law. In other words, the husband acts as the arm of the law for serious offenses in order to spare her public indignity. These interpretations, however, have not yet displaced the time-honored antifeminist versions.

For the Prophet's wives God had a special double-edged message. Proclaiming them Mothers of Believers, He ordered them to behave in a manner befitting their new title, which meant a considerable curb on their freedom. Like the wives of desert chieftains, they had mingled democratically with men and women in their community. Now they had to seclude themselves in their homes, as was customary among some of the aristocratic women of Mecca. Their apartments now became a true harem—quarters reserved exclusively for women. They could speak with men unrelated to them only from behind a curtain, and had to veil their bodies when they went out. God never commanded women to cover their faces, however, although the face veil was high fashion among the Byzantine and Persian ladies who were much admired and emulated throughout the Middle East at that time. "And say to the believing women," the Quran said, "that they should lower their gaze and guard their modesty; that they should not display their beauty and ornaments except what must ordinarily appear thereof; that they should draw their veils over their bosoms . . ." (xxiv,31). Another verse (xxxiii,59) asked women to "throw around them a part of their mantle" when they went out.

The timing of the introduction of these rules was perfect, for the wives were so disunited by the competing political factions within the Muslim community that they could not muster a strong enough opposition. Aysha, the one most likely to have led the rebellion, was temporarily cowed by the "affair of the slander," which had put her reputation in question. The others were either too aged to care one way or the other, or found themselves without allies. Wives of humble origin were likely to have been flattered by the highly visible mark of aristocracy imposed on them. Moreover, life in Muhammad's household did not change drastically, for harmony was restored in a typically Arab fashion by saving everyone's face. The wives bowed nominally to the rules. Having asserted his authority, Muhammad proved himself a good sport, and an even better lawyer against himself. Contending that foster relatives—that is, one's wet nurse and her family—as well as blood relatives were allowed into the women's presence, he directed his wives to give some of their or their sisters' milk to men they wished to see, thus making them foster sons or nephews. As the laws on seclusion remained, however, the seed of women's imprisonment was sown.

Very few people had Muhammad's flexible mind ruled by compassion. When he died about A.D. 632, women's right to participate in public affairs and even to occupy public space began to erode. Although Aysha and Umm Salama had been close advisers to Muhammad in both political and religious matters, neither they nor other women were invited to elect the caliph (spiritual and temporal leader) who would thenceforth guide the Islamic community. Within several years of Muhammad's death, women were barred from worshipping in the mosque despite his specific instructions to the contrary. Shortly afterward, they were forbidden to go by themselves on the annual pilgrimage to Mecca.

However, the relatively compact tribal nature of the early Islamic community acted in women's favor. As the first caliphs were Muhammad's closest friends and in-laws, they continued to behave on the whole like tribal chieftains, listening to everyone who came to them with problems. For the sake of communal harmony, they could not totally ignore women's petitions.

The caliphs were obliged to treat with special respect the

Prophet's widows, who were revered by Muslims as Mothers of Believers and dowager queens. These women thus formed a potent feminist force in the community, especially as they were now united peacefully in the memory of their departed husband, with no thought of remarrying. Under the widows' leadership Muslim women succeeded in lifting the ban on pilgrimage and public worship, although they had to accept segregated praying quarters in the mosque (from which their descendants have not yet escaped). Aysha and Umm Salama continued to act as imams for the women of their household, thus encouraging Umm Waraqah to lead the men as well as the women of her household in prayer. No one dared quarrel with her, since she had been appointed by the Prophet himself.

The Prophet's widows—Aysha and Umm Salama in particular—contributed heavily to the shaping of early Islamic dogma. Considered the best firsthand authorities on their husband's life and teachings, they were consulted in compiling the Hadith (Sayings),[12] which, along with God's revelations recorded in the Quran, formed the basis for the Shariah. Aysha also acted as judge. Since the widows relied on their memory rather than on written notes, it is reasonable to assume that they tended to recall what was favorable to them even if they were scrupulously honest. Unfortunately, they were not the only sources used. Moreover, unlike the Quran, which was compiled very soon after Muhammad's death and has not been changed in any important way since, the Hadith remained open to additions and thus highly vulnerable to "correction" by antifeminist scholars and powerful special-interest groups over the centuries, although efforts have been made to weed out Hadith of questionable authenticity. It is therefore remarkable that so many of Muhammad's statements upholding women's equality and dignity have survived at all.

According to what we know today, Muhammad did not specify women's right to hold political office. Aysha, nevertheless, helped herself into the main political arena by exploiting her triple prestige as the Prophet's favorite wife, the first caliph Abu Bakr's ablest child, and the foremost authority on the Hadith. Childless and still in her teens when widowed, Aysha had not been content merely to lodge a few complaints on behalf of women's rights and serve as a walking library of Muhammad's teachings. She liked to be in the center of action. She started out as a one-woman shadow cabinet to the ruling caliphs, a role reminiscent of the tribal poetess–social critics. Although she had no talent for versification, she had a flair for drama and oratory. When the flagrant nepotism of the third caliph, Uthman, stirred serious discontent in the community, she took to the podium. Holding up Muhammad's shirt and sandal for all to see, she lamented that the holy Prophet's example was being forgotten too soon. Aysha considered her mission accomplished when Uthman promised reforms, but she had unwittingly inspired the opposition to take more drastic steps. Uthman was murdered, and Fatima's husband, Ali, was elected caliph.

Ali was never implicated in the murder but apparently did nothing to bring the assassins to justice. Unable to forgive his attempt to depose her from Muhammad's favors many years ago during the "affair of the slander," and outraged by the violence committed against the sacred office, Aysha delivered a fiery speech to a crowd gathered at the mosque, denouncing the criminals and those who protected them by their indifference. "Keep yourselves safe by not associating with them so that others can inflict an exemplary punishment on them and scatter in fright those who are behind them," she pleaded. Her supporters fanned emotions further by exhibiting the blood-stained shirt of the dead caliph and the fingers his queen had lost trying to protect him. What Aysha had intended as a bloodless purge snowballed into the first civil war in Islamic history, which sparked a series of events leading to the division of Islam into the Sunni and Shiite sects. Having unwittingly started the war, Aysha participated in it fully. Seated in a camel-borne litter, she led her forces against Ali's in their first confrontation, known as the Battle of the Camel, in 656. Ali emerged victorious, and gallantly sent her home on condition that she retire from politics.

Aysha's defeat was the kiss of death for the women warriors of old. Antifeminists never tired of repeating the comment Muhammad—according to one report in the Hadith—made upon hearing that a queen ruled Persia: "No people who place a woman over their affairs prosper." In time they attributed to the childless Aysha the confessions of a reformed housewife: "I regret having gone to battle. If I had to do it over again I would have chosen to remain in my house. The wisdom of doing so would mean more to me than the honor of bearing ten noble and heroic sons to Muhammad."[13]

The indomitable Aysha did not remain at home, however, and continued to pull political strings backstage until her death at about sixty-four years of age. But without a clearly stated right to exercise leadership, the majority of women lost their political voice, especially when the Islamic community grew into an empire whose caliphs ceased to be tribal fathers who would listen to the humblest of women and heed the demands of the poetess–social critics. The unspecified rights that women had enjoyed during Muhammad's time were chipped away gradually. But the meticulously detailed laws on marital and financial rights were too specific to be ignored entirely, and gave women a modicum of security and independence in the patriarchal family, which survived as a mini-tribe in the sprawling empire. Within the family circle women exerted considerable influence, not only on their men but also on the blossoming of Arab culture in the Middle Ages. An exceptional few followed Aysha's example and ruled the caliphs and their empire, which spread Islam to lands and peoples far beyond the Arabian peninsula.

2

᠁᠁᠁᠁᠁᠁

Women in the Arab Caliphate

Say to the believing women that . . . they should draw
their veils over their bosoms.
—Quran xxiv: 30–31

But once a wife steps out of the house unbeknown to
her husband, he has his grounds and she's divorced.
—Plautus, *The Merchant*
(third century B.C.)

A woman should not leave her spindle or her private
apartment, nor look down on the street from her
terrace.
—Imam Ghazali (leading Moslem theologian,
eleventh to twelfth centuries), *Vivification des
sciences de la foi*

Maysun had everything a Muslim woman of the late seventh
century could wish for. She was the wife of a caliph and the
mother of a bright little crown prince. And she lived in a
sumptuous palace in Damascus, a cultured city that made
Mecca and Medina look like desert outposts. Yet she was
unhappy. She felt trapped in an idle existence that cut her off
from real life. To make matters worse, her husband did not

understand her, maintaining that he already gave her everything. Homesick for the simple but more meaningful life that
she had known in her desert home, she composed a song of
protest:

I love the Bedouin's tent, caressed by the murmuring breeze,
    and standing amid boundless horizons
More than the gilded halls of marble in all their royal
    splendor . . .
I prefer a desert cavalier, generous and poor,
To a fat lout in purple living behind closed doors.[1]

The queen got her wish, perhaps unexpectedly. The caliph
was so furious at being called a fat lout that he banished her
from her dollhouse to her beloved desert.

The incident marked much more than the end of one royal
marriage. Above all it highlighted the deterioration that had
been taking place in the Muslim woman's status ever since her
people united under Islam to conquer the wealthier lands beyond the Arabian peninsula. So successful were they that by
the time Maysun's husband became caliph Muawiya I in A.D.
661 they had extended their control over most of the North
African coast and the Fertile Crescent. These lands of abun-
dant orchards and bazaars had not only made them rich
beyond their wildest dreams but also introduced them to
old civilizations—Assyro-Babylonian, Egyptian, and especially
Persian and Byzantine. Dazzled, they had established their
capital in Damascus and begun to develop out of these new
influences a sophisticated culture that reached its full bloom
when the caliphate moved to the even more fabulous city of
Baghdad.

Great wealth made the Arabian Muslim woman who accompanied the conquerors to the new lands quite obsolete.
With more than enough men eager to march to battle for gold
rather than tribal or Islamic honor, the imperial ruler did not
need women warriors or cheerleaders. Nor did anyone want to

have his consciousness raised by poetess–social critics while
he was enjoying his nouveau-riche status. With slaves to look
after the land and the herds, the woman warrior stayed at
home. In keeping with their new station, her people eventually
adopted the status symbols of their Byzantine and Persian subject peoples and neighbors—the veil² and the harem. The
Prophet Muhammad had succumbed to these influences from
afar and recommended seclusion to his wives when he became
politically prominent, but the Mothers of Believers had usually hidden behind the curtain of their apartments only when
they felt it expedient to remain invisible to male visitors. The
Muslim community was too small and poor then for the full-
scale practice of such snobbery. Nor was the patriarchal insistence on women's sexual purity threatened much in a tightly
knit group. In the highly urbanized Damascus and Baghdad,
however, both the snob and the patriarch needed stronger reassurance. Accordingly, by the middle of the eighth century—
less than a hundred years after Maysun was banished to the
desert—the Arabian conquerers shut their women—sisters
and daughters as well as wives—into their own private apartments, complete with the paraphernalia of the Byzantine
harem. Eunuchs, mostly Greeks at first, came to guard the
harem doors, and let in no man except the inmates' owner and
those approved by him. Houses were built with central court-
yards to allow women to take fresh air without being exposed
to strangers. If they had to go out to the street, they were
required to veil their faces. These rules, rather flexible at first,
became more rigid when they were sanctified by Islam during
the Arab caliphate. The Quranic verses enjoining the Prophet's wives to stay in their homes and to speak to men across
curtains were eventually applied to most women. And through
an extraordinary acrobatic process of reasoning, God's message calling on women to "draw their veils over their bosoms"
and "throw around them a part of their mantle" came to be
interpreted as an order to hide the face. One of the best examples of how local traditions were absorbed by Islam, the

law of seclusion has occupied a nebulous realm between custom and religion and has not been as universally applied as the
more specifically worded Quranic precepts. Seclusion did not
affect peasants and other poor women who had to work for a
living, but it banished the well-educated and potentially most
influential women from the outside world and in so doing
turned them into sex objects. The long era of the "feminine
mystique" was born in the Islamic world.

Any Muslim woman who objected to her new status could
expect to share Maysun's fate, for she was dispensable not
only on the battleground but also at home. Gone were the
days when a Muslim considered himself well off if he kept a
few slaves taken in small-scale tribal forays. Though the
spread of Islam reduced intertribal wars in Arabia and discouraged Muslims from enslaving each other, conquests
abroad made ever-larger populations of non-Muslim slaves
available to them. Except for those taken as war captives, the
majority of conquered non-Muslims merely became vassals to
their Muslim lords by paying tribute-taxes in exchange for
protection, or they converted to Islam in order to escape the
tax and enjoy greater privileges. Muslim wealth, however, attracted slave traders from many lands with their best human
merchandise. The caliphs and the officials of the new empire
owned literally thousands of beautiful slave girls, who at first
replaced their free sisters in everything but bearing heirs to the
caliphate, which by then had become a hereditary kingship
rather than the elective leadership of the Muslim community
that it was during the first three decades following Muhammad's death. When the son of a concubine of Caliph Walid I
succeeded in becoming Caliph Yazid III in 744, the free
Arabian Muslim woman lost the last exclusive right that had
given her some bargaining power. She could not rally Islam to
her cause, for the Prophet had not outlawed slavery, which
was an integral part of his people's economy. He had tried
instead to phase it out gradually by encouraging his followers
to free their slaves in exchange for great rewards in the next

world. His offer did not interest the new Arab imperialists very much, however. "I enjoy this world / Rather than wait for paradise," sang Walid II, who ascended the throne in 734.

During the Arab caliphate the slave presented several important advantages over her free sister. She was subservient to her master's every whim and caused him no in-law headaches, a point which the caliphs looked upon favorably. Marrying a nonslave Muslim Arab woman often required the distribution of political plums to her kin, or at least the consideration of their sensitivities when making state decisions. Even the perfectly justifiable divorce of a royal queen entailed a fortune in property settlement, and the possibility of unpleasant political repercussions to boot. Such problems led the caliphs to contract fewer marriages and to rely more on slaves to produce heirs. Their offspring were legitimate according to a clause in Islamic law originally intended to prevent the perpetuation of slavery from one generation to the next.

Yazid's father, Caliph Walid I, preferred the company of his slave girls even though he had married eight wives of noble birth.[3] Sixteen of his nineteen sons were born to slave women, with seven of his wives bearing no children at all. The irresistible charm of these slaves lay not only in their subservience but also in their talents in music, dance, and poetry, which preoccupied the aristocracy increasingly as it became securely established in its power and luxury. Though every educated woman of the day knew how to compose a good verse and strum a pleasant melody on the lute, most were amateurs compared to slave girls trained in the best conservatories since childhood by slave dealers who hoped to recoup their investment through the astronomical prices these artists fetched on the market. Also groomed in refined manners, which the daughters of the Arabian women warriors might not yet have mastered, these slave girls knew how to stir the imagination of the most jaded prince. Beauty alone was not enough, for many of the princes were poets and musicians in their own right and insisted on an artistic dolce vita, not a simple orgy with brainless sex objects. Mahbuba[4] was one of those who filled the bill perfectly in the court of the Caliph Al-Muta-wakkil in the middle of the ninth century, when the Islamic culture had reached its zenith. She enchanted her master with her beauty and her knack for refined romantic gestures, such as tracing his name on her cheek with musk before improvising love songs in his honor. Above all the caliph was impressed with her talent. In fact, many of her compositions became the hits of all Baghdad. Her quick wit was particularly appreciated in the court's favorite pastime: the caliph would improvise a line or two of verse and challenge his poetesses to continue in the same meter and rhyme. The one whose response pleased him the most felt a bag of gold drop into her lap.

So indispensable did talented slave girls become to the aristocratic lifestyle that princely patrons of the arts vied with one another to collect Mahbubas. The most famous patron of them all, Caliph Harun al-Rashid, turned his palace into a veritable theater where he staged extravaganzas with a cast of thousands of slave and freelance artists. His sons and grandsons, including Al-Mutawakkil, continued the tradition, occasionally sailing with their artists on the Tigris River for a floating concert in the moonlight. The townspeople came out with torches to listen onshore or follow the party in their own boats. These were the magic moments which gave Baghdad its legendary fame and attracted ever greater talent to it during the Middle Ages.

With the caliphs so passionately devoted to culture, the slave artist could earn fame and fortune by her talent alone, but a more spectacular success could be achieved only through sexual charm. If she produced a son for a caliph, she could hope for the ultimate success—to be the mother of a caliph, which automatically made her the boss of the palace harem. Since the caliph traditionally respected and obeyed his mother more than he did his wives, and sometimes his counselors as well, the queen mother could be the most powerful person in the empire. What gave every concubine hope was the fact that any son or brother of a reigning caliph could be designated crown prince.

The free, or rather the nonslave, Muslim women eventually learned from the slaves. During the Baghdad caliphate many of them were in fact daughters of concubines who taught them to work within the system. The princess who followed her concubine mother's advice with the greatest flair and success was Zubaydah.[5] Her cousin, Harun al-Rashid, fell so deeply in love with her that he married her, for concubinage was forbidden to Muslim women. Conforming to the fashionable image of the ideal woman, Zubaydah became a charming caterer to her husband's pleasures and earned the main credit for perfecting the splendor of the court which enhanced Harun's glory in history and in A Thousand and One Nights, better known as The Arabian Nights, which was compiled in Arabic in the middle of the tenth century, about a hundred years after the queen's death.

Her parties for the caliph were feasts for all the senses. Not for her the crude style of those who would impress her husband with a centerpiece of conspicuous consumption, such as a dish of fish tongues. Reclining on low divans spread with Persian rugs and brocade cushions, Zubaydah's guests were treated to the haute cuisine of the day—delicately spiced pilafs, lamb stews, and chicken fed on almonds and milk. The beverage list included date and grape wines, as well as rose water and fruit sherbets for those who obeyed the Islamic prohibition against alcohol. The dessert trays were loaded not only with honey and pistachio pastries and locally grown fruits but also with fragrant melons imported from Persia in lead containers packed with ice. All this was served in gem-studded gold and silver vessels, by pretty slave girls wearing colorful silks. The olfactory menu was as carefully planned, with jasmine and myrtle strewn around the room and musk and ambergris burning in gold bowls. Throughout the evening musicians and dancers entertained the guests, who added to the

drama of the occasion by clever poetic improvisations. Zubaydah was always the star of her production in her opulent
garments and jewel-studded shoes, which set the fashion of the
day.

Aside from her tardiness in producing an heir to the throne,
she fell seriously short of being the ideal wife only once—by
involving her relatives in a domestic quarrel. One day she
complained to her uncles that Harun was spending too much
time with a songstress. Unable to ignore the queen's pleas, the
men broached the subject diplomatically with Harun. The
good-natured caliph took them to hear the singer in order to
prove that he was more interested in her art than in her sexual
charms. The men came back agreeing that the woman was
indeed a first-class artist and that it would be a shame to deprive any music-loving soul of her performances. Embar-
rassed, Zubaydah presented her husband with a kiss-and-make-
up gift of ten slave girls, among whom were the future mothers of princes who would compete against the queen's own son
for the caliphate. Zubaydah went along with what was expected of women by serving her husband's pleasure, even if
she had to do so by proxy.

Zubaydah was fortunate enough to keep, if not monopolize,
her husband's affections until the end of his days. Numerous
courtesans and princesses lived neglected and frustrated in the
harem. Many were kept merely as evidence of their master's
prestige and never summoned to his bed. On rare occasions
even the caliphs' sisters were condemned to celibacy or forced
marriage on their brothers' political or personal whims. As
illicit love affairs often brought death to the concubine and
divorce to the nonslave offender, they had to be conducted
with the utmost secrecy, which was difficult in the spy-ridden
palace. Money bought the silence of a few eunuchs. The veil
sometimes helped in evading the ever-watchful eyes of the
others, as the story of Princess Abbassa suggests. Her brother
Harun had forced her to contract a paper marriage with his
vizier, Jafar, in order to deflect scandalous gossip that stemmed

from the two men's very close friendship. Although the princess was never allowed to be alone with the handsome young minister, she fell in love with him. Disguised as a veiled maidservant, she finally managed to visit him several times in his chamber. So successfully did she hide her subsequent pregnancy that not even her husband knew of the birth of her child, who was smuggled out by her allies to a foster mother in Mecca. But rumors about Abbassa's child eventually reached the caliph, who ordered him back to the palace. Enraged by the resemblance he saw between the child and the vizier, he ordered both put to death. It was useless for the princess to plead her Islamic rights in marriage. Harun merely spared her the humiliation of a public execution by sending a eunuch to strangle her in her apartment.[6]

Lesbians were also punished by death, even though Islamic law called only for imprisonment for homosexuality (iv,15). Harun's harem shuddered to remember a variation on the biblical story of Salome and John the Baptist which had been enacted a few years earlier during the reign of their master's brother Al-Hadi. When Caliph Al-Hadi was entertaining friends one evening, a servant came in and whispered something in his ear. The caliph asked the guests to wait and disappeared. After quite a while he returned, extremely upset, followed by a slave carrying a towel-covered tray. When he calmed down, the caliph ordered the towel removed. On the tray were the heads of two beautiful young women, whose jewels sparkled in the pool of their own blood. "I was informed that they were lovers and set my spies to watch them. I caught them in the immoral act and killed them myself," the caliph explained, and ordered the party to continue.[7] The episode must have given the loneliest woman cause for hesitation. Totally dependent on a man and unable to defend her rights, she continued to live like a precious stone locked in a jewelry box and brought out only at her owner's pleasure, as testimony to his wealth and power.

The empire did offer women some advantages which even-

tually served the feminist cause. If imperial success taught
Muslims to adopt harems, it also exposed them to the world's
oldest civilizations. Their voracious appetite for studying these
ancient cultures and building on them harmonized conveniently with the Islamic commandment for women as well
as men to acquire knowledge. Better yet, wealth gave them
access to the best scholars, and the leisure to study for the first
time in their history. The aristocratic harem played an important role in the Muslim woman's education by freeing her
from chores outside the house and by exposing her to learned
courtesans, who were as sought after as the musicians and
dancers. Harun al-Rashid is said to have paid a fortune for
Tawaddud, a slave girl who passed with flying colors the
stiff examination given her by the foremost scholars on as-
tronomy, medicine, law, philosophy, music, history, Arabic
grammar, literature, theology, and chess. Even if the claim
smacks of *Arabian Nights* exaggeration, it does emphasize the
high level of general education expected of the upper classes
and the value placed on women scholars. Many an educated
noblewoman found her raison d'être as patroness of the arts
and sciences. By subsidizing the education of young slave girls
and princesses in her charge and by gathering the best scholars
and artists in her salon, she contributed to the blossoming of
Arab civilization in the Middle Ages.

A princess or a courtesan who could attract the caliph himself to her salon wielded much power as a lobbyist. Indeed, a
few made and broke caliphs. The most famous of these rare
few was Khayzuran, whose life reads like a composite of all
women of the Arab empire who attained success by exploiting
the harem system.[8] Her name, which meant "a slender and
graceful reed," described her figure aptly in her early teens,
when she was yet in a slave dealer's hands. Lacking musical
and poetic talents, she was sent only to a mosque school,
where religious scholars gave free classes to the public in the
Quran, Arabic, and whatever other subjects they knew. One
day her graceful and sprightly beauty caught the eyes of

Caliph Mansur, Harun al-Rashid's grandfather. He bought her for his young son Mahdi, who already had a harem of superbly talented musicians and dancers.

Although Khayzuran got along very well with her teenage master, she was shrewd enough to realize that she would not last long on luck alone amid such formidable rivals. She therefore studied with the best teachers in the palace and cultivated relationships with the most respected and influential members of the harem hierarchy. In music and poetry Khayzuran remained at best an educated amateur, but she applied her learning to practical situations with elegance and a sense of humor that the sunny-natured Mahdi appreciated. When Mahdi was indisposed, for example, she did not dispatch a long-faced messenger to inquire solemnly after his health, as was the general custom. She sent him instead an exquisite young girl bearing a crystal goblet of rare wine. As the patient sipped the wine, he could read the get-well message inscribed on the goblet: "When you have recovered your health and have improved it further by this drink from this cup, then be gracious to her who sent it, by paying her a visit after sunset." So delighted was Mahdi, it is said, that he called on Khayzuran soon afterward and spent two whole days with her—a rare honor for any woman in an overpopulated palace harem.

Frequent honors of this sort gave Khayzuran two sons— Musa and Harun—and eventually an unusual promotion to the status of legal wife and queen. But she was not yet assured of becoming queen mother, since many other women had also borne sons to the reigning caliph. Like an ambitious stage mother, Khayzuran exploited all of her connections to gain her end. She organized elegant literary and musical soirees to please the right princesses. Through them she hoped to gain the goodwill and support of important members of the royal house. But above all, she did everything to keep her husband charmed. She finally scored a double triumph. After Mahdi's death her elder son, Musa, succeeded as Caliph Al-Hadi, followed by the younger, Harun al-Rashid.

As queen mother, Khayzuran became the most powerful woman in the empire by virtue of her power over her son. Seekers of political favors hovered constantly at her door. So confident was she of her influence on her son that she often granted requests on her own authority and asked the caliph only to rubber-stamp her decisions. Although she was generally credited with a keen nose for talent, she did secure a governorship for her barely literate peasant brother, and occasionally succumbed to other acts of flagrant nepotism. Finally tired of being ordered around by his mother, Al-Hadi threatened to behead any man who loitered around Khayzuran's door, and warned his mother that "it is not dignified for women to enter upon affairs of state."

Her demotion was only temporary. When Al-Hadi fell seriously ill, Khayzuran forced his little son Jaafer to renounce his claim to the caliphate at swordpoint and arranged for the succession of her favorite son, Harun. There are even rumors that she sent her slaves to poison the ailing Al-Hadi.

Under her younger son's rule Khayzuran once again played Lady Bountiful to favor seekers, and shared the administration of the empire with the grand vizier (prime minister), who was wise enough to consult her on state and palace affairs. So powerful was she that only after her death did Harun raise to power a few persons whom his mother had disliked. He also inherited from her the greatest wealth that any woman in the Muslim world of her day had possessed. Indeed, she had been the richest person in the empire, next to her son. Her influence had extended so far beyond the walls of the palace during her lifetime that the royal cemetery where she was buried came to be called Khayzuran's Cemetery.

The larger-than-life adventures of Khayzuran and other palace women set the style for the women of the wealthy merchant and professional classes. But their chances of languishing unnoticed in a smaller harem were much less, and they were free from the all-consuming and often hazardous occupation of placing a son on the throne, since all sons shared more or less equally in the father's wealth in accordance with Quranic law. The paradoxically feminist advantages of the harem system emerged more clearly, therefore, among this group. They did not always have to achieve success through men, for the harem system opened careers in professions to them. Medicine was one of the most important, for obvious reasons, and it consisted of much more than basic training in midwifery.[9] Regarded as the most advanced by Christians and Muslims alike, Arab medicine of the Middle Ages required many years of training in anatomy, physiology, and botany, which women received in reputable medical schools.

Since medicine was usually a family enterprise in those days, as were rug weaving and other crafts, a woman medical school graduate often apprenticed herself to her father or uncle in order to learn their trade secrets and eventually entered group practice with them. But while her brother paraded down the main street in voluminous turbans and flowing silk robes, wearing the contemplative expression of a doctor of medicine, she was often indistinguishable from a midwife or any other woman in an anonymous veil as she scurried along the rear alleys to reach her harembound patients. She must have passed on to the male doctors in her family the fruits of her experience with women patients, but none of the Arab medical treatises which have survived to our day bear her signature, although some do cite women surgeons and mention that a few also taught in medical schools in Salerno and other Italian cities.[10]

One consolation for her anonymity was that no man could take away her job in the harem, whereas she was allowed to treat men as well. Her male competitors were allowed into the harem only if she could not help a patient. Since curing the master of the house usually brought a greater honorarium than curing his dearest wife or concubine, male doctors tended to earn more than their women colleagues, but a woman doctor's income was not negligible.

Although some women were trained as instructors of reli-

gion for girls, at least a few are known to have gone beyond
serving women alone to become professors and judges of Islamic law for both sexes.[11] The most famous among them is
Shuhda, who was considered one of the greatest authorities on
the Hadith in twelfth-century Baghdad. Prominent men came
to her lectures and honored her as "the scholar" and "the
Pride of Women." Amat al-Wahid, daughter of a Baghdad
judge, studied Islamic law under her father and gained fame
as a brilliant judge. Though it is not clear exactly how these
women influenced the shaping of the Shariah, it is doubtful
that anyone came to them to protest against harems and veils,
which would have been tantamount to lodging a formal com-
plaint against whalebone corsets or spike heels. Like those
Western items, the veil was worn mostly by those who did not
have to labor, regardless of how the Quran was interpreted.
Nor does the women's right to occupy public space for professional purposes seem to have been an important issue in bour-
geois circles, where a woman tended to enter her family's
profession and work under their protection.

This is not to say that the harem laws were accepted with
full complacence by nonslave women. There were many
gradations in observance of these rules, according to social
status and personal inclination. Famous artists and spoiled
daughters of wealthy aristocrats sometimes rebelled completely. Significantly, the latter group included the Prophet's
relatives, who were so honored and endowed with the right
family connections that men stumbled over one another to
marry them no matter how boldly the ladies flouted conven-
tion. Indeed, Ali's granddaughter, Sukaynah of Medina, is
said to have made complete freedom of action a condition for
accepting a marriage proposal.[12] The beautiful woman who
ran one of the most distinguished salons in the early eighth
century apparently did not lack suitors, for she married so
many times that the number of her ex-husbands "could not be
counted on the fingers of two hands." More restrained in her
marital activities but no less rebellious was Aysha bint Talhah

of Taif, near Mecca and Medina, the niece of the Prophet's wife Aysha. The younger Aysha categorically refused to obey her husband's orders to veil herself. "Since God hath put upon me the stamp of beauty," she said, "it is my wish that the public should view that beauty and thereby recognize His grace unto them." It may have helped these headstrong women to live in Arabia, away from the center of Persian and Byzantine influences and the caliphs' court, but being independently wealthy and socially well connected helped numerous women in Damascus and Baghdad, too. Many men depended on their wives' relations for political and professional advancement.

The liberated woman par excellence, the one who counted solely on her own talents rather than on family connections or sexual seduction, was the freelance artist. One of the best-known in Baghdad during the reign of Caliph Al-Mutawakkil was the poetess Al-Fadl.[13] Having come to Baghdad from central Arabia on her own in the hope of breaking into the glittering world of poetry, Al-Fadl made a brilliant debut in the aristocratic salons of the capital, which soon led to command performances in the caliph's court. So impressed was the caliph with the clever ways in which she capped the difficult verses he gave her that he rewarded her with hundreds of pieces of gold. With fees like that she was financially independent and did not marry, preferring to take lovers openly. Like today's Hollywood actresses, she was evidently beyond the pale of morality ordained for the rest of womankind. And the public was tickled by her free-spirited love affairs, which were like dramatic interpretations of other women's fantasies and of her much admired love poems.

Occasionally she was criticized for refusing to bow to the sexual double standard. At one party a man presented her with a verse: "I prefer a horse that has not been broken in. What a difference between an untouched pearl and one that has been pierced and threaded into a necklace." Al-Fadl retorted in the same rhyme and meter: "But it is not pleasant to ride a horse that has not yet been disciplined by the bridle nor known a rider. And pearls are useless unless they have been pierced and arranged on a thread."[14] During the Prophet Muhammad's time she might have been a warrior or a social critic. Among women living in gilded cages she had to devote her talents to the concerns of the boudoir. But she did so far more on her own terms.

Only saints managed to escape totally from the wine-woman-and-song tyranny of the day. One of them—Rabia al-Adawiya,[15] born in Basra (in today's Iraq) in 717—developed a mystic approach to the practice of Islam which eventually gained popularity as Sufism. Free from the pressures of marrying because she was an ex-slave without family, Rabia turned away from her contemporaries' fixation on the earthly paradise of the caliphs and retired to a life of poverty, chastity, and prayer—despite Muhammad's disapproval of monasticism. Unlike many other devout Muslims of the day, Rabia held that obsession with heaven and hell was time stolen from loving God Himself. "First the Neighbor, then the house," she stressed repeatedly, in preaching, during her eighty years of life, a totally disinterested love which would lead to union with the Divine Force. This is the ultimate goal of the Sufis, most of whom acknowledge their debt to Rabia's teachings and quote her as one of their highest authorities. Simple folk in need of miracles attribute her with the power to speak with wild animals and to make prayer rugs fly.

The saint's influence reached the palace, too. When Sufism took root after her death, princesses built convents which provided religious education for all women and refuge for the divorced and abandoned ones. Although Rabia's effect on the royal women of her day is not specified, both Khayzuran and Zubaydah responded to the thread of Muslim piety that ran through their materialistic society. Khayzuran worked hard to find the house where the Prophet was born, purchased it, and converted it into the Mosque of the Nativity. Zubaydah spent her personal fortune to make life safer and more comfortable for pilgrims to Mecca. She constructed and repaired roads leading from Baghdad to Mecca, and built wells and hostels along the way. Both queens also had wells dug and fountains, canals, and aqueducts built—all of them major projects, since they were hard to construct and maintain in the desert, where the wind and sand constantly threatened to erase them. As pilgrims from all over the empire quenched their thirst at these wells and peasants irrigated their sun-scorched lands with water from these canals, they praised the generous Khayzuran and Zubaydah.

Their bequest of water to the desert also lasted as a monument to the role that women played in the flowering of Islamic civilization. Their jewel-studded garments and wine goblets; their banquets in the jasmine-scented harem; their concerts and poetry readings on dolphin-shaped boats or in a courtyard of gold trees adorned with chirping mechanical birds of silver; their political intrigues; and their schools, hospitals, and libraries turned to ashes when the Tatars from Central Asia sacked Baghdad in 1258.

But the Islamic culture was not lost forever. The Ottoman Turks took over the vestiges of the Arab empire and recreated the splendors of the Baghdad caliphate on the shores of the Bosphorus. Non-Arab as well as Arab Muslims looked upon the Arab civilization of the Middle Ages as the golden age of Islam, and therefore a part of their own proud heritage. In a way they were right, since the Arab civilization was a composite formed by the natives of lands extending from the Mediterranean basin all the way to India. The place that women held during the Arab caliphate thus set the ideal for subsequent generations of Muslim women.

Subsequent generations did not always remember the whole picture, however. The brilliant women judges and free-living poetesses were trotted out only when needed to prove Muslim women intelligent, while the unveiled craftswomen and farmers who made up the bulk of the population faded into the background as part of the crew of millions who made genteel life behind veils and latticed windows of the harem possible for a few. It is these few who were remembered and emulated well into the twentieth century as the epitome of aristocratic femininity and Islamic morality. So strong a fascination did this ideal exercise on Muslims in many parts of the world that the less wealthy also clamored to follow at least its most visible aspects as their standard of living improved. If they could not afford to educate their women and shut them out of the world at the same time, they condemned them to an untutored existence behind harem walls. Yet seclusion was imbued with so many layers of meaning that the victims themselves often helped perpetuate the system. For many a poor woman who toiled in the scorching sun, "to sit at home" sipping tea with the ladies of the neighborhood was a fond dream, and continues to be in some of the remoter areas of the Islamic world, untouched by the fever of mass education. Early rebellion against the traditional ideal could therefore emerge only among the secluded but superbly educated aristocratic women of the Ottoman Empire.

3

𝍖𝍖𝍖𝍖𝍖𝍖𝍖𝍖𝍖𝍖

Women in
the Ottoman Era

Turkish Ladys . . . are perhaps freer than any Ladys
in the universe. . . .
—Lady Mary Wortley Montagu, 1718

Unlike our grandmothers, who accepted without
criticism their written fate, we analysed our life. . . .
—Zeyneb Hanoum, 1906

"A remarkable thing which I saw in this country was the respect shown to women by the Turks, for they hold a more
dignified position than the men,"[1] Ibn Battuta, a famous Arab
travel writer of the mid-fourteenth century, wrote upon visiting one of the small Turkish sultanates in Anatolia. He was
scandalized that these Central Asian people did not segregate
the sexes, even though they had embraced Islam as far back as
their nomadic days. Not only was the public square a be-
wildering sea of female faces, but the royal court was presided
over by the sultan and his khatuns, or queens, who issued
decrees jointly: "By order of the Sultan and the Khatuns . . ."
Nor was women's power an empty formality, the Arab discovered when the queens and the princesses invited him
openly into their private apartments to pose statesmanlike

questions on the lands he had seen. Less than a century later, these idyllic scenes remained only in Ibn Battuta's chronicle.

Turks eventually discovered the neighboring Byzantine and Arab civilizations. When they united under the Ottoman dynasty to capture Constantinople (Istanbul) in 1453, and within the following century most of the territories which were formerly ruled by the Arab caliphs, they had the power and the money to emulate more fully the ways of the conquered, including the harem and the veil. These old status symbols of the Byzantine and Arab societies had by then been sanctified as Islamic among many of the Arabs. The Turkish sultan eventually assumed the title of caliph and granted considerable power to theologians, who interpreted the Shariah more and more conservatively in matters regarding women. Through a religious "Supreme Court" sexual segregation was enforced in the cities with the convert's zeal. The palaces segregated women in harems guarded by eunuchs; the wealthy followed suit.[2] Edicts were issued periodically well into the nineteenth century, specifying the type of veil and garment to be worn by women outside their homes.[3] Transparent face veils and coats came in for official attack, and a decree of A.H. 1165 (A.D. 1751–52) even threatened to hang dressmakers who continued making the forbidden garments. Finally women were banned from certain shops and areas of the city, ostensibly to discourage prostitution. Nor were they permitted to walk or ride with men, not even with their fathers and sons.

It was impractical to enforce these commands in rural areas, where women toiled in the fields. Though they were not obeyed to the letter in the cities either, the laws effectively banished women from the masculine world of business and politics, confining them to weaving, midwifery, and other tasks compatible with sexual segregation. The few who ran shops and market stalls usually did so under heavy veils. The most rigorously secluded were concubines in the sultan's palaces and free Turkish women of the upper classes, who could afford the luxury of slaves and covered carriages.

Life for the Turkish woman in the sumptuous villas of Istanbul became an endless round of parties relieved only by study, good works, and an occasional business venture, as limited as the old world of the Baghdad princesses. It might have remained so had not the Western world begun its ascendance. During the Arab caliphate and a good part of the Ottoman era the Islamic world was the widely acknowledged fount of science and culture to which the most open-minded of the Europeans looked for inspiration. Even the Turkish woman's lot was admired and envied by European ladies. "Turkish Ladys . . . are perhaps freer than any Ladys in the universe" wrote Mary Montagu in 1718,[4] when she was the British ambassador's wife in Istanbul. Though she enviously catalogued her Turkish friends' "emeralds as big as Turkey eggs" and other fabulous jewels which would make the English queens' ornaments look mean by comparison, Mary Montagu herself was too wealthy and strong-willed to equate material luxury alone with freedom. What the lady, who used to match wits with Alexander Pope back home, admired was the Turkish women's enlightened approach to health care, which relieved them from many of the burdens borne fatalistically by European women. For instance, Turkish women resumed their normal activities shortly after giving birth instead of remaining needlessly in bed for a long time after each delivery, as was the custom among the wealthy English. Turkish women escaped the disfiguring smallpox because they accepted vaccination, which the English refused until Edward Jenner "invented" it more than seventy years later.

Lady Montagu saw an advantage in the harem system, too. Since the ultimate in feminine success at this time in both the East and the West was not to enter the professions but to be mistress of a wealthy home, she approved highly of the independence from men's authority that sexual segregation made possible. Contrary to popular Western belief, the master of the house was only a guest in the harem and rarely interfered in its internal affairs. He could not even enter his wife's apartment if he saw a woman guest's slippers outside her door.

Under such circumstances, Lady Montagu noted, "Turkish Ladys have at least as much . . . Liberty as Ladys amongst us." Although harem residents made each other's business very much their own and punishment for adultery could be severe, the ambassadress added that particularly determined women with trusted servants and friends had "opportunitys of gratifying their evil Inclinations (if they have any)."[5] They could, for example, travel incognito behind veils, and even send love tokens. Instead of resorting to incriminating letters, they dispatched objects which symbolized verses expressing their feelings. A match stick meant "I burn, my flame consumes me"; a blank sheet of paper "I faint every hour"; and a gold wire "I die; come quickly."[6]

About a century later another Englishwoman named Lucy Garnett applauded the Turkish woman's Islamic rights. The fact that polygamy was rare outside the palace harems was immaterial, Mrs. Garnett noted as she underlined the advantages of being wife number two rather than a mistress without any legal protection for herself or her offspring. Being number two in a Muslim marriage, she added, was actually better than being number one in holy Christian matrimony, for the Christian laws of Europe forced the wife to give up to the husband her rights over her own person and property in exchange for having her children declared legitimate and given the necessary sustenance. Mrs. Garnett shuddered to think that such an arrangement was the best her society could offer a woman. Mistresses and servants in Europe, she noted, were worse off than the female slaves of the Ottoman Empire. Not only was a slave girl treated kindly and married off with a pension after five to seven years of service, but any child she bore to the master was legitimate and could inherit from his father. Indeed, she concluded, women of every station were better off under Islamic protection.[7]

Meanwhile, Europe moved at a brisk pace from the Renaissance to the Enlightenment and to the Industrial and French Revolutions, which inspired new ideals of individual freedom and equality as well as new hopes for women. The Ottoman Empire was on the wane. With its vitality sapped by centuries of restrictive laws and customs as well as abandonment to luxuries, it could not effectively defend its vast colonies against the European powers. By the eighteenth century the Ottomans had fully realized that their way was no longer the best and that they would have to adapt to the times in order to survive. Accordingly, they looked to the West for technological help and education, which necessitated a knowledge of European languages. The fastest way up the Ottoman hierarchy was no longer through the knowledge of Islamic religion and culture, but of the infidels' tongues and sciences. The Islamic schools, which had had exclusive control of education until then, lost their most talented young men to secular schools at home and in Europe. The result was a new breed of highly Western-oriented leaders and intellectuals who shaped the *Tanzimat* (Reform), a forty-year period of reforms launched in 1839 with a decree providing for new penal and commercial laws based on the Napoleonic code, as well as a proclamation upholding the equality of all subjects regardless of race or creed.[8] These edicts naturally paved the way for the abolition of slavery, which eventually eliminated the system of concubinage, the Turkish woman's biggest competition for her husband's attentions and a drain on her children's inheritance.

Though the laws did not specifically touch on other aspects of women's status, the Tanzimat unleashed a passionate debate on the subject among the Westernized intellectuals. The Turkish woman, who had been considered very privileged not long ago, appeared a prisoner in the light of the new ideals. The most prominent male writers of the period published books and articles defending her right to go to school and to practice a wider variety of professions. The formation of constitutional governments in 1876 and 1908, though short-lived, raised aspirations and spurred even bolder demands for women. In a book entitled *Feminism in Islam* (*Islamiyette Feminism*), which he published in 1910, Halil Hamit argued for women's suffrage. Five years later Celal Nuri suggested in his book *Our Women (Kadinlarimiz)* that polygamy be formally abolished by the caliph. Ahmet Agaoglu, a highly respected intellectual of the late Ottoman era, summed up the most pressing argument in favor of these demands: that women's emancipation, along with public education, was the most important prerequisite to progress in the Islamic world. Moreover, these rights were in accordance with the tenets of pure Islam cleansed of misinterpretations. Another eminent intellectual, Zia Gokalp,[9] went one step further to justify women's emancipation in light of the Turks' ethnic roots, harking back to the free nomadic ancestors of Central Asia. His arguments would form the intellectual backdrop of the Turkish Republic in the 1920s.

But neither the Tanzimat nor the two constitutions went so far as to grant the liberals' demands. Reforms did not go beyond granting higher education to women. In 1858 this meant the opening of the first middle school for girls. In 1870 the government established the first teachers' college for girls, which was a post-middle-school training institute rather than a university. European and American schools also proliferated, but women had to wait until 1914 to be admitted to the university. At first very few families saw any use in keeping daughters in school beyond the primary grades, but as these pioneers gradually replaced the elderly schoolmasters who had been hired for lack of qualified women, they helped popularize education for girls.

Women teachers might have been available sooner had the privately tutored aristocratic ladies been willing—or allowed—to work outside their homes. But in the latter half of the nineteenth century many of them kept their daughters secluded in the harem with governesses. Nevertheless, it was these daughters who grew up to forge the intellectual groundwork for women's emancipation, much more boldly than did their brothers, and thus complemented the work of the humbler schoolmistresses devoted to teaching basic reading skills

to the masses. What inspired the daughters most was the intense exposure to new Western ideas that they received
through their European governesses.

Though Turkish fathers who had been influenced by the
Tanzimat had their women wear the best Paris fashions in the
privacy of their homes and took them to the most elegant
capitals of Europe, they expected the governesses to give their
daughters much more than charm-school training. They
wanted their daughters to have serious Occidental and Oriental education, as befitted the future spouses of important men.
The best European women teachers were attracted to the
villas on the Bosphorus by generous salaries and luxurious
living accommodations. English and German women were
considered serious and therefore good models for the Turkish
lady, although French governesses maintained the popularity
that they had won after Empress Eugénie's visit to Istanbul in
1869. Instead of debating the merits of each nationality, many
families simply engaged tutors for each subject of study to
supplement the talents of a live-in governess or two.

The phenomenal variety of courses that this arrangement
offered young women was described by Emine Foat Tugay,
the great-great-granddaughter of Muhammad Ali, the Ottoman pasha who came to be honored as the founder of modern
Egypt while he ruled it between 1805 and 1849. Growing up in
the early twentieth century, Emine and her brothers learned
German and basic academic courses with their German fräu-
lein. Twice a week a Scotswoman and a Frenchwoman came
for two hours each to give English and French lessons. A
Turkish teacher came on alternate days for Turkish, Persian,
and Arabic languages, as well as calligraphy and Islamic history. The children got a break from all these studies several
times a week through gymnastics drills and piano lessons from
European tutors. "In the evening we showed our homework to
my mother, who, after minutely inspecting it, would dispense
praise or reproof," Emine wrote in her memoirs.[10] As if this
were not enough, the music-loving parents took her to matinee

performances of ballet and opera every day while vacationing in Germany, so that before she was ten years old she had seen almost all of Wagner's operas.

Among the most fortunate results of European education were the frank records that many women left about their lives. Unlike their mothers, who expressed themselves through the nightingales and roses of formal Turkish poetry, the daughters wrote letters, memoirs, newspaper articles, and novels, thanks to the European literary influence. Indeed, prose freed women's thoughts to such an extent that it created a psychological climate for social change, all the more powerfully because their writings could be printed and circulated to help unite harembound women. (A ban on printing in Islamic languages —Turkish, Arabic, Persian—had been lifted in the eighteenth century.)

Emine was still too young at the close of the Ottoman era to have done much more than worry about her homework. But Zeyneb Hanoum (*Hanoum* means "lady"), a diplomat's daughter, was painfully aware of the contradictions in which her modern Occidental education trapped her. "If you only knew the disastrous consequences of that learning and the suffering for which it is responsible!"[11] she lamented in one of the many letters that she wrote to a Scots friend between 1906 and 1908. Irritated by the endless round of social visits as well as the quieter embroidery and storytelling evenings which kept her elders contented, Zeyneb abandoned herself totally to reading Western authors and critically reassessing her life.

She had enjoyed a perfectly happy and carefree childhood until at age ten she discovered what it meant to be female: a slightly older friend was suddenly withdrawn from their games and pony-riding excursions, to be allowed outside only under a thick black veil. "We cried for her as if she had died,"[12] recalled Zeyneb, whose turn came soon after. She was heartbroken at not being allowed to run outdoors whenever she fancied, without having to worry about the veil and the thousand other details intended to keep her cloistered even on the streets. She could no longer drop in at an open-air theater on her summer-evening drives without arranging first for a place in latticed boxes. Despite the better life promised by official reforms, it seemed to her that the condition of women was deteriorating. In her grandmother's youth, in the mid-1800s, women could get away with translucent white face veils. Fifty years later they had to wear the thick black shroud.

Unlike Mary Montagu and her Turkish friends who were content to be left to themselves in the harem, Zeyneb longed for a true companionship with men as she grew up. "The Turks have all the qualities necessary to make good husbands," she stressed, "and yet we have no opportunity of knowing even the men we marry until we are married."[13] Even then, a deep spiritual communion between husband and wife was difficult in a polygamous household. A pasha's wife who shared her husband with many concubines confessed to Zeyneb: "It would be easy to forgive the physical empire that each in turn has over my husband, but what I feel most is that he does not consult me in preference to the others." "She read a great deal in the evening when she was alone, alas, only too often,"[14] Zeyneb noted, thanking God that polygamy was quite rare except in the palace.

Other things could also be rivals for the husband's attention in a sexually segregated society. A young Turkish bride could be in for a rude shock if she waited for her husband to come home to a candlelit dinner for two in the fashion of the European romances she had read. He often arrived with his men friends and called for more places at the table. Not allowed to receive men unrelated to her, the wife was obliged to disappear into the harem. "To these Oriental women were given more jewels than liberty, more sensual love than pure affection."[15] Zeyneb wrote. The Turkish woman's traditional expectations of marriage which Mary Montagu liked so much had been shattered by Western romanticism.

Seeing Zeyneb restless, her grandmother remarked: "Your young days are so much sadder than mine. At your age I didn't think of . . . raising the status of women. Our mothers taught us the Koran, and we had confidence in its laws. If one of us had less happiness than another, we never thought of revolting. 'It was written' we said, and we had not the presumption to try to change our destiny."[16]

Zeyneb wanted to scream her agony to the world, and she found a most willing listener in Pierre Loti, the French writer-diplomat stationed in Istanbul. Unable to rebel openly against sexual segregation, she saw him secretly to give him the details of harem life that he needed for his book. These rendezvous produced the novel *Les Désenchantées* (1906), which describes the malaise of a Turkish woman whose brain had leaped to the twentieth century while her body remained imprisoned by medieval customs.

To avoid scandal, Zeyneb fled to Europe with her sister shortly before the novel appeared. She had been dying to taste Western freedom, which emboldened her further to ignore tradition that deemed it inappropriate for a Muslim woman to travel abroad without a chaperone. "For the first time in our lives we could look freely into space—no veil, no iron bars,"[17] she wrote exuberantly upon arriving in Nice. In Paris she felt like a child again as she wandered freely around the streets and rode buses.

Young, beautiful, and fresh from an exotic harem, Zeyneb naturally became a much-sought-after guest in Paris society. She in turn was equally fascinated by the strange female denizens of "le tout Paris." Try as she did, she could not be comfortable with the senselessly chattering ladies who rushed nervously about the soirees courting attention from men they hardly knew and falling into their embrace in front of everyone. "I suppose we Turkish women, who have so much time to devote to culture, become unreasonably exacting,"[18] Zeyneb noted. Sadly indifferent to the cultural treasures of their land, Parisians seemed obsessed with only one topic—who was sleeping with whom. "Everyone seems eager to get married," she added, "in spite of the thousand and one living examples there are to warn others of what it really is."[19]

All this foolishness was a tolerable abuse of liberty, however. What disillusioned her about the ideals of the French Revolution was a bout with illness in Paris. Unable to stand the pain, she asked the concierge to get her a doctor, only to be told that one risked being assassinated in the streets at 2 A.M. The refusal was followed up by a letter from her landlord the next day warning her not to disturb the concierge in the middle of the night. She remembered with mixed emotions her countrymen, who would not let women move about freely in the streets but would go to any length to help the sick and the needy.

In London Zeyneb looked forward to meeting the suffragists who worked so hard for the ideals in which she fervently believed. But they disappointed her too. They struggled all their lives to escape the tyranny of home and social conventions. They fought for the right to live on their own, to travel as they liked, to be responsible for their own lives. But they did not seem happy. "The only harvest they reap after a youth of struggle is that of disenchantment," she noted, "yet I ask myself, is a lonely old age worth a youth of effort? Have they not confused individual liberty, which is the right to live as one pleases, with true liberty, which to my Oriental mind is the right to choose one's own joys and forbearances?"[20] Women's emancipation, she concluded, would be a tug-of-war between working within a restrictive but lovingly protective patriarchal fold and rejecting it to stand alone in a man's world. For all their lofty political ideals, Europe offered no solution to the woman's dilemma. It gave mere palliatives—a lifetime of struggle for abstract principles of freedom which might turn out to be a mirage, or abandoning oneself to the ephemeral sexual "freedom" of the social butterflies.

Zeyneb's enchantment with Europe was over. She returned home, only to be unhappy with her old way of life. She had valuable insight into the problems inherent in the Middle Eastern woman's accepting her European sisters' version of emancipation,[21] but she was perhaps too far ahead of her time. She remained the symbol of the Turkish woman's bittersweet awakening to a new way of life without being able to escape the old, not only because she was forbidden to but also because she herself was confused. "What ought to have been accomplished in centuries we have done in three and sometimes in two generations,"[22] she said.

Unlike Zeyneb, who aired her complaints mostly to her friends and had her letters published only incidentally—and abroad—Fatma Aliyé wrote with the express purpose of publishing in her country. This in itself was revolutionary, tantamount to public unveiling, since in Turkey ladies were supposed to write only for the pleasure of their intimate circle. More significantly, Fatma Aliyé went on to earn public respect for women's brainpower by becoming one of the major professional writers of her day, proving herself equally at home with the "manly" subjects of philosophy and history and with feminist rights.

While she brought women out of the Ottoman era into the modern on the intellectual level, her private life remained strictly tradition-bound.[23] Born around 1862, a generation before Zeyneb, when Western education was yet the exclusive privilege of the empire's future leaders and technocrats, Fatma Aliyé had to prove her worthiness to study all that was taken for granted during Zeyneb's time. In the 1860s and '70s French was considered to be of doubtful merit for young ladies, who would not be dealing with foreign officials. The only other use for French, the clerics argued, was to open the way to Christianity or to novels, which were then a new and morally suspect foreign import. Why not stick to the time-honored harem education, consisting of the study of Islamic religion and poets and Middle Eastern music? Given the conservative climate prevailing during her childhood, it is all the more amazing that Fatma Aliyé grew up to be the prototype of the modern Turkish woman—without physically breaking out of the harem.

Trying to pinpoint the influences that shaped her, Fatma Aliyé's favorite tutor, an eminent writer named Ahmet Mithat, compiled her biography in the mid-1890s from her own essays and letters as well as his personal knowledge of her. What emerges from *The Birth of an Ottoman Woman Writer* (*Bir Muharrire-i Osmaniyenin Neseti*, A.H. 1311 [A.D. 1893–94]) and from the recollections of Fatma Aliyé's surviving relatives and friends is the overwhelming importance of men in the harembound woman's development. Even the poetesses of past centuries who looked to their hearts and gardens for inspiration had scholarly fathers who took more than a cursory interest in their daughters' studies. Now that education demanded a wider experience of the world, it was more crucial than ever to be guided by someone who had such an experience, which meant having the right men in one's life. Fatma Aliyé was fortunate in being the daughter of Ahmet Cevdet Pasha, a prominent statesman and historian, who always kept the doors to the men's quarter of his house open to her. He did not chase her away even when he had important guests. Little Fatma loved to listen to the men's conversation, which opened for her the new vistas about which the old generation of harem inmates knew little. Her favorite among her father's visitors was Mr. Eskin, an old British consul, who had a special rapport with children. He frequently invited her to visit him at his home. The friendship must have sharpened her appetite for more distant horizons, for she grew increasingly irritated with the precious manners and conversations of the harem. She followed a favorite manservant around if she had nothing else to do. "I never wanted to stay in the harem during my waking hours," Fatma Aliyé recalled.

Unwittingly perhaps, her father alienated her further from the harem by engaging the best minds of the day to tutor her. At first her education followed the traditional pattern, but when Fatma Aliyé learned French in secret and began to catch up with her older brother in his chemistry lessons, the pasha relented and ordered her to be educated on an equal footing with her brother. She thus joined the handful of Muslim girls who were pursuing a Western education at that time.

Her greatest fortune came with Ahmet Mithat, who nurtured her talent for writing not only for her own pleasure, as a traditionalist might have done, but also for publication, although she was clearly destined for the strict seclusion of the aristocratic harem.

Indeed, her father's iconoclasm did not extend beyond giving her French lessons, and the harem walls eventually closed in on Fatma Aliyé and shut men out of her life. She complained about the boring gossip and the endless social visits that she had to sit through with her mother. There was no one in the harem to discuss Descartes with. The outside world did finally come to her, in the form of a European woman, Mademoiselle Alfa, who smuggled in the forbidden novels. Having noticed that Mlle. Alfa had survived her voracious taste for novels, Fatma Aliyé wrote to Ahmet Mithat: "Shouldn't we also look for corrupting influences in the harem gossip about lovers?" She added that the traditional stories of boy meets girl and they live happily ever after misled the young much more than did the complex and often realistic plots of the good novels. On the contrary, she felt that novels were educational for women who were deprived of the chance to experience the outside world.

At eighteen, with her head full of novels describing ideal couples communicating spiritually with each other, Fatma Aliyé accepted an arranged marriage with Faik Pasha, aide-de-camp to Sultan Abdulhamid II. The matchmaker had reported that the groom knew French, which suggested that he might have liberal ideas. At worst he should be able to help her keep up with her French conversation or discuss Western philosophy, Fatma Aliyé reasoned. She was deceived. With his military training and high-school-level French, the pasha was no match for Fatima, either in French conversation or in philosophical discussions. His resentment of his wife's intellectual superiority finally exploded one day when he saw her reading the immoral novel. He snatched the book from her and tore it to pieces. True to tradition in the realm of personal relations, the obedient young wife put aside her studies for some years and devoted herself to the four daughters that she bore. The father and the teacher who had so lovingly nurtured her mind were powerless to intervene. Nor did Fatma find it suitable to complain to them.

She had not entirely given up hope of writing, however. Her chance came unexpectedly when she discovered that her husband had liked the novel *Volonté* by Georges Ohnet. "What if I translated it into Turkish?" she asked, as casually as possible. "Go ahead," he replied. Fatma could not believe her ears, but tested her luck further: "Would you let me publish it, too?" "Why not?" came the answer. In fact, the pasha himself planned to take lessons in French and other subjects in order to catch up to his wife. Perhaps the liberal ideas that the Tanzimat and the constitution of 1876 unleashed had finally affected him, too.

Her work caused a sensation when it appeared in the bookstores in 1890. The excellent translation satisfied the great thirst for Western culture, and the intelligentsia envied the translator's mastery of French, which was universally considered to be the key to the best in Western civilization. What intrigued the readers, however, was the translator's signature —"by a Woman." Despite this, they assumed the translator was a "he"—an exceptionally modest man or a joker. So sure were they that when the Woman's identity was finally disclosed, they simply laughed. Her father must have written it, some said, while others suspected her brother or her tutor to be the real author. In fact, Fatma Aliyé's conservative brother had disapproved of the venture from the start. Now what he had feared was happening: his sister was being talked about, and thus figuratively unveiled in public. Her father, however, had finally found his intellectual match. Permission to publish her work had unlocked talents that he had not suspected in her. "If my daughter were a man and had been educated accordingly in a more systematic manner, she could have been a genius," he declared, and he openly solicited her advice on his work thereafter. Whatever second thoughts her husband might have had about her "going public" he kept to himself when the great scholar began to spend hours each day with her in the library. She thus had the men of her family to help her with the logistics of doing business with the publishing world.

Having proven herself in a respectable manly literary endeavor, Fatma Aliyé lost no time in pouring out the frustrations that had been bottled up in her heart for so many years. The result was *Womanhood* (*Muhadarat*), a novel about a talented young woman who was prevented from realizing her full potential by backward traditions and laws. Published in 1892, the book made Fatma the first woman novelist in Turkey. In the same year she also published *Islamic Women* (*Nisvani Islam*), which was translated into both Arabic and French. Throughout her versatile career, which included books and articles on philosophy and history, the author returned again and again to feminist themes expounded in her first two original works: that women must be educated and allowed to participate in society and that Islam was being misinterpreted to deprive women of their rights.

She finally popularized her thoughts on the matter by establishing in 1895 one of Turkey's first and longest-lived newspapers for women by women—*A Newspaper for Ladies* (*Hanimlara mahsus gazete*). Fatma Aliyé's friends and relatives claim that she not only contributed articles to it under various pen names but also ran the paper under the name of Fatma Sadiyé (pronounced Shadiya). If this is so, Fatma Aliyé can be credited not only with a series of books on the free and powerful women of early Islam but also with encouraging Ottoman women to publish their books through the newspaper's printing house. In fact, her first book was encouragement enough, for its publication caused a veritable flood of novels and translations, as well as books on modern pedagogy and childcare. One woman, Behire Hakki Cendey, was bold enough to publish her autobiography in the early twentieth century. Women thus had a large hand in shaping the new Turkish prose.

Fatma Aliyé's newspaper also ushered in a flowering of feminist journalism. At least nine papers came out in Istanbul between 1908 and 1919. By then the number of French-educated women had proliferated enough to allow some of the papers to be published in both French and Turkish. Reflecting the editors' and writers' background, all of them looked resolutely westward for ideals of womanhood, harking back only to the days of the Prophet Muhammad to justify their demands in light of unadulterated Islam. So daringly did they pursue this editorial policy that, if stripped of the photos of veiled women and advertisements for corsets as well as instructions on complicated embroidery stitches, the Ottoman feminist papers could almost be mistaken for their American counterparts of today. For they also focused on:

THE NATURAL EQUALITY OF WOMEN

In order to prove this equality it is sufficient to show that man's and woman's brain are equal. If the woman's brain happens to be smaller, it is because she was deprived of mental exercise. An ordinary man is not considered inferior in status just because he is physically less developed than an athlete.[24]

CONSCIOUSNESS-RAISING

A good husband and an excellent father is one who knows how to do housework and care for children at least as well as do swallows and pigeons. . . . The couple must share in making and keeping the nest.[25]

We women blame our unhappiness on our idleness and want to help our men in their economic struggle.[26]

SUCCESS STORIES AND ROLE MODELS

In the U.S. it is now considered normal for women to work and participate in their society.[27]

Madame Marie Stopes, a suffragette leader, was named professor at the University of London.[28]

HEALTH

Health of the child depends on how the mother takes care of herself during pregnancy and postnatally.[29]

OPPORTUNITIES FOR THE READERS

Announcement of special university classes for women, offered for the first time.

Courses include one on women's rights and another on women's health.[30]

To this day women's liberation movements in the Islamic world echo the powerful arguments that the Ottoman journalists presented against:

THE LACK OF EDUCATIONAL OPPORTUNITIES

Islam gave women the right to education. Today we are deprived of that right.[31]

ARRANGED MARRIAGE

In a marriage contracted between two strangers, divorce is born at the wedding ceremony.[32]

UNILATERAL DIVORCE

When a man and a woman get married, they become partners in a business, so to speak. Business cannot flourish if it can be dissolved at any time at the whim of one partner. Why then should such a state of affairs be allowed to exist in marriage?[33]

The newspapers, sold either on newsstands or by subscription, enjoyed a wide circulation among literate people of both sexes. Letters to the editors indicated that the papers served a pressing need for women living through a difficult cultural transition period.[34] Not only did they interpret Western ideas for the Turkish woman's consumption, they also became a forum to unite the readers, each of whom had thought that she was alone in her frustration and confusion. The women enthusiastically took up the chance to communicate with one another. "For the first time I feel proud to be a woman," wrote one of them.

The Balkan and First World Wars catapulted these women into the outside world, to organize aid for the soldiers and fill vacancies left by men. True, the restrictive interpretation of the Shariah by the religious court held its grip on women's lives, and the sexes were still segregated. But the harem wall had cracked a little more. The woman who reached out to the world with her pen was giving way to one who would work freely in it.

Fatma Aliyé had been a symbol for Turkish women, as one who had freed herself intellectually from four centuries of harem tradition to prepare her people's minds for the modern era. She was succeeded by a new breed of woman, typified by Halidé Edib, a writer who defied the crumbling Ottoman regime and joined Ataturk's army to help establish a republic that would translate Fatma Aliyé's ideals into reality.

4

꠹꠹꠹꠹꠹꠹꠹꠹꠹꠹

National Liberation/
Women's Liberation

> Islam provides for the equality of the sexes.
> —Huda Sharawi,
> Egyptian feminist leader, 1925

> The weakness in our society lies in our indifference
> towards the status of women.
> —Mustafa Kemal Ataturk, 1923

"You are the first woman in Turkish history to be honored
with a death sentence for political treason," an officer arriving
from Istanbul told a fellow nationalist fighter, Halidé Edib, as
he bowed low to kiss her hand. An eminent writer and the
daughter of a palace official, Halidé was one of seven leading
nationalists to be condemned by the sultan for inciting the
Turks to resist his surrender to the Allied powers after World
War I. Glad to be rid of the cumbersome empire but determined to save Turkey from occupation, General Mustafa
Kemal had organized a rebel army in the steppes of Anatolia,
where Halidé had joined him. As an eloquent public speaker
and an adviser to Kemal, she was the most visible woman of
the revolution, but not the only one. Countless others left their

homes for the first time in their lives to fight for national independence—as nurses, ammunition carriers, and soldiers.[1]

Other parts of the Middle East had fallen into European hands after shaking off Ottoman domination, and there women played a no less decisive role in winning independence for their people. In Egypt, for example, aristocratic women stepped out of their luxurious harems on March 16, 1919, to demonstrate against the British occupation. They went on to organize more protest marches as well as strikes and boycotts while their poor sisters, working inconspicuously in the fields and factories, cut telephone wires and disrupted railway lines in order to hamper the movement of enemy troops until Egypt won independence in 1921–22.[2]

A quarter of a century later Algerian women joined their men to fight against the French colonizer. Covered by ample veils, they smuggled guns much more effectively than the men. Many of them unveiled for the first time in their lives to plant bombs in French cafés and shops, or to join the guerrillas. Two of them—Djamila Bouhired and Djamila Boupacha[3]— were tortured in a French prison, moving such famous Europeans as Pablo Picasso and Simone de Beauvoir to their defense and rallying world opinion to their nation's cause.

Throughout the Middle East and North Africa the story of women's liberation begins with their fight for their nations' independence, when they stepped out of their domestic roles for the first time in recent history. Once they had a taste of the larger world, they wanted to stay in it, but serious obstacles stood in their way. Sexual segregation, which had limited their educational and professional opportunities for centuries, could not be lifted totally so long as women's virtue was measured by their compliance with this practice. Nor did early marriage and abuses of Islamic family law favor woman's liberation, for the husband's right to take more than one wife and repudiate them at will condemned women to ulcerous insecurity. Fortunately, however, women's new hopes were compatible with their independent countries' efforts to catch up with the industrialized West. Since women were needed to work outside the home, influential men took up the feminist cause.

Women were particularly fortunate in countries that were led by powerful male feminists. The first and the most revolutionary of such men was Mustafa Kemal, who came to be honored as Ataturk (Father of the Turks) when he established the Republic of Turkey in 1923, with himself as its elected president.

Reasoning that over the centuries the Shariah had gathered too many barnacles of theological misinterpretation and local custom to be cleared away fast enough to meet the young nation's needs, Ataturk boldly separated church from state for the first time in Islamic history and eliminated all legal distinction between men and women. According to the new scheme, the Shariah was to remain within the bounds of the secular state law. Women's life was thus to be governed mainly by a civil code adopted from Neuchâtel, Switzerland, which abolished polygamy, set a minimum age for marriage, and gave equal rights to both sexes in divorce and child custody as well as inheritance. To his critics he stressed that he was not abolishing Islam but merely closing the loopholes which had led to abuse. "Nothing in our religion requires women to be inferior to men,"[4] he repeated, reminding them that Turkish women had been Muslim and free before the growth of the Ottoman Empire and that the new republic owed its very existence to women. By 1934 he had convinced his hesitant countrymen to grant women the right to vote and to stand for national election.

Although he hated the veil, Ataturk refrained from banning it outright or ordering women to do anything that might violate their husbands' sense of honor. He exploited instead his countrymen's sense of national pride. "I see women covering their faces with their head scarves or turning their backs when a man approaches. Do you really think that the mothers and daughters of a civilized nation would behave so oddly or be so backward?" he said in his speaking tours around the country, and concluded, "I firmly believe that the women of our country are by no means inferior to European women."[5]

Perhaps the more effective promoters of Ataturk's ideals were the aristocratic young Turkish women who had received a European education during the Ottoman era and were eager to make their mark on the outside world. The nation's first women professors, archeologists, and politicians came from their ranks. When a desirable role model was missing, Ataturk created it. One of his boldest moves was to talk Bedia Muvahhit, an aristocrat's daughter, into going on the stage. Asking women to follow in the footsteps of highly respected professional men was one thing, but asking an Ottoman lady to take up acting in public—an occupation which had been previously filled only by non-Muslim women of no particular social standing—was tantamount to stepping on her family's honor. Only three years earlier, in 1920, a Turkish Muslim woman had been arrested for acting on an Istanbul stage. Here, as usual, Ataturk selected his target from among those who were ripe for reform and would set a good example for the conservative public. Not only did the well-educated Bedia have impeccable social credentials, but as the wife of an eminent actor, she moved in a liberal circle. "I just did what was asked by our national hero and managed to learn my lines in one day. That very night I stood on the stage," Bedia recalled, adding that Ataturk attended her performances regularly throughout his life to show the public that he approved of her.[6]

In a still largely segregated society, he naturally turned to the women of his own family for promotable talent. Afet, an adopted daughter, who often accompanied him on his presidential rounds, was educated to be the historian of the early years of the republic. Another adopted daughter, Sabiha, became a pilot. And, showing a sense of humor, Ataturk appointed his sister Makbula, who loved to criticize him, to work for the opposition party.

Prejudice against the modern professional woman did not die overnight,[7] but Ataturk turned some of the cases into dramatic lessons for his people. Sureyya Agaoglu, the first woman lawyer, began to have her troubles with antifeminist attitudes as soon as she reported to her first job. The daughter of feminist writer Ahmet Agaoglu, she could handle all of her problems except one: where to have lunch. There was only one restaurant in the center of the newly created capital city of Ankara, which had always been a men's club and did not look kindly on Sureyya's intrusion. No one threw her out, but all eyes turned toward her whenever she came in, forcing her to swallow her food in the seclusion of the washbasin area. Since despite such treatment she persisted in her attempts to break the sexual apartheid, the annoyed men sent a warning to her father through the prime minister that it was not fitting for a young lady to lunch in restaurants. When Ataturk heard of her plight, he accompanied her to the restaurant. "This young lady is my guest today at my house," he told the customers, "but tomorrow she will be back to lunch here as usual." It became fashionable thereafter for men to invite their wives to lunch in that restaurant.

Such incidents convinced Ataturk more than ever that a total breakdown of the harem mentality on the social level was necessary to complete women's emancipation. As an example to others he had his wife, Latifa, a French-educated lawyer, stand unveiled beside him at public functions in the remotest and most conservative areas of the country, and did not permit her to be hosted separately by women. "There is to be an end to harems," he insisted. He played Professor Higgins to the nation's future leaders, grooming them in the European manners that he as a product of the Western-oriented constitutional period admired. His favorite lesson consisted of inviting his officials and their wives to a grand ball. Since most Turkish men had never exhibited their wives to one another before, they were as stiff as boys at their first dance. Ataturk coaxed and teased them to stop staring at one another and dance. These ordeals created a new line of work: ballroom dance instructor.

Ataturk's instructions and reforms fell on fertile ground, at least in the cities, not only because the most influential families had received a Western education in the late Ottoman period but also because Turks had been the superior power in their relationship with the West throughout the greater part of their history. Even when their power waned in the eighteenth century, they continued to present an opulent front to Europe, and imported Western technology and culture on their own initiative. Neither the loss of the empire nor the extremely brief foreign occupation of their country before it became a republic dampened the enthusiasm for Westernization among the educated elite, for Turkish pride had been saved by the founding of a republic against incredible odds. When the Arabic alphabet was replaced by the Roman and the Turkish language was purged of Arabic and Persian words, the younger generations were severed from their Ottoman past. With dissent quelled by the abolishment of religious courts and powerful religious orders, there was little to disturb the new national identity.

Although Ataturk's work has elicited keen interest in the rest of the Middle East, none of the other Muslim countries have chosen to separate church from state, for Islam had governed every aspect of life politically as well as personally since the time of Muhammad. The former European colonies were particularly eager to return to this tradition as soon as they became independent. Even if they adopted secular laws on modern commercial or criminal problems which the Quran did not treat in detail, a matter as close to home as women's status had to be defined within the Islamic framework.

It was again a national hero, Habib Bourguiba of Tunisia, who took the most radical approach to this task after he led his country to independence from France in 1956 and became its president. Taking advantage of every learned person's Islamic right to interpret the Quran for himself without priestly intermediacy, Bourguiba reexamined the scriptures with a lawyer's eye to suit the text to a feminist purpose. The resulting reforms, which he set down in the Code of Tunisian Personal Statute in 1957, were remarkably similar to Ataturk's. Polygamy was banned outright. Marriage was to be performed with the informed consent of the bride and registered by the state, which had the right to set the minimum age at which marriages might be contracted. Women were to have equal rights in divorce proceedings and child custody, and both sexes were to have equal educational and professional opportunities, although the veil was to be shed gradually, through persuasion rather than legislation.

In his ceaseless campaigns to promote his reforms Bourguiba became an Ataturk armed with the Quran, so to speak. Whereas the Turkish president muzzled the leading clerics by abolishing the religious courts, Bourguiba used the religious establishment to propagate his reforms, discussing them on the radio with Islamic scholars and addressing worshippers in mosques.[8] If he spoke of the need to catch up economically with the West, he also took care to justify his action in light of a purified Islam. The Quran allowed polygamy only to men who could treat all of their wives equally, he pointed out. Since it was humanly impossible to treat all wives equally, he argued, the Quran actually prohibited polygamy. By the same token, unilateral divorce by the husband was incompatible with Quranic verses requiring arbitration by an objective third party in cases of marital conflict.

Bolder reforms have followed over the years to broaden the scope of women's rights in Tunisia. These have included not only equal political rights but also the right of every woman, married or single, to free abortion within the first three months of pregnancy, with the only condition being that it be performed by a certified medical doctor. Permission from the husband or male guardian is not required. Not even Turkey has such a liberal abortion law. Along with Turkey, Tunisia is one of the few Muslim countries that permit women to be judges; others contend that women may not judge since the Quran rules them to be worth only half a man on the witness stand. Bourguiba's feminist reforms are thus closer to Ataturk's than to those promulgated within the Shariah in other countries, but by justifying his laws within the religious framework Bourguiba has served as an Islamic radical—rather than the religious outlaw that Ataturk was—in contrast to whom other Muslim reformers could feel safely moderate.

In countries without male feminist leaders women have had to struggle longer for their legal rights. Egyptian women made remarkable progress on their own, because they had organized well among themselves during their national independence movement. When the men dragged their feet in rewarding their liberators, the women had no trouble in reuniting to form the Feminist Union in March 1923, the first of its kind in the Arab world. Their leader, Huda Sharawi, formally declared war on the sexual status quo several months later by tossing her veil into the sea as she disembarked from the ship that had brought her back from the International Conference of Women in Rome. This Egyptian version of bra burning naturally caused a scandal, particularly as Huda was an eminent pasha's wife. Undaunted, other prominent women cast off their veils, one after another, to become visible fighters in the feminist struggle.[9]

True to the Middle Eastern feminist tradition, the members of the Feminist Union gave top priority to the closing of the loopholes in Muslim marriage and divorce laws and the improvement of educational opportunities. Though this was not the first time congressmen had received petitions on the subject—Malak Hifni Nasif, a teacher and writer, had presented one on her own in 1911—they expressed surprise that respectable ladies would try to corrupt Islamic morality. But Huda shrewdly convinced the Grand Qadi, the head of Egypt's Islamic court, that the Quran did not oppose setting a minimum age for marriage and that maturer girls produced healthier offspring. The Grand Qadi agreed, and a law was passed in 1923 establishing sixteen as the minimum age of marriage for girls, eighteen for boys. The rest of the Feminist Union's petition on family law was politely ignored for decades. Unable to win over the Qadi, who insisted that abolishing polygamy outright was against the letter of the Quran, the Union called on women to take advantage of their Islamic right to add special clauses to the marriage contract. A woman could save herself from polygamy, for instance, by stipulating that she would get an uncontested divorce if the husband took another wife. A number of Muslim countries have chosen the Feminist Union's path to liberation. Their laws specify what many brides may fail to in their marriage contract, out of ignorance or romantic notions: that the husband's taking wife number two gives the first spouse legal grounds for uncontested divorce.

Although the Egyptian constitution granted equality of education in 1924 and the Feminist Union sent the first class of women to the University of Cairo with great fanfare in 1927, professional opportunities were slow to materialize except in the traditionally approved fields of teaching and midwifery. Unlike the Turks, who had to accept women at work when large numbers of men were at the front during the Balkan and First World Wars, Egyptians were not yet accustomed to seeing many women in the professions. Women graduating in the nonfeminine field of law had to work as journalists and writers at first. There was powerful social prejudice against a woman's taking almost any type of paid work. The Feminist Union responded by stepping up not only its consciousness-raising campaigns but also the volunteer work members had done during the national independence movement. They founded and ran clinics as well as childcare centers and orphanages. They set up schools for girls of poor families and rehabilitation centers for prostitutes. When cholera epidemics broke out, it was the respected ladies who broke down the villagers' resistance to vaccination. In fact, the feminist volunteers were the social welfare department of Egypt until the government nationalized many of their services in the 1960s.

Although Huda and her aristocratic companions were embellishing on the tradition of philanthropy started by their grandmothers, they approached their work more as a career than a mere change of pace from harem life. Inspired, like their Turkish counterparts of the late Ottoman period, by the changes in women's status in the West, they gave work a respectable image by their participation and paved the way for the younger generation of professional women. Huda herself was the best example of this transition from the old order to the new. When she became, at thirteen, the second wife of a pasha whose children from his first marriage were older than she, Huda seemed destined to a life of luxurious seclusion relieved occasionally by good works. Seven years later she returned to her parents in order to complete her education, after which she plunged into political and feminist activities with a keen awareness of the Muslim woman's place in the context of international feminism. She attended women's conferences abroad and visited the homes of suffragists. She particularly admired American women, because they were active outside the house apparently without sacrificing their duties as wives and mothers. In order to mold such a well-informed and well-rounded new woman in Egypt, as well as to publicize her crusade for legal reforms, Huda founded in 1925 a magazine named *L'Egyptienne*, under the editorship of Céza Nabarawi, who had attended the Rome conference with Huda and joined her in the unveiling ceremony at the port. The magazine was published in French in order to consolidate the Feminist Union's relationship with feminists abroad. An Arabic version, *Al-Masria* (*The Egyptian Woman*), was not published until a dozen years later, but its tardiness was not felt acutely, for the feminist leaders were the multilingual elite. The poor could not read anyway, and were too busy earning their daily bread to have time for consciousness-raising. The elite were to be the catalysts for sweeping social reform, according to Huda's scheme.

In educating the elite, Huda did not ignore Egyptian reality. In every issue of her paper she and Céza justified their ideas in light of the uncorrupted Islam of Khadija, Aysha, and the poetess-warriors. "We, the Egyptian feminists, have a great respect for our religion," Céza wrote in 1927. "In wanting to see it practiced in its true spirit," she continued, "we are doing more for it than those who submit themselves blindly to the customs that have deformed [Islam]."[10] Perhaps it was as much in deference to the conservatives as to the close ties that had existed between the Egyptian and Turkish elites since Ottoman times that the magazine examined the women of the Turkish Republic as possible models for Egyptians, for as pioneer feminists Turkish women were the Muslim filters for Westernization in the Middle East. The conservative majority, however, thought that any woman tainted by Ataturk's reforms made a dubious model for Egyptian Muslim women.

Though Céza defended the Turkish leader as a man who merely cleared the religion of obscurantist interpretations that did not exist during Muhammad's time, she was above all a skilled politician with a mission to convert rather than antagonize. She conceded at the same time that "the overly rapid emancipation of the Turkish woman has not at this moment yielded all the happy results that were expected." Taking the evolutionary path herself, she refused to demand the vote before enough women were educated.[11] She chose instead to run articles on politics entitled "How would you decide if you could vote?" and printed the sophisticated responses she received from her readers. Her subtle approach paid dividends. Men wrote to the paper in support of suffrage and other rights for women, and a few volunteered their legal services to the Feminist Union.[12]

These men were not the first sympathizers, however. In the latter half of the nineteenth century a number of Egyptian men had called out for one improvement or another in women's status, mainly for the sake of a better family life or social progress. It was in Judge Qasim Amin, the disciple of a religious scholar and pioneer feminist named Muhammad Abdu, that these ideas converged and developed into a manifesto for women's liberation. The two books which he published—*The Emancipation of Women* (*Tahrir al-Mara*, 1899) and *The Modern Woman* (*Al-Mara al-Jadida*, in 1900)—are the first known works in Arabic on the subject and remain on every Arab feminist's reading list to this day.[13]

Starting from the premise that woman's emancipation was an essential prerequisite to national development, Amin argued that uncorrupted Islam provided for full equality between the sexes. In his second book he justified woman's rights in secular terms, referring to her natural human rights and freedom as essential in strengthening society. Though he stressed the value of woman's liberation to the society as a whole, he was one of the rare men to worry in print about her psychological well-being. While arguing that the Quran effectively forbade polygamy, for example, he detailed the agonies every wife suffers upon seeing her husband bring home a number two. He did not advocate higher education, but he did urge that women be given enough training to free them from their economically and emotionally parasitic existence, which made of every marriage a tyranny. By the same token, the veil was an insult to a woman's sense of responsibility. Moreover, it was perfectly useless in preventing adultery, serving only to keep the sexes from developing a healthy attitude toward each other. "If men fear that women might succumb to their masculine attraction," he added slyly, "why did they not institute veils for themselves?"

Amin's books were rabidly condemned as un-Islamic and un-Egyptian when they first appeared. But they inspired upperclass women to action almost immediately and eventually became an important part of the "feminist tradition" to which younger generations of Egyptian women harked back in making their demands. The demands were met very slowly. The right to vote and to stand for political election was not granted until 1956, while marriage and divorce laws were liberalized to feminist standards only in 1979. But the latest laws rank among the most progressive in the Middle East, thanks largely to the aristocratic feminists' successors, the university-educated women who entered prestigious occupations in large enough numbers to influence significantly the general attitude toward women.

Egyptian women were lucky to have started out with a strong feminist tradition and the organizational genius of Huda and her determined companions. Algerian women, who did not have these advantages, have traveled a particularly difficult road toward emancipation, though they helped their men fight one of the longest and bloodiest wars of liberation in the Middle East.[14] In fact, the war itself and their very past worked against them. Unlike Egyptians, whose relatively short bout with French and English occupation did not destroy their native language and culture, Algerians suffered a century of Western colonialism—one of the longest such periods in recent Middle Eastern history. Not content to dominate the political and economic life of the country, the French colonizers imposed their language and culture, discouraging the teaching of Arabic language and Algerian history. When the French teacher asked Algerian children what their capital was, he expected to hear "Paris." So thorough was the gallicization campaign that Algerian pupils speaking Arabic among themselves at recess were reprimanded and made to feel backward.

Home was the only sanctuary from foreign control. Not surprisingly, therefore, it turned into a conservatory of never-changing old traditions, with the women as curators and teachers. Anything that could possibly detract from this sacred feminine mission was vehemently rejected. Fadela M'Rabet, an Algerian writer who has produced radio programs for women and young people in Algiers, recalled that her mother had been pulled out of school as a child because her teacher forbade her to wear the traditional head scarf in the classroom. "Today they tell you to bare your head; tomorrow they will make you eat pork," the grandmother had said, preferring to have her daughter remain uneducated rather than violate the Muslim way of life as she understood it. The daughter led such a strictly secluded life thereafter that she left home alone for the first time only at forty-five years of age.[15]

With such a siege mentality, Algerians interpreted every French attempt to improve women's status as a scheme to corrupt the last bastion of native culture. The French administrators may occasionally have been sincere (if clumsy) in their indignation at the veil and their urging Algerians to bring their wives to mixed parties, but all such projects were doomed to failure, because they were not initiated by an Algerian Ataturk. To make things worse, the French did corrupt some women through a highly visible prostitution venture. They formed a corporation, Bordel Mobile de Campagne, to recruit Algerian women for their chain of brothels in the colonies. Prostitution had existed for centuries among Muslims; but seeing the infidel conqueror take his women, the Algerian harked back regretfully to the one native example of fairly dignified prostitution, or courtesanship. Among the Ouled Nail tribesmen, some of the women, called Daughters of the Nail,[16] customarily spent a number of years dancing and entertaining men in Bou Saada and neighboring oasis towns of the Sahara—often in houses run by their own relatives. Far from being ostracized, these gaily attired and bejeweled girls coiffed with heavy braids of black wool were invited to dance at sacred village festivities and eventually retired to a respectable marriage. The French tourist trade is said to have transformed them into vulgar strippers-cum-prostitutes.

When Algerians finally took up arms against the French in 1954, women joined in order to drive out the enemy and not strictly for feminist ideals. They did not organize themselves into a group. It might have been unsafe to do so, since theirs was guerrilla warfare. The few feminist fighters had little opportunity to communicate and form a united front as each went about her lonely mission of smuggling and bomb planting. Besides, most of the men who masterminded these operations were avowedly fighting to guard traditions. Nowhere was the point made more succinctly than at a meeting with revolutionary leaders Ahmed Ben Bella and Muhammad Khider arranged by Tunisian lawyer Gisele Halimi on behalf of Djamila Boupacha and other imprisoned Algerian women resistance fighters whom she was defending. When the discussion turned to Algeria's future, Djamila interjected: "And how about us women? Our status must change now that—" Khider interrupted the young woman, who had been raped and tortured by the French for her role in the war: "Women after independence? Why, you will return to your couscous, of course."[17]

That is what happened to most women. When national independence was won in 1962 and the medals were given out, along with constitutional guarantees of equality in the political and educational spheres, women were asked to go back home to their old job as cultural custodians. Women were far better off than before, but the high hopes kindled by the revolution were not fully realized. The liberal laws on personal status and the family which were drafted in 1966 were never passed. "We want a free Algerian woman, not a free Frenchwoman," announced Colonel Houari Boumedienne,[18] who took over the leadership of Algeria three years after independence. At a time of high unemployment, he was motivated partly by a wish to reserve the available jobs for men, but he was also summing up his country's desperate search for identity at a time when most people knew the French culture and language better than their own.

Assia Djebar, a young novelist who maintained a bird's-eye view of her countrywomen's situation as she watched the independence war from exile in Tunisia, warned that the average Algerian's knowledge of the West was meager and harmful, especially on matters concerning women's status. To many Westernization meant nightclubs and mini-skirts rather than schools and women's rights.[19] Arguments over the superficial aspects of Westernization and Islam tended to blur the basic issues of women's rights and destroy a golden opportunity to sweep away the old order. "Fatma of the feudal system who exchanges her robes for a dress from Paris and wears it cut too low," Assia lamented, "enjoys in fact no more rights than her veiled sister."[20]

While the search for identity has inspired some of the most powerful novels and essays by and on women to come out of the Mediterranean Islamic world, on the popular level the colonel's slogans merely legitimized the mummifying of women in the past, with the ironic excuse of escaping psychological colonialism. "We have used Islam to survive; now we must pay back our debts to it," Fadela M'Rabet's father told her as soon as the independence celebration was over. But Fadela noted that after a century of an involuted existence her father's Islam had been reduced to a few prayers and to fasting during the month of Ramadan, both of which seemed to be peripheral to the long list of antifeminist taboos. These included such un-Islamic practices as pulling young girls out of school to protect their virginity and marrying them off without their consent. What good were political and educational rights if women were chained to their homes by medieval customs, Fadela cried repeatedly in her books and articles as she appealed for laws to curb the patriarch's power over his women.

These problems are not unique to Algeria, although Algerians have discussed them with particularly bitter eloquence and insight borne of their history. In fact, the Algerian experience embodies some of the greatest obstacles and most painful conflicts of women's liberation throughout the Middle East. While other countries were not as culturally annihilated, they also stagnated under adverse economic and political conditions. Modernization thus meant borrowing from the West and somehow resolving the clash that this invariably caused between the old ways inherited from the Islamic past and the new ways imported from the non-Muslim foreigner. Laws in some countries may be fairer to women, but they have so far benefited only a minority of women in big cities. Even in countries with a long tradition of equal educational opportunities, girls lag far behind boys in school enrollment, especially after the onset of puberty—partly because of poverty but also because of their parents' wish to protect their daughters' virtue and marriageability. In 1975[21] only 34 percent of Turkish girls between the ages of twelve and seventeen were enrolled in school, compared to 57 percent of the boys. In Egypt the figures were 27 percent versus 49 percent; in Tunisia 24 percent versus 44 percent; in Lebanon 55 percent versus 70 percent. Married off early, these girls know neither their rights in marriage nor modern birth control methods. Under such conditions equality of professional opportunity remains theoretical. So do political rights. The female voter turnout is dismal everywhere, due both to ignorance and to the demands of traditional modesty. The number of women in political office is equally low. Even profeminist Tunisia elected so few women to the National Assembly in 1979 that the liberal press has launched a soul-searching campaign. Egypt decided in 1979 that the only way to ensure adequate representation of women in the Peoples' Assembly was to reserve 30 of its 392 seats for them. In such a context the election of 12 women to the 250-seat Iraqi parliament in 1980 has been hailed as a feminist milestone, as has the appointment of a few prominent women to ministerial posts in many countries, even though their duties are generally confined to social and cultural affairs.

Nor have the educated urban women escaped emotionally crippling traditions. A woman who is entrusted with the construction of a bridge or the healing of the sick may not be trusted with her own sexuality. Afraid to lose their patriarchal privileges, men expect her to be educated and sophisticated and yet chaste and submissive. She cooperates in perpetuating the conflict-ridden image out of desire for security as well as fear of ostracism. Locked in their own uncertainties and contradictions, men and women try to sort out what they want from the indigestible avalanche of new influences in their lives, and to reconcile them with the old ways that they cannot or will not abandon.

Their dilemma is watched with particular interest by conservative oil-rich countries, which may be in line for the next wave of women's liberation. Although they can now hire expensive foreign labor in order to catch up with the industrialized world, they must plan for the day when oil reserves will run out. Men alone could not possibly fill all the posts. How can women participate in national development without violating the traditions? So acute is the need for trained personnel that even in Saudi Arabia, which observes strict sexual segregation, the question is no longer whether women should work, but how and where. For the time being they are educated exclusively to serve the needs of other segregated women, mostly in schools and hospitals. But education and travel abroad have time and again proved potent catalysts of change. A solitary voice here and there has already cried out for modifications in women's opportunities in Saudi Arabia.[22]

In less rigidly tradition-bound countries, petrodollars and education have produced rapid changes in women's lives. Recent developments in the minuscule state of Bahrain in the Persian Gulf are indeed like a speeded-up film on the story of women's emancipation in the Middle East. Bahrain is especially motivated to replace imported labor with local talent as soon as possible because it is one of the poorest of the oil-producing countries and expects to run out of oil in twenty years. Accordingly, girls' school enrollment in the last five years has been among the highest in the Middle East and has caught up with boys', with practically no dropping out at puberty. Very few Middle Eastern countries can boast of such a record. With no sexual segregation on the job, women graduates have begun to occupy posts in the oil industry, hotels, and the police force as well as in the "feminine" professions in schools, banks, and government offices. Their private lives are still governed largely by tradition, but educated women of the elite families have begun clamoring for legal reforms.

The cultural conflicts generated by such rapid changes will invariably converge on women's rights in private life, as they have in the more slowly evolving parts of the Middle East. Though they have been guinea pigs in their societies' attempts to resolve these conflicts, Middle Eastern women are also well placed to mold their own destiny. The fact that their first steps toward emancipation were closely linked with their countries' liberation or development means that they are dealing with a male establishment in a state of flux and dependent on educated women's support.[23] It is this potential for dialogue that adds unexpected dimensions to the story of the Middle Eastern woman.

PART II

5

𓊝𓊝𓊝𓊝𓊝𓊝𓊝𓊝𓊝

Childhood

Whoever hath a daughter and doth not bury her
alive or scold her or prefer his male children to her,
may God bring him into paradise.
—The Prophet Muhammad

When the Prophet Muhammad was walking toward paradise
one day, he saw an old woman preceding him to the gates.
Muhammad was hurt, since God had promised that he would
be the first of Adam's children to enter heaven. "What does
this woman have that she goes before me?" he asked. "O
Muhammad," came the thundering voice from the clouds,
"this woman was beautiful and graceful. But when she became
a widow, she devoted herself fully to her two daughters until
their future was assured. God wanted to show her that He was
grateful."[1]

Thirteen centuries after this parable was first told (reportedly by the Prophet himself), and more than half a century
after the first Muslim feminists reasserted the equality of the
sexes, girls are still second-best. Parents no longer bury their
daughters alive at birth in Arabia and other regions where
infanticide was common before the advent of Islam. But, like
their counterparts in the United States[2] and elsewhere, parents prefer sons. It is said that a man with a son is immortal,
whereas a girl is brought up to contribute to someone else's

family tree. There are much more compelling reasons for wanting a boy, however. Since at least 60 percent of the Middle East and North Africa is rural, and adequate social security has been instituted so recently in many areas as to cover only a small segment of the populace, employed mainly in large industries, sons are indispensable as musclepower on the land and as insurance for old age. Moreover, boys do not have to be supervised very closely, since their sexual behavior cannot dishonor the family or compromise their chances for marriage.

Given the overwhelming advantage—indeed, the dire economic necessity—of having a son, the prospective mother's responsibility is heavy. Even royal princes aware of the latest discoveries in genetics do not hold themselves accountable for the sex of their child and may divorce their wives or take a second wife if the first does not bear male heirs. The masses who know nothing of X and Y chromosomes readily blame the mother if she fails to produce a boy, silent or explicit reproaches growing more intense with the birth of each successive girl. Even if the wife is not threatened with divorce or polygamy, she has little hope of rising in the pecking order of her husband's family. Thus, if she has had no sons she cannot help but greet the arrival of her baby daughter with disappointment.

But the fate written by Allah must be accepted. The disappointment is usually pushed into the back of the mind and the infant girl is welcomed joyfully. The feasts staged in her honor may not be as grandiose as they would have been for her brother, but they serve nonetheless to remind the parents of the hundred and one advantages of having a daughter. She is far more lovable and pliable than a boy, and a better assistant to her mother. In fact, her nurturing qualities are supposed to manifest themselves so early in life that the Moroccan version of "Hansel and Gretel" has the sister protecting the brother from the wicked witch.[3] Nor is she lost to her parents after marriage. The Islamic world also believes in the adage that a son is a son until he marries but a daughter is a daughter forever. According to a Moroccan proverb, parents without a daughter will have no one to attend them on their deathbed. One Moroccan father took a second wife upon learning that his first, who had given him two sons, could have no more children, so badly did he want a daughter. Very few would go to such extremes today, but most parents hope for at least one daughter.

Though the woman is viewed as subordinate to men but vital for nurturing throughout the Middle East and North Africa, there is no one way to mold little girls to that ideal. Islam offers only general guidelines and goals, which parallel and enhance the kinder versions of folk beliefs. A daughter is entitled to only half as much inheritance as her brother and will be worth only half a man on the witness stand when she grows up, but she must be loved and educated just the same. Muhammad promised the best fruits of paradise for parents who treat their daughters as kindly as their sons. However, since the sexual double standard persists despite Quranic prohibition of adultery (premarital as well as extramarital sex) for both sexes, the parents must also do everything in their power to keep their daughter chaste until marriage, taking special care to train her for her most glorified role—motherhood.

How this is done depends largely on the parents' socioeconomic background. Among the propertied and the professional classes, who do not have to depend on their sons' labor in old age, a woman is less threatened if her baby is a girl—unless she has to produce heirs to a royal prince or an important dynasty. She is also likely to be well educated, which makes her fear divorce much less than would her counterpart without marketable skills. Accordingly, the mother is not prone to transmit her own insecurity and resentment to the daughter who arrived in lieu of the much-hoped-for son. She may try again and again for a boy, ending up with a few more children than she initially intended to bear, but the family budget allows for extra mouths to feed. And if she still fails to produce a son, her husband is not likely to follow the example of Iran's ex-shah Muhammad Reza Pahlavi, who married three times in quest of a male heir.

Now that the top professions are open to women of this class, it is possible that parents who have only daughters influence, consciously or otherwise, at least some of the girls to take the role of a son. A thirty-five-year-old physics professor in Istanbul who was an only child recalls that her parents never pushed dolls on her but encouraged her to play with puzzles and science equipment, although neither of them was a scientist. She showed an early inclination for the sciences, and when she went on to win top prizes in the field in high school and college, family friends praised her as "a girl who is like a man"—a Turk's supreme complement to a woman's intelligence. "With a daughter like that," they said, "who needs a son."

She has never been called upon to look after her parents, although she stands ready to do so, but another young woman from a less wealthy family in Morocco works to support her widowed mother and several younger sisters. She is treated with all the respect due the head of a household. When she comes home from work she is greeted at the door by her mother. Leaving her jacket with one of her sisters, the breadwinner looks over the day's mail in the living room while the "housewives" set the table and bring in supper. "Of course my daughter will marry," the mother insists, without being asked, holding up a bedsheet that she is embroidering for her trousseau. The middle-aged widow does not worry about her own future, for her younger daughter is almost finished with her schooling and ready to take over the breadwinning duties. The plan is to have all of the daughters chip in to support the mother after the youngest child is married.

Unless economic need or exceptional scientific talent forces them to bring up a girl "like a man," however, most parents enjoy turning their daughter into a doll. They fuss over her toilette and shelter her from the rough-and-tumble world, which they expect their sons to confront without crying too often for mercy. Her daily life is essentially quite similar to that of any other privileged girl in the world: training for her future role as a dependent housewife, the only rehearsal for motherhood being her games with dolls. Although overprotection implies that she is weaker than her brother, most educated parents are too enlightened to bring up at an early age the matter of her being worth only half a man.

There are far more important religious basics to master first. Along with her first lessons on charity, honesty, and other virtues so dear to the Judeo-Christian code of ethics, every child learns the Islamic profession of faith: "There is only one God and Muhammad is His prophet." For adult converts this statement constitutes the equivalent of baptism. For a child born of Muslim parents it is a confirmation of her faith. As she grows older, the child memorizes a few short passages from the Quran attesting to God's creation of the universe and His justice and compassion, as well as the existence of heaven and hell in afterlife. These are incorporated into the five required daily prayers, but first the ritual of ablution must be mastered. No haphazard washing will do. Each part of the body must be cleansed in the prescribed order, intended to prepare the mind to commune with God. The prayers consist of physical movements, such as bowing and prostrating, as well as Quranic recitations. Each of the five prayers requires a specific combination of these movements and recitations and must be performed facing in the direction of the Kaaba in Mecca at specific times—the first between dawn and sunrise; the second at noon; the third when long shadows begin to form on earth; the fourth at sunset before the last rays of daylight have gone; and the fifth in the dark of the evening. The routine is not as complicated as it sounds and is learned gradually, with the child imitating an older person in her family when it suits her fancy. The various combinations of a few basic movements give just enough variety to the otherwise hypnotic monotony to relax the worshipper as it sets her in harmony with her body and environment, as well as with God, much as yoga would. And women's prayers are exactly the same as men's.

At the mosque, however, the child will notice that women never lead the prayers or deliver the sermon, and that they are the only ones to cover every part of their body except the face, hands, and feet. What irked me most when I grew too old to roam freely in the men's section was that women are banished to the least attractive corner of the mosque during prayers. As a result, they are denied the privilege of contemplating the full splendor of the greatest architectural masterpieces of the Islamic world—just because men are supposedly so weak as to forget God if women joined them in the main hall. Women prayed alongside men during Muhammad's lifetime.

Such a footnote to the Prophet's biography does not concern little girls, who have complete liberty to cross harem boundaries before reaching puberty. For them Muhammad's history is a tale of God's last messenger and successor to all of the biblical prophets. Good teachers of Islam do not preach hatred of Judaism or Christianity, their only quarrel with the latter having to do with the divinity of Christ, whom Muslims recognize as a prophet. The rest of the story about Moses and his Ten Commandments and the compassionate Jesus and his good mother is all there in textbooks of religious history— along with the adventures of an orphan who had the good qualities of both Moses and Jesus and went on to hear the last revelation from God on a mountain near Mecca.

The patriarchal values of the Old Testament were also transferred intact into these texts. The prophets were fathers in whom one had to believe blindly or risk burning in hell. Their wives always believed and obeyed, except one who was punished by being turned into a stone. Mothers were always self-sacrificing and longed only to multiply as God bade them. Failing that, they went fishing for baby Moses set afloat in a basket. Khadija and Aysha, however, were much more ambivalent figures. No instructor failed to mention their "masculine" talents in trade, politics, and war. In fact, a few rhapsodized them. But one of my teachers of religion said: "And Aysha saw the error of her ways and left war and politics to men and retired into a saintly life as befits the Mother of Believers."

My girlfriends and I were sorry that Aysha was shooed so unceremoniously off center stage, for she had entertained us by doing something more than just sitting around to weep or babysit. I imagined that she looked something like the Chinese Opera's woman warrior, decked out in enough banners and plumes to make a peacock jealous. Being Arabian, Aysha probably rode a similarly adorned camel. But I was not sure, for our texts were not illustrated. Islam forbade drawing pictures of holy personages, in an effort to discourage idol worship.

I turned to Harun al-Rashid and other caliphs who brought the Islamic civilization to full bloom. The imperious Khayzuran, whose power rivaled the caliphs', and Rabia al-Adawiya, the inspirer of Sufis (to mention but two heroines of the age), must have figured very little in my lessons, if at all, for I was desperate enough to people this apparently all-male period of history with dancing slave girls salvaged from *Arabian Nights* films and comic books. Only in secular schools did I learn of Halidé Edib fighting alongside Ataturk and Huda Sharawi tossing her veil into the Nile. At last I, a woman, had a part in my history again.

Huda in particular caught my fancy when I was eight years old. Like my grandmother, she had contracted a polygamous union, but unlike my grandmother, she threw her veil into the river. My grandmother wore only the head scarf, but she kept it on even inside the house. I had grown up viewing this custom as normal for old ladies, but now I itched to liberate her from the chador, which was surely uncomfortable in warm weather. One spring afternoon my younger sister and I gathered up all of her scarves and veils into a basket and marched down to the nearby Bosphorus. We stood ceremoniously for a moment at the edge of the water, each holding an end of her black Spanish lace mantilla. Then we flung it to the breeze, which caught it and carried it over the waves, the lace etching floral patterns on the frothy whitecaps before floating away to meet Huda's veil somewhere at the bottom of the Mediterranean Sea. Inspired, we went to work like flower girls at a wedding, scattering petals of bright silk and lace on the water. That evening Grandmother looked in vain for her favorite Spanish mantilla to wear with her lace-trimmed dress. We told her where it was. She was furious. Some women just do not want to be liberated.

Yet it is a luxury to mind other people's liberation or to search for a meaningful role in history. Though it is a luxury that is becoming more accessible as the middle classes grow and education and the benefits of oil wealth reach more people, the Middle East and North Africa have far to go before wiping out the effects of centuries of economic and cultural stagnation. Except in the oil-producing countries, the GNP per capita averaged less than $1,000 in 1975 and in some countries dipped as low as $151, while it was at least $7,000 in the U.S. Public education being a recent arrival, the overall illiteracy rate in the region hovers at 60 to 65 percent among males and 85 to 90 percent among females. Although governments consecrate a much larger proportion of their budget to education than do the Western countries, the trouble is that children under fifteen make up 40 to 48 percent of the population and must look to their illiterate parents for support while they study.

To be born female into the wrong side of such statistics means to get life's last crumbs, not because of Islamic precepts but because of crushing poverty. A destitute mother who needs a son in order to ensure her own survival is likely to wean a daughter from the breast as early as possible in order to enhance her chances of becoming pregnant again. Commercial baby foods and adult diets are nutritionally so inadequate that many more girls than boys die early in life. In fact, neglect of female babies is one of the main causes for the high child mortality rate reported from this area. Ten to 14 out of every 100 babies born in 1975–76 died before celebrating their first birthday. Only those born in Kuwait, Lebanon, and Bahrain did better, with 4.4, 5.9, and 7.8 deaths per hundred, respectively. The rate for the U.S. was only 1.5, and for Scandinavia almost nil.[4]

If a girl survives infancy in the poverty-stricken areas of the Middle East, she is saddled with work as soon as she can walk. A typical sight in the urban slums and countryside is that of small girls trying to eke a few games out of their day while carrying their youngest siblings on their backs or hips. Busy and debilitated with frequent pregnancies, mothers charge their little daughters with everything from housecleaning to fetching water. No mere rehearsals for motherhood with dolls and tea party sets here. Woman's nurturing duties begin early in life with real babies and kitchen utensils—and as often as not with real farm equipment and weaving tools. Girls are economic assets from the start, though not always counted in surveys because they are usually unpaid helpers to their parents. If they were counted along with their brothers who hire themselves out as farmhands, sweatshop assistants, or peddlers, the prevalence of child labor would be staggering. The picture is already quite grim. In 1975 children under fifteen years working to support their family constituted 1.5 to 3 percent of the total population in Iran, Afghanistan, Pakistan, and Turkey, and 0.5 to 1.5 percent elsewhere, compared to 0.1 to 0.5 percent in the U.S. The picture is bright only when compared to the more than 3 percent found in certain countries of sub-Sahara Africa. Everywhere girls form only a small fraction of these figures. Egypt, for instance, reported 4.5 percent of girls and 18.2 percent of boys in the labor force.

Elementary school enrollment figures are perhaps a better indication of how many girls help their families survive. Only about half of the girls in the region attended the primary grades, while over two-thirds of the boys were excused from work to study. Although at puberty many girls are pulled out of school in order to protect their chastity, the main reason for the lower attendance of girls in elementary school is poverty. Education is usually free, but supplies are not always so. Poor parents usually choose to invest their limited resources in their sons' future. At this social level education is considered to be of little value for a girl, since she marries and begins her long childbearing years shortly after she reaches her teens.

When desperately poor parents consider putting some of their children up for adoption, they invariably choose to part with their daughters. Adoption in many parts of the Middle East has traditionally taken a peculiar form. A girl is not formally adopted but is taken in by a better-off family as an "adopted maid," usually between infancy and puberty. The term is apt, since she is a cross between a foster child and a maid. She is different from other domestic servants in that she is not salaried, because she is "too young to be of much use." She is merely fed and clothed, and trained to do simple domestic chores. In her spare time, she goes out to play with her master's children, whom she may call "brother" and "sister."

Ideally, adopted maids are also to be schooled, but very few are that lucky. In one Moroccan family the little maid's education boiled down to a few lessons given by the master's daughter, who was barely a year older than she. The adoptive family had hoped to have their unscholarly daughter learn better by trying to teach her own assignments to the maid, Rashida. The two children naturally took to gossiping and giggling at their desk, with disastrous academic consequences for both. The daughter was ordered to do her homework alone in her room, and the maid was taught to embroider so that she could help the grandmother with her young mistress's trousseau.

Aside from the family's reluctance to send her to school, Rashida was well treated, eating with her "parents" and being dressed up for festivities. But there was always something unchildlike about her. She was too good, too obedient, and never threw a tantrum. All it took was one word from the "mother" and she dropped her games immediately to do her bidding. Though only ten years old when I first met her, and sincerely loved by her adoptive family, she knew her place. Several times a year her real family came from the country for a visit. I often wondered what she thought when she saw their scrawny, weather-beaten faces.

Rashida was one of the lucky ones, more daughter than servant. It took an exceptionally strong personality like Nagwa not to grow sheepish in her servile post. A peasant's daughter who had grown up with a wealthy Cairo family since age seven, Nagwa at sixteen was an energetic and sharp-witted mother hen who took complete charge of the house. On a visit to their home I complimented her on her lovely new dress. Pulling herself up, she informed me that it was one of the better ones on the market. She had made her mistress buy it. "This is to make me look my best. After all, what will the neighbors say if I remain an old maid?" she said with mischief brimming in her enormous dark eyes.

Nagwa was astute in counting on pressure from her master's peer group. I have seen a five-year-old adopted maid in ill-fitting hand-me-downs carry water buckets as large as herself and be made to eat alone on the kitchen floor, but social disapproval usually discourages such overt abuse of child maids. Moreover, the demand for these little unpaid maids is high enough that poor parents can shop around for families who will give their daughter the best possible future. It is said that there are no girls in Moroccan orphanages since the few who are brought in are adopted in no time at all.

Although many people argue that the best-treated of these maids are victims of child labor, this form of adoption is one way of keeping poor children from starving. In a wealthy family even the leftovers that an adopted maid eats are often more nutritious and plentiful than what she would get in her own home. She is clothed and housed better. If she is not always taught reading and writing, she learns more sophisticated housekeeping methods—how to care for fine furniture, use modern appliances, cook. As a result, her adoptive parents, who take upon themselves the responsibility of finding a husband for her, have little trouble in marrying her up the social ladder. True, she may not be considered by young men of her master's circle, but she is a good match for aficionados of well-bred young ladies from the slightly lower classes, and also for older men who are willing to "marry down" for the privilege of having a very young and pretty wife. That is what happened to Nagwa, who is now the apparently satisfied wife of a middle-aged barber whose purse is reputed to be as fat as his belly. Rashida, who is almost sixteen today, is so exquisitely beautiful that a medical student has fallen in love with her. "She is, after all, a maid. We'll see what his parents will say," noted a cynical neighbor.

Some families go beyond the call of strict duty and actually send their adopted maids to school. One Moroccan carpet merchant trained his as a bookkeeper because none of his own children showed as impressive a head for figures as she did. She is now married to one of her "father's" employees and keeps the firm's accounts. Needless to say, her own parents benefit enormously from her luck. Not only does she send them money, she helped a younger brother land a job in the firm.

Despite the promise of a better life for their daughters, the poor are not giving them up for adoption as readily as they used to. In Turkey this trend started with the peasants' mass migration to work in Germany, where salaries were good enough to allow families to stay together. Moreover, migration has unexpectedly turned the daughter into a long-term investment. As sons left for Germany or to larger Turkish cities in search of work, old parents moved in with their married daughters. The arrangement has reportedly proved so agreeable, especially to old mothers, that in some villages daughters are virtually taking over one of the son's most important traditional roles.

Whatever form the extended family takes, it plays a crucial role in the life of the little girl of any economic class in the Middle East and North Africa. The girl who is deposed early from her mother's breast feels less rejected than might be expected because an older sister, aunt, or grandmother adopts her, providing her with a secure lap from which she can watch the preferential treatment given her brother. Halidé Edib, growing up in a tension-ridden polygamous household at the end of the Ottoman Empire, writes in her memoirs of how her grandmother represented stability for her. In fact, grandmothers star quite frequently in biographies and novels about women.[5]

The ubiquitous presence of grandmothers assures the continuity of some marvelous childrearing practices. In the famous carpet-making region of Gordes, Turkey, a newborn is never exposed at once to the harsh glare of natural or artificial light in which adults function. He or she is born in a semidark room and placed in a crib surrounded by layers of curtains, which are removed one by one each day to accustom the baby gradually to the extrauterine environment. All adults, except the one who is directly responsible for the baby's care, are asked to relax away from the crib for five or ten minutes before approaching the infant so that their nervousness will not rub off on him or her.[6]

Everywhere in the Middle East traditional social graces are mastered very early in life, again thanks to the grandmother's insistence on tradition as much as to the absence of age segregation. Families often visit with each other in multigenerational groups, where little girls are encouraged to say welcoming words and serve the guests. Stories lauding hospitality as a sacred duty are frequently told. A well-known one among them has a poor couple sitting down to dinner when two visitors knock at the door. They invite them in but have no extra food in the house. Accordingly, the wife sets two empty plates for herself and her husband and discreetly blows out the candle before inviting the guests to the table, so that they may dine without ever suspecting that their hosts have no food in front of them. The moral of the tale is absorbed extremely well. An American friend has not yet gotten over her amazement at a five-year-old Lebanese girl who entertained her a few years ago while her mother was detained unavoidably on the telephone. The little girl brought out fruits and nuts for the guest and sat down patiently to keep her company, even though the two had no language in common. When the mother tarried longer than expected, the girl ran out, to return minutes later with a jigsaw puzzle for the guest.

While most families lovingly train their little girl for her nurturing role without thinking about her sexual future until she reaches puberty, a few begin to worry right away. They may resort to the very un-Islamic custom of genital mutilation[7] to abort sexual awakening, in order to assure her chastity until marriage and her fidelity thereafter. Genital mutilation was a medically accepted treatment for masturbation and nymphomania in the West in the nineteenth and early twentieth centuries. In the Middle East and Africa the operation comes in three main varieties today. The simplest form is the Sunna circumcision, in which only the tip of the clitoris is sliced off. More radical is clitoridectomy, calling for the excision of the entire clitoris and the labia minora.[8] Even more harrowing is the practice of infibulation. Called Pharaonic or Sudanese circumcision, it involves sealing the labia majora together after the entire clitoris and the labia minora have been removed.

Edna Adan Ismail, who has served in the health ministry of Somalia, describes how this is done in her country. The village midwife, who performs the operation with razor blades and knives, scrapes the skin off the inner surface of the labia majora and "staples" them together with strings and thorns of dwarf acacia. A matchstick or a small bamboo wedge is inserted into the tiny opening left at the lower end to allow the passing of urine and menstrual blood. When the procedure is completed, the patient's legs are bound together down to the

ankles, and she is placed on a mat until she urinates, in order
to ensure that the opening is adequate. A week later the thorns
are removed, but the legs remain bound together until the
chastity belt of flesh has healed completely. If the girl survives
hemorrhage and infections to get married, she must, of course,
be cut open for intercourse and childbirth—often without
benefit of even primitive forms of anesthesia, such as cauteri-
zation with fire or rubbing with a special kind of nettle.
Modern medicine contributes to this crime against women. It
is a crime that pays, for the victims must be sewn up after
delivery, only to be cut open again later. This causes untold
numbers of medical complications—urinary retention, incon-
tinence, pelvic infections, frigidity, and obstetric complications that also damage the fetus, to mention but a few.[9] Some
women's genitals are so maimed and scarred by repeated
operations that normal intercourse and childbearing become
impossible. If they cannot satisfy their husbands' sexual appetite in another way, they may lose their place to younger,
healthier women. Despite such tragedies, infibulation is practiced to this day in most parts of the Horn of Africa—Somalia,
Ethiopia, and Djibouti as well as certain regions of Sudan,
Kenya, Egypt, Nigeria, Mali, and the Arabian peninsula.

The most widespread genital mutilation, however, is clitoridectomy, affecting some thirty million women in more
than twenty-six countries in Africa, including certain regions
of Egypt, Algeria, and Libya. It has also been reported from
some parts of the two Yemens, Saudi Arabia, Iraq, Jordan,
and Syria. Its practice among non-Muslims as well as Muslims
suggests its non-Islamic origin. In fact, Greek scholars have
noted the existence of clitoridectomy in the Upper Nile valley
since the time of the pharaohs. The Quran makes no mention
of the practice. Muhammad disapproved of it, since it renders
a woman frigid for life, but he apparently could not eradicate
it—which may shed light on one curious tradition which
claims that the Prophet stopped a matron one day from performing the radical operation on a little girl by ordering her:

"Reduce but don't destroy." Some Muslims take this statement as an order to perform the Sunna circumcision on little
girls. The Sunna type is certainly the least damaging, since it
does not completely kill the ability to respond sexually or cause
as many serious complications as the other forms, which are
also referred to euphemistically as "female circumcision" but
are effectively equal to penile amputation. So absolutely essential to a good marriage are the radical operations considered
that they survive in the hinterlands even in Sudan, Egypt, and
Somalia, where laws forbid them.

In more enlightened urban areas the crippling versions have
given way to the Sunna circumcision, but this is no less psychologically traumatizing for the young victim, and may lead
to sexual frigidity in adulthood. Since it is called "the cleansing operation," parents do not always appreciate its harmful
effects. Nawal al-Saadawi, an Egyptian doctor born to educated parents, recalled the terror she experienced when she
was circumcised at age six.[10] As she lay cozily in her bed one
night, cold hands grabbed her and carried her to the bath-
room. She thought that thieves had broken in and were going
to cut her throat—a fear confirmed by a rasping metallic
sound that reminded her of a butcher's knife being sharpened.
Dazed with fright, she saw only blurred adult figures busying
themselves about her as if preparing to sacrifice a sheep. The
knife did not touch her throat, however. Instead, it reached
for something buried deep between her thighs. A burning pain
shot through her body from her intimate center, blood pooled
around her hips, and Nawal found herself freed from the
medieval rack of hands. A greater shock awaited her as her
eyes focused more clearly—her own mother stood over her,
smiling at her daughter's executioners! "For years," she wrote,
"the memory of my clitoridectomy continued to track me
down like a nightmare. I had a feeling of insecurity, fear of the
unknown, waiting for me at every step I took."

When Nawal graduated as a medical doctor in 1955, she
joined a growing number of people dedicated to the eradica-

tion of genital mutilation. After treating numerous circumcised patients in cities and villages, she has written books boldly asserting women's sexual rights and condemning doctors and midwives who defend circumcision for their own lucrative ends. *Women and Sex* (1972), her first book, scandalized her compatriots and quickly climbed to the best-seller list in some Arab countries, while it became the most popular under-the-counter item in others. "The irony is that society looks at the woman as a tool of love and deprives her of the one organ which will make her be good at it," she comments in *Women and Neuroses*, which she wrote in 1977.

Circumcision is declining among enlightened people in larger cities, according to Dr. Saadawi. But it does not mean that parents who refuse to mutilate their daughter care less about her chastity. They just use other ways when she reaches puberty.

6

𐎟𐎟𐎟𐎟𐎟𐎟𐎟𐎟𐎟𐎟

Growing Up in a Traditional Society

Whoever doeth good to girls, it will be a curtain to him from hell fire.
—The Prophet Muhammad

With the first drop of her menstrual blood, every Muslim girl becomes a temple of her family's honor. She must remain chaste until marriage and faithful to her husband thereafter. Otherwise she not only shames herself but also destroys her entire family's honor, the highest virtue of the ancient Arabs, which has come to represent everything a respectable man in the Islamic world should have—truthfulness, courage, loyalty, generosity, ability to protect his family, and above all his women's chastity. Small wonder, then, that a young girl's freedom is curtailed abruptly at puberty as parents and relatives rush to protect her virginity at all costs.

When Safya* came of age about a dozen years ago in the oasis of Tozeur in the Tunisian Sahara, she was no longer allowed to play in the palm groves or run to the bazaar on errands. Whenever she had to step out of her house, she veiled herself, and she refrained from speaking with men on the

*All names in this chapter are fictitious unless otherwise stated.

street. I pitied her at first, as another victim of an antiquated tradition who was no doubt dying to be liberated—my way. To my surprise, she did not consider herself imprisoned at all, even though she knew of my less restricted life in Paris. She had no real choice in the matter, but she accepted the harem[1] and the veil cheerfully, as if they were privileges. This is the story of how she lived when I shared her world with her for three months and of how she shaped her future—in her own way.

When I arrived in Tozeur in the summer of 1970, I viewed harems and veils strictly as jails for women. Even checking in at a respectable hotel was not as simple for a woman as it would have been in the U.S. The young innkeeper's jaw dropped when he discovered that no man followed me in with the rest of my baggage: "Alone? You traveled the Sahara all alone? And you are Turkish? And a Muslim?" He gave me a room near his own family's living quarters, where, he assured me, the few Frenchmen who had begun to trickle into the oasis would not bother me. I could not bring myself to admit that I would welcome the company of a male tourist with whom I could do the sights and sit in restaurants unselfconsciously. The good innkeeper seemed to have foreseen the problem of a single woman in a conservative village, for he advised me to stay in my room until he found time to take me sightseeing.

But I had to stretch my legs after the long journey. Moreover, on my way to the oasis from the Algerian Sahara I had skirted the Chott Djerid, an immense dried-up salt lake, which reflected mirages on the horizon. I needed to touch the palm trees and plunge into the springs to make sure that they would not fade under my gaze. I walked out into the main square, a sandy lot bordered by the hotel, the souk (bazaar), and a coffeehouse or two—all of them occupied by men only. A shrouded figure who scurried past a side street to disappear quickly into one of the windowless adobe houses impressed on me all the more that I did not belong on the street. "You're alone, miss? Can I help you?"—a friendly young man underlined my alien status. Too tired to socialize, I walked on to find a place where I could quench my thirst. Hordes of men staring out of the coffeehouses intimidated me enough so that I continued on my way toward the springs.

I desperately wanted to splash in the cool water and bite into a pomegranate or any other fruit that was ready for plucking. Tozeur has been famous since Greco-Roman times for the nearly two hundred springs that feed its verdant orchards, and for the palm trees which yield many varieties of highly prized dates. The local people, anxious to use every bit of arable land around the springs, had built their homes away from the oasis. I still had a long way to walk, and the sun had risen high enough to rob the desert of all its shadows. My destination shimmered over the horizon as if it were a mirage, once more arousing doubt about the reality of the world around me.

"Ah, you are going to the oasis, miss? I invite you to my orchard," another young man called out, suddenly appearing in front of me. I refused politely, but he did not give up. "But you are alone," he insisted, "and I invite you. A woman like you should not be walking alone." *Alone.* I had heard the word, pronounced half solicitously and half accusingly, so many times during my trip across the Sahara that it reverberated like an echo in my feverish brain, reducing me to tears. Maybe I should not have stayed behind my safari companions to see more of the desert on my own. But what was wrong with a woman's traveling alone, anyway? Was I supposed to miss the chance of a lifetime to see the Sahara just because its inhabitants liked to keep their women locked up in their homes? Could I not enjoy even a moment of communion with nature in solitude?

I turned back to the village and took refuge in my hotel, cursing men's scheme to guarantee the legitimacy of their heirs by imprisoning their women at home. It was sneaky to link chastity to honor and pass it off as an Islamic ideal. Not only did men seem to have conveniently forgotten that Islam forbade adultery to both sexes, but they interpreted the Quranic injunction on covering the breast as a command to incarcerate women in their homes and behind shrouds. If God did not want women to run freely against the wind and quench their thirst wherever they wanted to, He would have created them with vestigial legs good only for shuffling about their cramped harems.

To make matters worse, I overheard the innkeeper talking about me excitedly to another young man as I fumed over my glass of mint tea in the hotel's courtyard: ". . . and she is all alone." Predictably, the young man approached me. "I hear you are Turkish and a Muslim and traveling alone," he said. His comment was incongruous for a man in a French outfit who looked like a vacationer from Tunis, where thousands of local women go about their business alone. But the young man turned out to be a native of the oasis who had gone to college in the capital. He was Khalil Shelli, Safya's older brother.

The following morning he returned to the hotel to tell me that everything was arranged and I would live with his family. He had his little sister Fatima in tow as proof of his honorable intentions. "This is a respectable hotel," the innkeeper piped in, "but it is better for a Muslim woman to be with a family." He would have invited me to his house, he explained apologetically, but he was a bachelor with no unmarried sisters to keep me company; staying with him might incite gossip. His bosom friend Khalil, on the other hand, had three sisters, who would be happy to welcome another into their home. My ands, buts, and ifs fell on deaf ears. The matter seemed to have been settled without my being consulted. "Yes, yes, you're right, some women are staying here," said the innkeeper, "but they're French." "And I'm a Turk, another ex-imperialist," I pleaded, unwilling to be whisked off to the unknown even though Khalil appeared to be a decent man. "But you're a

Muslim, and so are we," they repeated. The local policeman
and the postman had joined the chorus by then. "Please, my
family invites you in the name of our village," Khalil tried
once more. "Please come, miss," Fatima added shyly. Exhausted and ill from the physically punishing journey across
the Sahara, I could not resist any longer. I gave in, allowing
Fatima to lead me by the hand as Khalil walked ahead quietly
with my bag toward a cluster of flat-roofed adobe houses
hardly distinguishable from the infinity of sand that surrounded them.

The Shelli family welcomed me as if I were their long-lost
daughter come home. Fatima and her older sister Safya ushered me into a room and helped me wash my hands and sand-
covered feet, one girl pouring the water from a pitcher while
the other caught it in a basin. I changed into the fresh loose-
fitting long cotton gown they held out to me and stepped out
into the shady courtyard, where a feast was spread out on the
low round table. The rest of the family sat on cushions on the
floor, as if posing for a portrait—the oldest sister, Faiza, obvi-
ously pregnant and surrounded by her four small children,
although she appeared to be no more than twenty-one or -two;
the mother, with blue tattoos on her forehead and chin, which
the older generation of women wore to keep away the evil eye;
and the father, his only son, Khalil, and Faiza's husband, Ali.
All of them showed traits of their Arab-Berber heritage, and a
few suggested a touch of black Africa as well. Perhaps the
blood of the Greeks and Romans who were attracted to the
fertile oasis centuries ago also ran in their veins.

Only when the mother beckoned me to the table did I realize that I was to be the guest of honor and eat alone. As an
educated woman from abroad, I might also have been accorded the honor of sitting with the men, but they had already
eaten. Sensing my embarrassment, however, Khalil joined me,
while the women hovered over me, ready to offer a spoon and a
fork in case I failed to roll the semolina grains well enough in
my palm to pop them into my mouth, or found the flatbread a

clumsy tool for picking up the meat and the gravy. They asked me to tell them of my trip. "You are very brave," the mother exclaimed, without pointing an accusing finger at my venturing out alone. "We're honored you came to us. You are a Muslim and my daughter. This is your home, and we hope you stay," the father pronounced ceremoniously. Desperately in need of rest, I gladly accepted the offer to stay through the summer.

Home life quickly improved my health, but the adoption also locked me into the cloistered world of the Shelli women. Their whole life seemed to revolve around half a dozen windowless adobe rooms which opened only on an inner courtyard, where the women took fresh air as they cleaned and cooked. They rose before sunup so that they could dust and sweep the house and do the laundry while it was still cool. These chores never ended, because the sand crept in constantly and clung to everyone's clothes and sandals. The couscous, a staple at almost every meal, was made at home. At fourteen, Safya was already a master in the delicate task. During her summer vacation from school, she spent hours pouring water over the semolina drop by drop and rolling the crumbly dough until tiny pellets of couscous formed. These were steamed like rice over a pot of spicy meat stew—a clever way to cook two dishes at once over the same fire and also flavor the grains with the aroma of the spices and vegetables in the stew. When the men came home for lunch they consumed Safya's masterpiece so heartily that after the midday siesta she had to start the couscous rolling and steaming process all over again for supper. When she had a free moment, she amused her sister's children or wove silk belts.

Despite their ceaseless labors, the Shelli women were underworked by Tozeur's standards. Most of their neighbors made long woolen capes as well as the belts, to be sold at the bazaar, while Mrs. Shelli and her daughters busied their fingers only occasionally; the family did not need the extra money. In fact, Khalil's salary as a teacher and his brother-in-law's as a bookkeeper added so much to the family's income from the sale of dates that the women did not even work in the orchards and vegetable gardens, as did their poorer sisters. That job, along with the ancestral masculine occupation of date-palm cultivation, was relegated to hired workers. When the installation of modern plumbing in the house made it unnecessary for women to fetch water from the springs, their last traditional excuse for going outdoors was gone. They could not even shop for themselves, for the bazaar was an exclusively male territory. Only the eight-year-old Fatima, who did not yet count as a full-fledged woman, could run out of the house freely to play or buy groceries. Because of the economic reasons behind their seclusion, however, the Shelli women's objecting to their lot would have been like preferring crowded subways and public beaches to chauffeured limousines and private swimming pools.

So unequivocally did seclusion mean high class and a man's concern for his women that even the less fortunate women who toiled in the brutal sun insisted on their right to be excluded from certain places in the oasis. Women who contributed substantially to their families' income through farming and handicrafts had no direct control of their income, because only their husbands could sell the products and spend the money at the bazaar. But no one seemed to resent the arrangement. "Thank God I still have a man to go to the bazaar for me," said Khalil's old aunt. Her young grandchildren usually shopped for her daily grocery needs, but the bigger transactions had to be conducted by her husband or sons, who knew the bazaar's intricate web of business relationships. When he got a good price for his goods, the old man would buy fabric and jewelry for the women. At such times even the normally imperious aunt, who wore a perpetual frown on her blue-tattooed brow, smiled as coyly as a young bride, and draped the fabric on herself to show her audience how she planned to cut it. Judging from the artistic sensibility she displayed in weaving silk belts, I suspected that she would have chosen a fabric of another color, but never mind. She would have considered it degrading to buy the cloth for herself.

Accustomed to coming and going as I pleased, I had to keep reminding myself that the Shellis were giving me the red-carpet treatment when they effectively isolated me from the world with their loving care. I wanted to take a walk? The mother dispatched Fatima to bring Khalil home from a teachers' meeting or his transactions at the bazaar so that he could accompany me. I needed medicine? Fatima ran out to buy it for me. I wanted to go to the bazaar to buy a silk belt? No problem. Safya was an expert in the craft and gladly made one for me. It seemed that Mrs. Shelli was bent on socializing me into the respectable niche of the Tozeur women. When I expressed an interest in learning how to roll the couscous, an approving smile spread over her face, and she sat me beside her for many tutorial sessions. At this rate I feared that it would take me a lifetime to see the Roman ruins and the legendary orchards of Tozeur. As a temporary resident of the harem, I could tolerate its demeaning intention of containing women's sexuality, but its walls made me claustrophobic. The yard was large enough for jogging, and the windowless adobe rooms kept out the desert heat more effectively than air conditioning. But I wondered how Safya, who had been as free as Fatima not very long ago, could so cheerfully confine herself to the courtyard day in and day out without wanting to burst out into the wide space beyond the walls. Did seclusion mean so much as a status symbol for a fourteen-year-old? Didn't she ever long to plunge into the cool springs shaded by palm leaves? "But of course," she replied, "and all I have to do is ask."

She asked her mother, who in turn discussed the matter with her husband and son. The men agreed to take the family to Al-Hamma for a picnic and a swim. I thought that we were going to pack a basket and walk over to the nearest palm grove the following morning and wade in our street clothes. Instead, we awoke at dawn and spent hours on maddeningly elaborate preparations. Khalil went to borrow a delivery truck from his innkeeper friend. His brother-in-law disappeared to their garden to slaughter the lamb, which the family had surely been keeping for a much more special occasion than a mere picnic. Little Fatima was dispatched to buy spices. Her mother filled goatskin bags with water and packed nearly all the kitchen utensils, while Safya rolled the couscous and Faiza collected her children, with her father's help. Everything was finally ready by the time Khalil arrived at the door with the truck, laden with the meat and vegetables from the garden. We climbed in with our provisions and took off into the desert.

Al-Hamma turned out to be a small oasis fed by hot springs which were frequented long ago by the Romans. We drove past the inviting palm grove where I thought we were going to picnic and stopped at a tiny version of the Shellis' house. With a waterless kitchen and two small rooms leading into a court-yard, this was not only a beach cabin where we would change into bathing suits, but also where we would cook and dine in private.

While the others prepared the meal, Khalil took me and his two young sisters swimming. Along the canals we passed all-male and all-female groups picnicking and wading in the water strictly among themselves, as if invisible screens sep-arated the sexes. Seeing women dunking themselves in their street clothes, I wondered why we had been allowed to wear bathing suits. Khalil walked on until we reached a house topped with a dome, and left me and the girls at the door, explaining that he would be swimming in the men's section. There was a large pool of hot spring water in a marble hall, which we had to ourselves. My young friends slipped out of their outer garments and frolicked in the water like nymphs among forgotten ancient ruins. When they were thoroughly exhausted, they washed and massaged each other and then turned to work on my muscles.

As two pairs of hands kneaded my back, I realized how tense traveling alone in the desert country had made me. Although it was usually the women's duty to fetch water from the springs and cultivate the vegetable gardens in most of the oases, they were confined to their homes whenever their services were not needed outside. No facilities existed to serve their needs in public, not even teahouses, all of which were men's clubs. Hotels in some of the out-of-the-way oases had nothing but tiny cells without doors, clearly meant for men only. A European woman traveling alone in such a place might be regarded as a crazy foreigner who did not know the harem laws, but a Muslim woman who ventured out alone was assumed to have no family and be in need of protection. Many men obliged, as honor required them to do. Even where a good number of tourists were seen, word of a Muslim woman arriving alone spread fast. Some of the local men insisted on my lodging with their family; others invited me to dinner or to weddings; a few offered to adopt me or to marry me. Although I was a descendant of their former colonial masters, they considered me one of them because of common cultural and historical roots and a sense of brotherhood that Islam had bequeathed us.

On rare occasions I had to deal with the most unpleasant facet of harem laws, the one which judged a Muslim woman on her own as lacking in sexual integrity. "But you are alone," a man protested when I told him I was not looking for illicit adventures. He advised me not to look directly into men's eyes if I wanted to keep out of trouble. Indiscriminately gazing at everything and everyone as a tourist, I had inadvertently met the young man's eyes for a second too long. Shaken, I toyed with the idea of buying a veil. But each region had a differently colored and textured veil, which ascribed to the wearer certain characteristics peculiar to her people. In Tozeur, for instance, married women always wore black, while the unmarried sported a white head veil striped with brilliant colors. Both drew the cloth only momentarily across the lower half of their faces when encountering a man not related to their families; the gesture signaled that the women were not out to flirt.

Most of the Bedouins who camped near Tozeur, on the other hand, dressed in all colors of the rainbow and did not always bother hiding their faces. If you behaved like a Bedouin while clad in black, your intentions could be mistaken. Merely covering the face in all cases, just to be on the safe side, did not always guarantee immunity either, for the veil was a potent silent language. A woman who let her veil glide down just so over her hair or her shoulder even as she covered her face might be flirting rather than saying no. (In fact, prostitutes in Istanbul exploited the veil's seductive possibilities as recently as the 1960s.) I opted for dark glasses instead. At least no one would know where my gaze was directed. In Morocco, looking up and then down encouraged men's advances. Perhaps other ocular signals for the same purpose existed in the Saharan oases. I did not want to take any chances.

In my dismay over being cloistered, I had almost forgotten what it was like to be alone in this part of the world. After weeks of being mistaken for either a waif or a whore, it was a relief to belong to the Shelli household and have a respectable place in the community. As the weeks passed, I found myself more passively and even willingly submitting to the restrictions on my freedom which had so irritated me at first. The male-dominated outside world was too uncomfortable for me. It was so much easier to accept the harem system and work within it, as the women around me did.

For those who knew the rules the harem doors were in fact open. As Safya explained, all she had to do was ask to go out or be taken out wherever a male escort was necessary to legitimize her presence. Not even an adult woman considered the requirement insulting to her maturity. On the contrary, she was proud that the men took elaborate precautions on her behalf. Those who could not afford "beach houses" and swimming pools allowed their young sisters and daughters to splash in a secluded corner of the springs under an older woman's supervision. Though they never took women to such a rigidly male domain as the teahouse, men did their best to keep their women content, in the interest of domestic harmony, insisting only on being kept informed of their whereabouts. Accordingly, the cardinal rule was to go through the motions of clearing the outing with the head of the house. For major or unusual requests girls preferred to use their mothers as mediators. As respected advisers to their husbands and sons, mothers enjoyed so much influence that a girl in love often confessed her secret to her mother. Unless the young man's credentials were totally unacceptable, the mother defended the daughter's choice successfully against an older but richer suitor preferred by the father.

Such quarrels over marriage partners were rare, according to Mrs. Shelli. A Tozeur girl usually settled happily on one of several cousins proposed to her by her family. Since custom forbade dating, she preferred to marry a cousin, whom she had known since childhood, rather than take a chance on a stranger. Having a loving aunt for mother-in-law was equally important, as she would be spending most of her waking hours with her. Perhaps it was because they could not have boyfriends and did not have to look for husbands on their own that young women took as much delight in the social functions of the harem as they did in outings arranged by their fathers and brothers.

Women organized many fascinating activities on their own. Among the most popular were religious, or rather parareligious, functions. Although Mrs. Shelli prayed at home and rarely went to the mosque, she visited the local saints' shrine with her friends. "They're like sacred picnics," she told her young daughters. She also took an occasional evening off from family duties to attend women's prayer meetings of one of the many religious sects which flourished in the oasis. "We have among us a very holy woman who can see into the future. She predicted that my niece was going to have a baby boy, and she did. She also predicted that my own Faiza, who was miserable in marriage, would not need to seek divorce because her husband would suddenly become good to her, and it really happened that way," Mrs. Shelli whispered in awe as she led me along the narrow streets toward the source of the drumbeat. Devotees had already assembled in the courtyard of a house when we arrived. Swaying in rhythm to the drumbeat, they chanted. One of them suddenly threw herself into the middle of the circle and started dancing. Lost in her private world of spirits, she moved slowly at first and then followed the crescendo of the drumbeat until she quivered like a leaf and fell exhausted on the floor, mumbling incoherently. A few guests fanned her, but attention was already focused on the holy woman, who took her place in the circle to repeat the dance and mutter prayers. Foreheads glistened with perspiration in anticipation of the message that the holy woman would deliver to the mortals as soon as she established communication with the spirits. On the evening I attended, the jumbled words that Mrs. Shelli interpreted for me were fairly noncommittal. "Your grandchild will be born in good health and bring honor to your family," the holy woman told Mrs. Shelli. It was a reasonable prediction to make for the healthy young Faiza, who had had four easy deliveries, but Mrs. Shelli, remembering the infants she herself lost long ago, was so relieved to hear the good verdict that she did not mind the spirits' refusal to answer whether the child would be a boy or a girl. For me the holy woman predicted a long and happy life if I respected my health. Everyone knew that I had dragged myself into Tozeur emaciated with fatigue and illness, but it would be unfair to dismiss the woman as a charlatan. She gave good psychiatric help. The magic and fortune-telling were just props to lend her words authority in a village with a long tradition of voodoo-like rituals. They also had cathartic value. Faiza's main problem, for instance, had been her mother-in-law. Through the holy woman's inspiration Mrs. Shelli had maneuvered to have Faiza and Ali live in her home, where the young couple's relationship blossomed.

Influenced by her city-educated brother, Safya would have none of the "old-fashioned mumbo jumbo." But she did tag

along to the harem celebrations of weddings and circum-
cisions. Safya met all of her girlfriends there and was seen by
matrons on the lookout for daughters-in-law. Although local
custom favored marriage between cousins, Mrs. Shelli liked to
impress the right cousin's mother. Accordingly, she transformed her daughter into an exotic princess for these occasions. With a brilliantly colored fabric draped over her long
tunic and fastened at the shoulders with cross-and-crescent
pins, Safya would have looked like an ancient Greek goddess
had she not also been covered from head to ankle with the
massive silver jewelry of her Berber ancestors. It would have
delighted a choreographer to see her and her similarly dressed
friends emerge from the plain veils like butterflies from their
cocoons and stretch out on cushions in their hostess's courtyard. Eventually the drums coaxed many of them to dance,
while the rest swayed to the hypnotic rhythm and threw out
compliments. Suggestive of what is known in the West as the
belly dance, their movements trained the muscles needed for
natural childbirth. Women were encouraged to learn to dance
at a very young age and continued well into their middle
years. So well coordinated were they that they could keep a
pitcher balanced on their heads while performing intricate
steps. Stuck in duller celebrations in their own quarters, men
were eager for a peek at the mirage-like splash of tropical
colors dancing in the desert night.

To think that I'd once felt imprisoned in the harem! As my
knowledge of the community's events and gossip widened
along with my circle of friends, thanks to these parties, I
ceased to notice the four walls enclosing me in one house or
another most of the time, to be inconvenienced by the advance
planning needed to venture into men's territory. Like my host-
esses, I began to accept jealous protectiveness as my privilege
and to like the feminine world of parties, religious outings,
and simple cooking and weaving sessions at home. It might
not have fulfilled me for life, but it temporarily satisfied my
huge appetite for physical and mental activities, including

being in touch with the world around me. If I were a permanent resident, I could also have exercised great influence over the affairs of the oasis, for the harem was a powerful decision-making, social welfare, and public relations center. Not only were marriages made there, help for neighbors in need was organized with remarkable speed. The support was psychological as often as it was material. For example, harem pressure inspired many a mean husband and mother-in-law to shape up. It was also through the women that the latest news on every aspect of oasis life was disseminated, as were new remedies and ideas. Men who ignored harem power risked their domestic tranquility and public dignity.

Cooperating with women was also a matter of honor for men. In the desert honor was basically a feudal system with a whole series of mutual obligations between the sexes that helped the community survive. A woman produced heirs only for her husband and thus increased his clan's number. In return, the husband supplied her material needs and protected her against the harsh environment—and against the enemy in the old days of tribal warfare. So sacrosanct was this marital arrangement that it was considered every man's civic duty, or honor, to contribute to the pool of acceptable brides by protecting his sister as well as his daughter. "At my age most bachelors in the West worry only about themselves. I use my salary and my free time to help my father care for all the women of our house," the twenty-four-year-old Khalil said.

A brother looked after his sister's welfare long after she moved to her husband's house, for her behavior reflected on her natal family's honor throughout her life. However selfishly motivated, the brother's altruism deterred a less than kind husband from mistreating her. When it did not, the divorcée was taken back into her own family. Khalil and his parents had gone so far as to take both Faiza and her husband into their house in order to save the marriage from the mother-in-law's destructive influence.

If a woman did not live up to her end of the bargain and

committed adultery, punishment involved more than loss of protection. In many strictly traditional communities the only way to erase the dishonor that she brought on her family was to kill her. Although this custom has waned considerably, it is actually permitted by law in some countries today and is punished only lightly in most others. Since Islamic laws protecting women reflect the ancient code of honor in many respects, some people mistakenly believe that the Quran also ordained the murder of adulteresses. The survival of this form of punishment, which has been reported since biblical times, illustrates perfectly how today's Muslims often meld pre-Islamic custom with the Shariah in governing their behavior toward women.

Ironically, Safya's future in the modern world also hinged on her submission to the ancient lord-vassal relationship. As one of the first generation of women to go to a coeducational middle school—the only type the government provided—she was watched nervously by her family, although most of her classmates in this small oasis were her relatives. Any indiscretion on her part which threatened the family honor would have interrupted her education. She had to please her brother above all, not only because he taught in her school and was always on hand to chaperone her but also because her semiliterate parents had left it to their son to direct her future. Spurred by his country's commitment to women's rights during his college years, Khalil never tired of impressing on his sister the importance of education: "There were no schools during Faiza's time, but now you have no excuse for leaving your brain idle." Actually, middle-school education was still the highest that the oasis offered to both boys and girls. What had changed since Faiza's adolescence was the Shelli family's attitude toward letting their unmarried daughter stay with distant relatives in a neighboring town which had a high school and a teacher-training institute.

Behind the idealistic move, however, was a far more practical reason. The handful of local girls who had earned teach-

ing certificates were much sought after as brides because they
drew good salaries which helped make up for inflation and the
splitting of date-crop revenues among an increasing population. "A woman who has been to school brings more than a
salary, actually," Khalil added, explaining that he and his educated friends hoped to find wives whose minds would meet
theirs.

But like their semiliterate older sisters, educated women
were expected to stay at home when they were not studying or
working outside. Even after several years of advanced study
Safya saw no contradiction in dividing her life between seclusion at home and a career in a school with a mixed faculty.
Indeed, living in a conservative little town with relatives who
hovered nervously over her virtue had made her only too
happy to return home to the wide-open desert and her old
ways. She felt that women were best suited by nature for
homemaking and childcare. Teaching was both a modern extension of that role and a chance to train girls for better motherhood and for such careers as midwifery and nursing. Teaching alongside men should be no different from working in the
orchards practically side by side with the men who tended the
palm trees, Safya said, pointing out that women did not veil
themselves while farming. "A piece of cloth alone won't protect anyone's virtue anyway," she added.

Though the veil was a superfluous screen from colleagues
and relatives, it was a useful symbol of respectability among
strangers—when a woman walked alone in the "downtown"
area, for example. "Don't you also have dress codes that tell
others that you are not what is called a loose woman? You can
bare your breast in some parts of Africa, for example, but not
in Europe," Safya noted. The veil's practical uses overshadowed its sexual implications, for all of the Shelli women considered it a most effective "hat" against the merciless sun.
Even men covered their faces completely during sandstorms in
order to protect their eyes. My resistance to the veil dissolved
as the sun cooked my shoulders to the point where the pain

kept me awake at night. When I learned to wear Faiza's old white veil without getting my feet tangled up in it, I finally understood why some women preferred to wear the veil. It is a great equalizer, covering rags as well as envy-provoking rich garments, fat bodies as well as lean. Draped properly, it can enhance any woman's grace and lend her an alluring mystery. The Iranian poet Iraj Mirza called it the cloud from which the moon peeked out, inspiring men to court her ardently for the privilege of beholding the rest of her charms. No wonder the beauties of Teheran before Ayatollah Khomeini's reign often hid themselves teasingly behind diaphanous silks.

In fact, the opaque veil permitted a woman to modernize her wardrobe much faster than she might otherwise have been able to do. Many daringly low-cut Parisian evening gowns emerge from behind veils at Saudi Arabian parties, for instance. Although Mrs. Shelli preferred the traditional long tunics for herself, she sympathized with her young daughter's eagerness to have mini-skirts and figure-revealing slacks like the ones which so-and-so's older brother brought back from Tunis. She let Safya wear such outfits on condition that she veil them in the street in order to avoid scandalized gossip. When a large enough number of girls wore their novelties long enough around the house, the mother pointed out, the conservative elders eventually gave in to the new fashion.

These youthful revolts against the establishment tended to remain within reasonable bounds, with no one demanding to parade down the street in shorts and halter tops. The minor changes satisfied the adolescent girl's thirst for novelty and kept her cheerfully obedient to the restrictions in her life. The remoteness of the oasis spared her from an undigestible avalanche of outside influences that would throw her into cataclysmic conflict with her traditions. French magazines and films were not readily available ten years ago, and even the television programs from the capitals of the Middle East seemed curiously unreal in the desert, where the elements demanded attention in all their harsh splendor. We started watching an Egyptian soap opera on television one evening, out in the courtyard. About fifteen minutes into the program, the air resounded as usual with the drumbeats of a religious meeting, and the weeping of the TV heroine sounded like noise interference on a bad shortwave radio. Before the program was over, the first blast of the sandstorm blew. We gathered up the television set and the rugs and took refuge in one of the rooms to continue watching the program. We could not hear anything over the whistling wind, but no one was interested any longer. We switched off the television and turned our full attention to the raging wind and sand. The desert is like the sea. Its moods and its power rule those who live with it.

Perhaps the isolated life of the oasis kept sexual mores relatively conservative among the young. Taught by their mothers that physical proximity to boys would bring dishonor, girls played in the school courtyard by themselves, mingling with boys only in groups. In fact, they were convinced that any girl who met a boy alone had in mind only one thing. A tangible proof occurred during my first visit to the oasis. One girl grew a belly of unmistakable proportion and was pulled out of school into a shotgun marriage. She was lucky compared to adulteresses in other remote areas of the Middle East and North Africa—no one at Tozeur demanded her blood to wash away the dishonor. But the moral of her fate was not lost on Safya and her girlfriends who hoped to be teachers and nurses, the salaried elite of Tozeur womanhood. "She was a good student. She could have made something of herself. It's too bad," muttered Safya.

The incident jolted the entire oasis out of its calm. Gossiping women visited one house after another, embroidering details into the pregnant girl's story, speculating on its whys and wherefores, and driving its moral home to the young. With women like them one did not need newspapers or survey takers in Tozeur. A few suggested that the girl might have been sexually too naive to know what she was getting into. Nonsense, replied the others, surely she had learned about the birds and the bees from her mother or from other older women. Of course the girl knew what she was doing. "What was wrong with the old Quranic schools, where boys and girls were separated?" clucked the old aunt with the blue tattoo on her face as she dropped in to visit the Shellis after making the rounds of the neighborhood. "I tell you," she continued, without giving anyone a chance to break in, "that's how life is around here—men and women live in separate worlds. So what are the new schools trying to do, throwing boys and girls together for a few hours a day? After that they go back home to separate worlds anyway. Some families suddenly found husbands for their daughters. Do you know what that means? No school for girls. I tell you, they would have been better off in all-girls school." She made sense. It was risky to tear the veil from a woman's body without also tearing it from her society's mind.

The girl's seducer was returned to the village's good graces simply by marrying her. The adulteress, on the other hand, continued to suffer verbal stoning even though she was respectably wed. She had dishonored the clan, and her marriage was only a bandage over the sin. Nobody thought the sexual double standard unfair, reasoning that she deserved worse for threatening both the conservatives' sense of honor and the liberals' educational ambitions. I wondered if the poor woman would not have preferred death, but before the end of the summer the gossip subsided. The lesson had been driven home, and the community returned to its all-consuming occupation of surviving in the desert. It was as if a sandstorm had swept the crime clean out of the oasis's memory.

With the building of an airport and more hotels, Tozeur had exploded into a major resort by the late 1970s. Only men deal directly with the tourists, however, leaving women pretty much in their traditional space. The relationship between the sexes continues to be governed by honor, with the woman remaining chaste in exchange for her father's and brother's material support, protection, and help in finding a husband. Increased affluence has made it possible for many more girls to follow Safya to school. Unfortunately, the small oasis cannot absorb all the women who train for teaching and social and paramedical work. Nor can these women migrate on their own to cities, as their brothers often do when they cannot find a suitable job at home. Few of the sisters follow these brothers to the city. And no one openly challenges the code of honor that puts such a premium on their chastity that they cannot strike out independently to forge their own destiny.

Though they may be on the verge of taking yet another step away from the harem, most of these young women envy Safya, who thrives peacefully in the sheltered world of her adolescence. She has fulfilled herself in the dream which continues to inspire young women. She is educated and enjoys a good teaching post at the local middle school without sacrificing the security of her traditional life, which is considered particularly sweet in her case because of the understanding and devotion that both her brother and her husband show toward her. Unlike many brothers, who stay in the city and send money home as absentee protectors, Khalil returned home to guide his sister toward a modern career and an educated husband. Though he is married and has children of his own, Khalil still watches over his sister's psychological and material welfare, as does her husband. Now that she has a baby, she is doubly content to rush back home from school and let the men manage her salary and do the shopping. She no longer veils herself as consistently as she used to, because the blouse-and-skirt combinations that she likes are considered respectable enough these days. But she often carries around her new black married woman's veil, mainly to shield herself against the sun.

Western-educated women may find it all too easy to view Safya's life through an outraged feminist perspective,[2] but her world suggests how the concept of honor may function under close-to-ideal conditions in small isolated communities, and how some men may be tempted to romanticize that world and try to re-create it in big cities—often with bitter results for women. Not every neighbor is a cousin in the city. Nor is the pace of Westernization slow enough for a comfortable integration with the traditional system of values. Seclusion of women may rigidify in such circumstances, which is all the more painful for women who must live isolated in tiny apartments rather than spend their days amid a large clan in the wide space of the hinterlands. Deprived of education and a chance to participate in the life around them, these women come to view honor merely as a tyrannical outmoded macho obsession with virginity. In many countries feminists of both sexes are trying to redefine honor in modern urban terms. Muslim girls growing up in cities today are heavily influenced by this process.

7

᠊᠊᠊᠊᠊᠊᠊᠊᠊᠊

Growing Up in a Transitional Society

The honor of woman lies in her being educated
Her veil should be her good breeding.[1]
—Maruf Rusafi, Iraqi poet (1875–1945)

"We want a free Algerian woman, not a free Frenchwoman,"
former president Boumedienne of Algeria was fond of saying.
He might as well have rephrased his slogan to speak for urban
parents everywhere in the Islamic world who want to educate
their daughters for a modern society without losing her completely to Western influences that inundate the cities: "We
want a free Muslim woman, not a Western woman." The only
trouble is that after centuries of being shut in, a free modern
Muslim woman has yet to emerge. And today's young women
are guinea pigs in that experiment.

This soul-searching does not call for a return to Islamic
fundamentalism, but rather tries to resolve the questions national liberation movements in Algeria and other Muslim
countries raised when they championed women's educational
rights without managing to topple the harem mentality. How
can a woman study and work away from home without compromising her virtue and her chances for marriage, especially

since she must delay marriage well beyond puberty in order to complete her studies? Will she be content with the old constraints on her life once she has been educated in a modern school which trains the mind to reason and question the status quo rather than simply memorize the Quran and submit to tradition, as the old schools did? If she goes on to hold a job, how will her financial independence affect the lord-vassal relationship between the sexes decreed by the ancient code of honor? In other words, the main problem in the search for the modern Muslim woman is to reconcile her rediscovered Islamic right to education with the tradition of honor. *Reconcile* is the key word, for there is yet no question of throwing out the tradition of honor on which the patriarchal society was built. Few have solved the dilemma, and many are facing it for the first time as education and industrialization reach them.

Overwhelmed by the cultural tug-of-war, some parents keep their daughters out of school altogether. About six years ago Amina Laribi of Algiers was earmarked for a semiliterate life for just such a reason. As soon as she "became a woman" her father announced that she had had enough schooling and must now stay at home to refine her domestic skills in preparation for marriage.

As a humble clerk, Mr. Laribi could support his large family only with the supplementary income that his wife earned by sewing at home, but he could well afford to keep Amina in the free public girls' school. Yet so afraid was he for his daughter's virtue on the streets full of young men who acted "like Frenchmen" that he was ready to ignore the state law requiring him to keep his child in school until she was sixteen. Such a law was fit only for the rich, who could chauffeur their daughters to school, he reasoned.

Even if her chastity could somehow be protected, he was not convinced of the value of educating a woman too much. The first woman to be educated in his family had turned out badly. His oldest daughter, Zohra, had been an exemplary

Muslim girl who cheerfully submitted to the veil despite the rage for mini-skirts that swept the city shortly after independence in 1962. When he married her off at age fifteen to a cousin working in France, however, she went to nursing school and took a job, thus exposing herself to such corrupt French customs as smoking, drinking, and provocative fashions. Her husband would surely have packed her home had he not died. In fact, it might have been far better if he *had* sent her back to Algiers, for when she was widowed she insisted on living alone in her Paris apartment instead of returning to her family or her in-laws. It did not matter that she worked during the day and went to school at night, which gave her precious little time for lovers. The point was that everyone back home knew of her living arrangement and could speculate on the virtue of the childless twenty-four-year-old widow, which cast a shadow on her family's honor. As upset as if he had actually been dishonored, the father indiscriminately blamed Zohra's iconoclastic habits on the French, on her modern education, and, when he dared speak ill of the dead, on her husband for having failed to put his foot down on her. Old Mr. Laribi knew that women deserved certain rights because they had helped fight for their nation's independence from France, but he was not willing to sacrifice his honor for them.

Amina wanted to stay in school, because her best friends did and because she viewed a good profession as a passport to the personal freedom that Zohra enjoyed. Her situation was even more difficult since her family did not share the middle and upper classes' long tradition of educating their daughters. The only Muslim "culture" which her barely educated father displayed, other than his daily prayers, consisted of the code of honor and the custom of veiling. These he guarded jealously against the French, suspecting every innovation as the enemy's plot to undermine his Algerian identity. Reports of Frenchmen who corrupted Algerian women into prostitution and compelled their Algerian employees to bring their wives to drinking parties had made Mr. Laribi cling all the more desperately to the outer trappings of traditional respectability. In the light of his experiences, modern education was deeply suspect—and Zohra's case proved him right.

Amina tried to win her mother, Rabia, to her side. Mrs. Laribi, who had stepped out of her home unveiled for the first time in her life to work for the resistance movement against the French, sympathized with both of her daughters' ambition to do something more than housework, although she herself had been only too happy to return to her children at the end of the war. She also recognized the more practical reasons which would soon end the Algerian woman's days of sitting at home making couscous. The War of Independence had left half a million widows, each with children and old parents to feed. Many did not have sons to take care of them and turned to their daughters for help. In fact, it was the checks which Zohra sent home from Paris that kept her brother in college. With the cost of living skyrocketing, even married women had to work. She herself was a good example. "Ah, those government schools came too late for me," she often muttered as she strained her eyes embroidering beads on the tunic-like traditional garments which wealthy women wore as evening gowns. "If you don't study, you will end up blind doing this kind of work," she told her daughters after recounting episodes of her revolutionary adventures. Zohra and Amina had absorbed her idealistic faith in education, but how could she convince her husband that the old feminine mystique did not work for new Algeria?

Somehow she succeeded in coaxing her husband out of his old reflexes. Amina could continue her studies on the condition that she be escorted to and from school by one of her brothers. So well recognized is the role of the brother as the guardian of his sister's honor that her ten-year-old brother was considered a proper chaperon when the older ones were busy. Rich Saudi Arabians reconciled the harem tradition with modern education by transporting girls in private cars and buses with one-way-view window panes to sexually segregated schools. Mr. Laribi had found a poor man's version of that approach.

Throughout the Middle East so many parents have failed to resolve the conflict that girls' enrollment in secondary school consistently has been much lower than in primary school. In 1975 an estimated 61 percent of Algerian girls aged six to eleven were in school, as opposed to only 24 percent of those aged twelve to seventeen. The enrollment declined from 30 percent in the primary level to 20 percent in the secondary in Morocco; from 72 percent to 22 percent in Libya; from 71 percent to 45 percent in Jordan; from 54 percent to 28 percent in Iraq; and from 26 percent to 6 percent in both Oman and Pakistan. Even Egypt and Lebanon, long considered the educational capitals of the Arab world, reported a drop from 52 percent to 27 percent and from 85 percent to 55 percent, respectively. Nor have the liberal feminist reforms in Turkey and Tunisia stopped parents from pulling their teenage daughters out of school. The female enrollment figures dropped from 66 percent to 34 percent in Turkey and from 63 percent to 24 percent in Tunisia.[2]

The high dropout rate is due as much to widespread poverty in the Middle East as to concern for feminine virtue; even though schools are free, many boys also leave school at twelve or thirteen, when they are old enough to help their parents scrape together a living. As the family's future breadwinners, however, sons are pulled out of school only as a last resort, after all the daughters have been put to work or married off. The boys' 1975 secondary-school enrollment rate thus exceeded the girls' by an average of 20 to 25 percent in most countries. The gap might have been narrower had coeducation been allowed, but girls have been trapped in a vicious circle. Parental concern for their virtue has forced the authorities to build separate facilities for teenage boys and girls, except in a very few countries. Where the budget was limited enough to force a choice between a boys' school and a girls', community fathers had no trouble in reaching a decision.

However, the 1975 enrollment figures for girls indicate that the concept of honor is being redefined in more and more areas to include education whenever the economic situation permits.[3] When older women who grew up before this change are counted, the percentage of women who have ever been to school drops dramatically. The overall female literacy rate in the 1970s was estimated to be 35 percent in Turkey, 20 percent in Egypt, 18 percent in Tunisia, 15 percent in Jordan, 13 percent in Iraq, 6 percent in Morocco, and 4 percent in Libya and Saudi Arabia. Only Lebanon boasted 80 percent.[4] The male literacy rate in these countries was 15 to 35 percent higher.

In light of such statistics the rise in university enrollment highlights even more eloquently the extent to which Middle Eastern women's role has changed since their countries gained independence or started benefiting from oil revenues. In 1954 the number of Muslim women in Algerian universities was negligible. Today Algerian women comprise about 20 percent of the university student body, with their government allocating as much as 11 percent of its GNP to education—far more than what the U. S. and the U.S.S.R. spend on schools. There were no women in Libyan universities in 1964, but they went on to take 10 percent of the seats in 1969 and 18 percent in 1976. Kuwaiti women have made the most phenomenal progress—with none of them enrolled in college in their own country in 1970, they constituted about 60 percent of the student body by 1975. Even Turkish and Egyptian universities, which started admitting women more than fifty years earlier, cannot boast of more than a 30 percent female enrollment.[5] The Kuwaiti track record hides only one discrimination against women: unconstrained by the business of honor, men find it easier to go off to Harvard or Oxford, where they can taste the Western way of life. But women's progress is real, just the same, and reflects the advantages of living in a wealthy and small city-state when it comes to effecting change.

Wealth also helped the Saudi women move ahead in education once their government saw the advantages of training women to fill the country's acute worker shortage. When the first Saudi Arabian elementary school for girls opened in 1960, thanks to strings pulled by Queen Mother Iffat, only the bravest few went escorted by the police, for the guardians of public morals threatened to flog them. Ten years later girls made up almost a third of the elementary school enrollment. Their oldest predecessors have now gone on to take about 7 percent of the places in the universities. About six thousand female university students ventured abroad in 1979, three thousand of them in the United States alone—a good third of the total number of Saudis in American universities. In 1970 only twenty women had ever made it to these shores, although their brothers numbered about one thousand. Along with their sisters studying in Cairo, Beirut, and Europe, these women are the elite of the elite, and the only ones who listen to male professors, lecturing in person, in the same room as their male classmates.

Those who have to listen to male professors on closed-circuit television and ask them questions by telephone feel fortunate compared to their illiterate mothers, and point out that women's education in countries now considered relatively liberal also started out with scrupulous respect for harem traditions, for fear of offending the powerful conservatives. When a teacher-training school for women opened in Istanbul in 1911, the oldest and ugliest men were chosen for its faculty, as no educated aristocratic woman was available for the post. Leaving nothing to chance, the principal cloistered the men behind a partition in the classroom and required them to be chaperoned by older women from their own families.[6] In 1924, three years before Cairo University opened its doors to women, an Egyptian woman dared cross the line of sexual apartheid and enrolled in the coeducational American University of Beirut. As if having her husband tag along to babysit her were not enough, she wore two layers of veils.[7] Not that women ever mingled with their male classmates—they sat apart in the classrooms, and played tennis and swam only when the men were not nearby.

Today men and women study, discuss politics, and socialize more freely in Beirut and Istanbul as well as in Cairo. A more relaxed attitude toward sexual integration is reflected in the increasing enrollment of women in "masculine" fields. In 1971–72 one-fourth to one-half of the places in law, business administration, medicine, chemistry, and pharmacy were taken by women at the University of Istanbul, the oldest in Turkey and the first to accept women. Its forestry department has women students, too. Ten enrolled, for the first time, in the academic year 1971–72. Al-Azhar University in Cairo, the most prestigious theological center of the Islamic world, for a long time a male stronghold, not only has accepted women students since 1962 but also has women professors of Islamic law on its faculty. And already one of the first crop of Saudi women students has published a poem criticizing her sisters who do not spend their time in college seriously, just marking time until marriage and blindly submitting to the status quo. "To tell me you accept the Tribe's traditions and prescriptions," writes Fawziyya Abu Khalid, "is a concession to being buried alive."

Because the harem mentality has remained an important part of the code of honor, education has invariably thrown Muslim women in conflict with their traditional culture. School opened their eyes to wider horizons and prepared them to take active roles in their society, while home restricted their freedom in order to guard their reputation and marriageability. The best career in the world was tangential to the sacred feminine roles of wife and mother. Amina bitterly resented having her merit judged by her chastity. Why should an intact hymen be more important than intelligence and kindness, she asked. Why should Djamila Boupacha, the Algerian war heroine, have had to worry more about her "honor" than her safety when she was raped with a bottle in a French prison? Shouldn't she have held up her head high instead, since her suffering inspired Simone de Beauvoir and Pablo Picasso to rally world opinion to her nation's cause? Didn't she prove that personality was more important in a woman, by eventually becoming a good wife and mother? Amina did not object to remaining a virgin until marriage, but she wanted to be responsible for her virtue without external controls imposed on her as if she were a bitch in constant heat. She wanted women to be treated as adults, answerable only to their conscience.

But she shared her thoughts only with fellow heretics at school, knowing full well that the time had not yet come to express them at home, much less translate them into reality. One threat to her father's honor, she feared, would jeopardize the educational rights for which she had fought so hard. Pinning her hopes on the day when she would change her destiny from a position of influence and financial independence, she learned to submit patiently to a schizophrenic life. Every day she commuted between a school for modern women and a home where the couscous pan and the mop awaited her. Her brothers not only refused to help her, they ordered her to fetch snacks for them while they watched television. They had to watch the important news or do their homework or go out for an important meeting with friends. She had to stay at home to be groomed for her future role as housewife. Only her mother saw to it that she had enough time to do her school assignments.

Although Mrs. Laribi did not fully comprehend the ideas stirring her daughter, she sympathized with youthful restlessness and tried to channel it into such acceptable social activities as women's wedding parties, visits to relatives, and shopping expeditions, which acted merely to distract Amina temporarily from her silent envy of the apparently freer lifestyle that she saw in French magazines and in the elegant quarters of Algiers itself. Their small modern apartment, without even an inner courtyard for women, was not made to contain an adolescent's energy, but the new building design that did not shield women altogether from the outside world occasionally worked to Amina's advantage. She liked to exchange a few words on the staircase with a neighbor's son or sit out on her balcony whenever the young man who lived across the street emerged on his. But her ultimate escape to the world of young lovers seemed to come from the pulp romances that she borrowed from her school friends and read between the covers of her literature and algebra texts.

The world of women from more liberal families may be larger, but it is never as large as their brothers'. Limited physical space remains a condition of virtuous femininity. In her autobiographical novel *I Live* Laila Baalabaki writes of how she entered a cinema alone in Beirut as an act of defiance against the narrowness of the Lebanese woman's space in the 1950s. Her courage almost failed her when the ticket seller repeatedly asked, "One ticket, miss? Only one?" "Alone? You are alone?" the usher repeated, eyeing her suspiciously. She was made so self-conscious that she could barely concentrate on the film.

Laila was doing the Middle Eastern equivalent of a woman's entering a man's pub or a porno theater alone and hearing echoes of "What's a nice girl like you doing in a place like this?" Unwilling to brave stares and gratuitous remarks, most women accept the public space unofficially assigned to them even today. If none exists, they may even demand it. A public beach near Alanya on the Turkish shores of the Mediterranean put up a special tent for ladies only about ten years ago—at women's insistence. I had considered it a blatant violation of the ideals of sexual equality to which Turkey was committed until my sisters and I went to the beach unescorted. We were literally besieged by a crowd of young men who wanted to become our friends simply because we were the only unescorted young women in bathing suits in a part of the country where women usually swam in large groups, wearing long underwear. The following day we gladly accepted our aunt as chaperone and sat willingly under the "ladies' tent," which no Romeo dared invade on pain of expulsion from the beach by a well-built lifeguard. Since our chaperone did not want to ruin her alabaster skin in the sun, however, she found a private beach harem for us, complete with a guard. Every day we entered the kitchen of a teahouse on the edge of a cliff overlooking the bay and climbed down the rocks to a platform which the owner, Mehmet Bey, had made for himself. No one from the shore could ever suspect our presence as we sunned lazily or dived into the sea. If young men on boats spotted us and approached the platform, the eagle-eyed Mehmet Bey came down, ostensibly to offer us more tea. Twirling his thin black mustache, he stared at the intruders until they left. We did not mind his supervision, especially since any man on our "approved" list was permitted to stay.

"Almost any man" would be a more correct way of putting it, for the Westernized intellectual and professional families of Turkey, like their liberal counterparts elsewhere in the Middle East, prefer to have their daughters socialize with men on *their* "approved" list—usually cousins and sons of their close friends. Any man outside their urban tribe (based on socio-economic ties) must pass the family's rigid scrutiny before qualifying for the list. A Turkish college student whom I know fell in love with a classmate who is not on her physician father's list. She arranges to be picked up by her friend at her sympathetic young aunt's home.

The most popular tools of courtship among women who are too closely supervised to meet men at will are the mail and the telephone. The facelessness that a telephone confers may in fact make a girl boldly flirtatious. In the late 1960s, when the village near Alanya had single-digit telephone numbers, the handsome son of a well-to-do cotton farmer received several phone calls from a mysterious young woman who rhapsodized on his Adonis-like features and asked him to meet her late at night in the nearby banana grove. With so few households that had both a telephone and a husky-voiced woman with a well-bred Turkish accent, it was not difficult to figure out who the caller was. The daughter of a banker on summer vacation, she was smitten by the villager, whom her father would never permit her to see. After much deliberation the young man went to the banana grove at the appointed hour, but found only bananas there, according to my brother. Throughout the summer the romance continued over the telephone, with the platonic lovers managing to chat by themselves at the beach once, only to have her irate parents remove her to a more respectable distance. The village telephones have three digits now, and Adonis finds it more difficult to guess who some of his anonymous admirers are. Only from their accents can he tell that village maidens are also after him. If their fathers find out, either they or he will be done for. Or he may end up a groom at a shotgun wedding, he boasted to my brother with pleased resignation.

To the banker's daughter, whom I shall call Selma, the episode underlined a painful lack of communication between her and her mother at a time when she most needed guidance and understanding to sort out the many contradictions in her life. She went to a coeducational school, traveled abroad, and attended mixed parties with her parents or with young men approved by her family. Every aspect of her life threw her into men's company. Yet she was bound to the old rules of chastity as firmly as Amina, whose all-girls school and secluded life at home at least gave her a clearer message of what was expected of her. Selma enjoyed the broader, modern definition of honor that Amina wanted—she had a greater opportunity to be responsible for her own behavior—but she needed an understanding adult who would discuss the problems that she encountered along the way, for which she had no precedent to guide her. Well-intentioned and educated though she was, the mother could not help but cling to her old values whenever her daughter's behavior baffled her. Having attended a girls' school in the 1940s and let the elders arrange her marriage, she had never grappled with the intricacies of surviving in mixed company as a single woman. "I wish Mother would have talked with me at first, though, instead of rushing to tell Father when she saw me talking with the young man. She knew that I did not believe in sleeping around and that I was very serious about becoming an architect," Selma reminisced some years ago, adding that she would never have dreamt of inviting Adonis out to the banana grove had she been permitted to speak to him openly at the beach.

Amid the dizzyingly rapid social changes taking place in the cities, so many mothers are failing in their traditional role of confidante and adviser to their daughters that numerous articles have recently taken up the issue. Talk with your daughter with an open mind even if her life is not a rerun of yours and you cannot understand her, pleads the Tunisian weekly *Dialogue pour le progrès.* "The adolescent girl is afraid, unsure of herself, and shut in on herself, and she feels profoundly alone in facing her problems. Loneliness can easily degenerate into despair,"[8] it goes on to say, warning that poor study habits, difficult behavior, and emotional outbursts as well as destructive reactions against tradition are due to this desperate loneliness and confusion. If this sounds like timeworn advice to Americans, it is a new message for many parents in the Islamic world, who are dealing with older, unmarried, and comparatively free teenagers for the first time in recent history.

Turks have gone one step further, publishing a magazine which tells parents how to talk with the young generation. *Elele,* launched three years ago in Istanbul, discusses all aspects of man-woman relationships that need to be redefined or at least brought out into the open after centuries of sexual segregation. A typical issue may feature anything from how to discuss sex with sons and daughters to sexual fantasies and jealous spouses. No topic is taboo, although sex is discussed strictly within the context of marriage. Because it was for so long mistakenly considered Islamic and genteel to shun frank talk on sex, all articles are carefully prefaced by a note that sex is not shameful and good mental and physical health and a successful modern marriage depend on being informed about sex at an early age. To help bashful parents, photographs and illustrations are provided as teaching aids. It is one of the first popular Turkish publications on sex education to get away from the sleazy voyeuristic approach and make frank discussions of sex respectable between a man and his wife and between parents and their children of all ages.

Perhaps it was a tone of respectability as much as the authoritative information that was badly needed as a bridge between the harem and the modern world. The magazine implicitly reconciles honor with women's education and professional rights by portraying women who have responsible jobs outside the home and happily return home each afternoon to share the joys of sex and childrearing with their husbands. For example, to convey the message that a woman who can be trusted on the job can be trusted with her own body, a husband-and-wife dental team are shown caring for their little daughter together and dropping her off at a day-care center on the way to their office. A nursing supervisor or a psychologist equates a morally healthy and lasting marriage with total trust and sharing between husband and wife. A pretty songstress who enjoys a nice-daughter image glamorizes such a union by announcing that she too hopes to marry a true friend rather than a rich sultan.

Unfortunately, their price and sophisticated language keep such intelligent publications as *Elele* beyond the reach of the semiliterate poor. A reader points out that migrants from conservative villages, who comprise a large percentage of the urban poor, would be outraged by the glorification of the nude body. "And what parent would show his own sexual organs to teach his child about sex?" she writes to the editor, calling for an approach that would be better adapted to conservative mores, which cannot leap from veils to nudity even within the privacy of the home. Her remark confirms a recent survey of high school seniors that revealed young rural migrants' great thirst for information suited to their needs in the city. Friends, parents, and the media often left the young not only with a feeling of shame but also with incomplete or wrong information, according to the survey by Ankara's Academy of Social Services.

Public schools, which reach a large cross section of society, increasingly are being called upon to provide sex education in Turkey and elsewhere. Dr. Adel Malek, a journalist with television station Tele Orient in Beirut, found that both teenagers and their mothers preferred to have the schools offer sex education. The majority of the middle-class Beirut teens whom he interviewed in the mid-1970s told him that they obtained their first information on sex from friends and the media and that they never discussed any questions related to sex with their parents.[9] Inspired by this finding, several schools launched a sex education program, but found themselves squeezed between supportive parents and those who feared that such courses would lead their daughters to experiment.[10]

Despite such difficulties, the debate in the more liberal countries centers less on whether sex education should be given than on how it should be presented to suit the needs of modern Muslim teenagers. Instruction on anatomy and birth control must be balanced with proper admonition to practice sex strictly within marriage. This seemingly straightforward and acceptably Muslim educational goal can be fraught with difficulties, as Egypt found out in its initial attempt at sex education in high schools during the mid-1960s.[11] To placate the conservatives, the course emphasized the moral issues in such a way that it ended by surrounding sex with unpalatable dangers—hardly what Islam decreed.

Keeping in mind the pitfalls that their colleagues in other Muslim countries fell into, Tunisian teachers set up one of the most successful high school sex education programs in 1974. First, they cleaned its image by removing the taboo word *sex* and named their program "Population Education," which parents associated with serious talks on employment and GNP. Anyone who did not like the syllabus could stay away, for the course was purely elective. The teachers were invited to teach only if they wished to, in order to avoid Kuwait's unhappy experience with instructors who transmitted their own acute embarrassment to the students. In Tunisia the courses are taught by volunteers who undergo special training to enable them to discuss without preaching the various aspects of the relationship between the sexes.

According to Dordana Masmoudi, who gave up her post as high school principal to head the program, no irate parent or Islamic theologian has come knocking at her door. Although very few teachers can truly transcend their old prejudices, Masmoudi considers it encouraging that 80 percent of the faculty have volunteered. To anyone who argues that teenagers are already getting too much exposure to sexual matters from Italian television and French films and magazines, Masmoudi points to the record classroom attendance and to the Population Clubs which students have organized in order to invite lawyers, physicians, and psychologists to discuss various problems of interest to them—a clever way for boys and girls to talk of common teenage problems without embarrassing themselves or compromising their parents' honor. "What they lack terribly is the opportunity to talk with someone, preferably someone who really knows the answers to their questions," Masmoudi said. Since the program was enthusiastically received in the sixty high schools covered so far, she plans to introduce it to all of the high schools by the end of 1980.

Such rare programs fostering greater equality in sexual and social relations have to compete against old values reinforced by the rest of the school curriculum as well as by the media. So busy have schools been in opening their doors to women that they have not yet clearly defined their goals for the modern young Muslim woman. They expect girls to live up to the same academic standards as boys, and know that the girls' chances of being co-breadwinners as adults are increasing dramatically. Yet textbooks are imbued with the attitude that boys will be breadwinners and head of their family, girls will be helpmates and mothers. Even religion is used—perhaps inadvertently—to buttress this philosophy in some school systems. The Islamic law of inheritance may be included in math problems, for example, without emphasizing that it was formulated when women did not have to support their families. A man dies and leaves a total of one thousand pieces of gold to his two daughters and one son. How much will each of them get? Three hundred and thirty-three pieces? You flunk. The correct answer is five hundred for the boy and two hundred and fifty for each girl. The Institute for Women's Studies in the Arab World based at Beirut University College is taking a critical look at the educational inconsistencies in several Middle Eastern countries and will soon publish its findings in a book entitled *The Image of Women in Arabic Textbooks.*[12]

Films have already received critical appraisal in Egypt, the Hollywood of the Arab world. Egypt has regularly produced some highly acclaimed films of the feminist consciousness-raising genre. But Muna al-Hadeedy of Cairo University, who analyzed 410 Egyptian films shown between 1962 and 1972,[13] concluded that much more should be done to upgrade the image of women in films: the majority of those she studied portrayed women as beautiful but brainless creatures whose sole mission in life was to catch the most eligible bachelor. So helpless were these women that as soon as the hero stepped out of sight they pined away, fell into the hands of villains, or wandered into prostitution and belly dancing in order to earn their keep (and offer the sexy musical numbers believed to be so dear to the hearts of the moviegoing masses). Even career women and students did not escape stereotyping, their worthy activities serving mainly to create new opportunities for meeting men. "In at least six of the films," Hadeedy reported, "the university campus was described as the playground of moral degradation rather than an intellectual center."

Since she pleads for a more realistic representation of

women in the media, she does not object to the frequent portrayal of women as housewives. That's what most women are today, she agrees, but objects strongly to the fact that they are often depicted as illogical, if well-meaning, incapable of self-sufficiency outside their small domestic sphere and able to attain dignity only in service of their menfolk.[14]

Although the divorce rate is quite high in Egypt and many housewives bravely raise families on their own through decent means, divorcées in films often fall into sexually degrading means of livelihood. It is the same old message: a woman must remain man's vassal in order to survive morally as well as physically. The modern setting of these films makes their message all the more insidious for the young, since the West is so closely associated with modernization and emancipation.

The old patriarchal values are carried over into television, too, although not with the sexual titillation favored in the film industry. Commercials often feature women as dependent consumers rewarding their husbands with loving smiles for buying a certain brand of furniture or washing machine. Women are usually housewives in soap operas, too. In conservative countries they are rarely cast as professionals except as teachers or nurses in charge of young children.

Yet the television industry in the Middle East is not rigidly set in its ways, since it is still young and heavily dependent on foreign imports. As the networks begin to create their own programs in the light of other countries' experiences, they have a unique potential to be responsive to women's needs. Because television was introduced in most countries no more than twenty years ago, when there were enough qualified women to pioneer in the industry alongside men, the ranks of producers and directors include a significant number of women today, and women are highly visible as announcers and newscasters in all but the most conservative countries, serving as more acceptable role models for young girls than belly-dancing film stars.

It is difficult to pinpoint the influence of women on programming since the ratings of viewer reaction and the policies of the governments that own the networks largely determine the nature of the shows. However, government ownership brings one bonus: the television industry is relatively free of the economic need to bow to the cinema world's success formula or to the soap manufacturers' dictates. This has produced politically safe but good cultural and educational programs, often featuring women experts. Iranian television before Khomeini, for example, ran a widely applauded science program produced and hosted by a woman. Perhaps the relatively large representation of women among media workers has encouraged the expansion of women's roles in soap operas, too. An increasing number of programs feature women as serious workers in a wider variety of professions, with romance only as a secondary interest.

A few programs speak openly for women's rights—President Bourguiba of Tunisia has appeared frequently on television to promulgate his feminist reforms—but television in countries without strong feminist leaders may opt for programs along the lines of *The Letter*, broadcast by Egyptian television since 1960. Under the guise of educating both sexes in their legal rights, it touches on many feminist issues. People who have no money to see a lawyer or are too shy to do so can write to the producer of the show asking for advice on such problems as divorce and wife abuse. Each week one of the letters forms the basis for a drama which concludes with the protagonist's asking, "What can I do?" A panel of experts offer several possible solutions.

However few and mild television programs that upgrade woman's image are, they have a wider impact than the few excellent feminist films shown in theaters. In larger cities television is found in almost every neighborhood, if not every home, and is generously shared.[15] The most secluded and illiterate women have access to it. Moreover, TV producers have captive audiences because so few channels are yet available. Someone who does not like *The Letter* can switch to only one other channel in Egypt. If Amina's brother does not want to watch a girls' basketball match, he can only leave the room. He cannot even write to the network demanding that the program be reserved for daytime female viewers, since Algerian television broadcasts only in the evening hours on weekdays. Therefore, television's message to women in such programs has a good chance of reaching its targets.

This message suggests the direction which the definition of the modern Muslim woman is taking today: she must be educated and contribute her professional talents to social progress. To enable her to do so, responsibility for her honor has begun to shift increasingly to her shoulders, although responsibility does not mean freedom of choice in the matter.[16] The double standard still prevails, and man's honor still hinges on woman's virtue. Laws of many countries uphold this contradictory ideal. They grant equality in wage and opportunities to the professional woman, for example, but demand that she obtain her husband's formal consent before she can be employed. In some countries women may not marry or travel abroad without their male guardians' permission, even if they are television producers or ministers of state.

Amina, who is now studying biology at a local university, has found an apt image to describe herself and other young women who live the contradictions imposed by their society in transition.[17] Today's young Middle Eastern woman, she says, is like a hermit crab that crawls into an empty snail shell on the beach because it has no shell of its own to protect its soft underbelly. Like the hermit crab, which outwardly assumes the identity of the invincible snail, the young woman seems to be master of her destiny, judging by the impressive educational and professional rights that she has gained. But she is vulnerable, because she does not yet have full control over her own body.

8

꧋꧋꧋꧋꧋꧋꧋꧋꧋꧋

Love, Sex, and Marriage

The best of you are they who behave the best to their wives.
> —The Prophet Muhammad

He created for you mates from among yourselves, that ye may dwell in tranquility with them, and He has put love and mercy between you.
> —Quran xxx:21

Yasmin had a better reason for being nervous than did most Middle Eastern brides. Although a reputable plastic surgeon had reconstructed her hymen, she wondered if she would pass for a true virgin on her wedding night. With repeated assurances from her mother, who shared her secret, she went off on her honeymoon. A week later she came back with her proudly smiling husband. She had passed the test of virginity.

Yasmin's experience dramatizes the uncertainties confronting a small minority of young women who explore the most sensitive frontier of women's liberation in the Middle East. They are the privileged ones who have come to take for granted their rights to education and work and now want exclusive responsibility over their own bodies, not as a license for casual sexual adventures but as a means toward full adulthood. As long as honor is equated with woman's chastity, so that the Yasmins among them are compelled to keep up a front, they contend that all women will remain vulnerable to society's gossips and whims which conspire to keep them from participating fully in life. The phrase "What will the neighbors say?" is a frequent refrain impeding many an adolescent woman's burst of energy and curiosity about her world, and a father with an old-fashioned sense of honor can interrupt his daughter's education. The argument has succeeded only in stirring up more questions, which are all the more difficult to resolve because they touch on the most painful contradictions burdening the Middle Eastern concept of woman's sexuality.

The conflicts lie in the double legacy which shaped this concept. Islam decreed that a woman was neither a mere childbearing machine nor man's toy but rather a person with God-given rights to sexual fulfillment as modern science understands it. "You must not throw yourselves on your wives as do beasts, but first there must be a messenger between you," Muhammad said one day. "What messenger, o Prophet?" his followers asked eagerly. "Sweet words and kisses," he replied.[1] The only condition he imposed was that women enjoy them strictly within the institution of marriage. He recommended modest dress and comportment in order to discourage temptation, but women were expected to be responsible for their own behavior. Otherwise, he would not have insisted on hearing from four reliable eyewitnesses to the sexual act itself before condemning an adulteress to public whipping.

Islam's liberal naturalistic view of sexuality, however, has been overshadowed by the patriarch's traditional awe of woman's power. He saw woman as a creature of mysterious, unlimited sexual drive,[2] which, if allowed free reign, would cause social chaos. Since she was too irresponsible to control herself, he had to build fences around her, not only to ensure the legitimacy of his heirs but also to maintain the social order. Modest dress was no longer enough—a woman's face had to be covered and her whole existence cloistered within the four walls of her home, if her husband could afford it. Her apparent good behavior was not enough—her virginity had to be vouched for on her wedding night. According to this fear-ridden attitude toward women, virginity was important in guaranteeing not only the legitimacy of heirs but also the bride's innocence; husbands feared being compared unfavorably to other men. Imam al-Ghazali, one of the most eminent theologians of the eleventh century, mentioned this point: "The virgin will love her husband and get used to him, which will favorably influence marital relations. . . . A woman who has had experience with other men or one who was married before will often compare her husband's peculiarities to those of other men and be dissatisfied."[3] This line of reasoning reduced the woman's Islamic right to sexual fulfillment to a mere tool for containing her wild passions: if she was appeased by her husband, she would not run elsewhere. If she did, she would be punished, while an adulterous man often escaped the public whipping Islam decreed for him. His passions did not endanger the patriarchal social order.

Like other Middle Eastern women, Yasmin was affected by the tension between the patriarchal and Islamic concepts of sexuality.[4] Though her liberal parents subjected her to no more supervision than was customary among their Western counterparts, they impressed upon her the importance of remaining chaste, in deference not only to God's will but also to the prerequisites of marriage. Also influenced by the ideals of romantic love,[5] Yasmin scorned men who judged a woman's merit by her intact hymen; she regarded sexual relations as the ultimate expression of love, with or without benefit of matrimony. But she did not object to obeying her parents, since she intended to marry the man she loved. Her life would have proceeded according to her plan had not the man with whom she fell in love asked to wait for marriage until he had finished his studies. She agreed, but saw no reason to postpone the consummation of their love. They were abroad, where neither her reputation nor her family's honor would be jeopardized. Their eventual wedding would be only a public acknowledgment of their private pact. However, she eventually decided against marrying him and terminated the relationship.

Her dilemma began when, back home, she decided to marry another young man. Since he appeared to be liberal-minded enough to value her for her intelligence and personality rather than virginity, her first impulse was to tell him her secret, but after much deliberation she decided against it. Birth, marriage, and other major landmarks in people's life elicited gut reactions that could not be easily changed by a few years of modern university education. The sexual double standard was nowhere near extinction. Though a few men transcended it, most could not. What if her fiancé, outraged, called off the wedding? Even if he offered a harmless excuse, others might jump to the worst conclusion. Yasmin would be hurting not only herself but her family, especially her unmarried younger sisters, whose morality might also be questioned. Even if she were willing to take the consequences of her rebellion on herself, she had no right to jeopardize her sisters' welfare and her parents' good name. Since her fiancé loved her, she also felt compelled to protect him from the secret, which could hurt his male pride. It was difficult to be a lone rebel in such a family-oriented society. Therefore, Yasmin finally decided to undergo the seemingly hypocritical operation for the sake of social responsibility.

Yasmin had to account only to her husband on her honeymoon, but weddings in more strictly traditional circles in the Middle East often call for public proof of the bride's virginity, as ordained by pre-Islamic custom. A wedding I attended in a Moroccan village was a typical example. The bride sat on her throne like a doll in her bejeweled kaftan and head veil while women guests stood up one by one to dance in her honor, until the entire courtyard shimmered with the brilliant colors of kaftans and jewels. Even the servant women balancing

huge trays of sweets and mint tea on their heads deftly danced
among the guests. Men were supposed to be celebrating in
their own quarters, but most of them were clustered around
every doorway and window giving a view of the bride and her
friends. By the time the party was in full swing, some of the
younger boys had infiltrated the party and were encouraging
the dancers by clapping and singing in harmony with the
music.

Toward midnight an ululating voice pierced through the
music and silenced everyone. The bride was placed on a plat-
ter, hoisted up on women attendants' shoulders, and twirled
around to the hum of incantations. The groom came in and
received the same treatment, after which the couple were led
to the nuptial chamber and left alone to complete the defloration ceremony while their parents waited anxiously outside the
door and the party in the courtyard buzzed expectantly. After
a while a woman let out a ululation of joy. The music picked
up tempo and the women abandoned themselves to dancing
and ululation. The groom had reported that the bride had
spotted the white kerchief with blood.[6]

In this case only the couple's families stood by to examine
the bloodstained kerchief. In some remote villages it may be
exhibited to all of the guests, who may actually hang around
the nuptial chamber, cheering the groom on with drums and
songs and teasing him good-naturedly about taking so long. A
few young men lose their nerve in such a circus atmosphere
and tarnish their image of virility.

At least the groom is given another chance to prove himself: the testing time is either extended or postponed to another day. The bride who fails to pass the test enjoys no such
tolerance unless the groom cheats for her, which he may do,
especially if he was her first lover.[7] If he was not and he did
not know of her past before the wedding, he may void the
marriage contract. No matter how discreetly he does so, suspicion spreads, and the bride might as well wear a scarlet
letter on her breast if she stays on in the community.

In ultraconservative areas failure to stain the sheet with virginal blood may bring death to the bride at the hands of her brother or father, whose honor she sullied. No allowance is made for the approximately 50 percent of women who are born with "irregular" hymens—that is, those which are too elastic to bleed at first intercourse and those which are fine enough to tear easily during exercise. No one in areas where crimes of honor tend to occur is aware of such modern scientific findings.[8] Nor do laws always take such findings into account; they continue to be lenient toward those who "wipe out the shame in blood," as they say in Arabic. Public sympathy sides so fully with the savior of honor that he usually gets away with the minimum sentence, if any, and is said to be treated royally in prison.

These crimes against women occur mostly among ultraconservatives, as they do in the remote corners of southern Europe, but their frequency is not important. The very fact that they can happen at all, with the acquiescence of law and custom masquerading as Islam, makes every woman feel as vulnerable as Scheherazade of the *Arabian Nights*, who awaits her husband's scimitar on her neck every day for real or imagined sexual offenses.[9] Figurative though the image is for a woman like Yasmin, it roots itself in her psyche, reminding her of the double standard which passes for honor, sends her to the plastic surgeon, and makes her lie to her husband and family.

Since so much hangs on the outcome of the virginity test, women have developed cheating into a sophisticated art.[10] Only wealthy women can afford plastic surgery, but every mother will help her daughter insert a pouch of chicken blood in the vagina or suggest other tricks. Women's refusal to be victims is celebrated in a Berber folk song from Morocco about a young woman who gives in to a handsome young shepherd's charms although her sister warns her that the ecstatic nights are not worth the headaches of the morning after. Unrepentant, she assures the sister that she has visited the local medicine woman, who knows all about plants and minerals to flatten her belly and make her a virgin again. Gleefully she concludes: "Oh, how would we survive against men / If we didn't have these tricks and smiles."[11]

Some marriage customs are changing to give women greater control over their destiny, but all are peripheral to the central issue of the woman's right over her sexuality. As more women attend school and work outside the home, more of them choose their own husbands, though their parents may still have much say in finalizing the marriage contract. Laws in many countries actually forbid an adult woman to marry without her male guardian's formal consent.[12] But even where no such laws exist, women and men tend to consult their parents, for marriage is still a union between two extended families. Whether or not the bride lives with the in-laws, she interacts heavily with them in a family-centered society. The groom's mother is therefore especially interested in having the young woman fit into the family. In turn, the bride's parents must assure themselves that she will be well treated and supported. Most have their daughter's happiness in mind, but the poor also think of their obligation to take her back—sometimes along with her offspring—should the marriage fail.[13] Young women want their parents to approve the marriage in order to ensure their support during marital crises.

The father's cooperation is also useful in drawing up the marriage contract and in bargaining for the dowry that the Shariah requires the husbands to deliver to their wives in whole or in part upon marriage, with the balance payable in the event of divorce. In some countries the dowry is the only alimony a divorcée gets. As a financially independent professional, Yasmin decided to accept only a ring as a token dowry, but she welcomed her father's involvement for another reason: she wanted him to undertake the seemingly crass business of stipulating in her marriage contract that she would have the right to divorce her husband.[14] She was not being cold-blooded, but sensibly taking advantage of the legal opportunity her religion offered to equalize her rights with her husband's, for without such a stipulation many Muslim authorities do not recognize the wife's right to initiate divorce,[15] although they permit the husband to divorce her at will without showing any cause. Yasmin intended to work hard to make the marriage a success, but strictly as an equal partner, not as a vassal.

Women who are less independent-minded and educated than Yasmin may not want to confront the ambivalence expressed toward those who socialize freely with men. These women may actually prefer arranged marriages, provided they enjoy veto power. In effect, the family acts as a private matchmaking service, presenting men of appropriate qualifications to their daughter until she picks the one she likes. "It beats looking for Mr. Right among strangers in a singles bar or at a crowded cocktail party," said an Indian Muslim woman, educated in the U.S., who married a man she had met through her parents. "What kind of a woman do you expect me to be taken for?" another university-educated Indian Muslim woman retorted to her oldest brother when he urged her to look for a husband on her own. Since his father had died, he was responsible for marrying off his sisters, and he did not relish the nerve-racking experience, even with his mother's help. "It is frightening to play God with someone else's happiness," he said. But his outspoken sister had a point, too. Muslims in India, as minorities everywhere tend to do, cling to old ways, in order to preserve their identity in a predominantly Hindu country. Although the sister had attended a coeducational university and did not veil herself, she had belonged to a group of Muslim women who voluntarily sat apart from men in the lecture halls and the cafeteria. Brought up in segregated circles, she was simply too shy to mix with men on and off campus as some of her classmates did. Later, as a kindergarten teacher, she met only children and other women. She had no choice but to depend on her elders for introductions. "I think men respect you more when you meet them through an elder," she said.

What gives arranged marriage a bad reputation are parents

who force their choice of men on their daughters, despite the Prophet Muhammad's strict orders to the contrary. Statistics on girls who run away from home or harm themselves in order to escape forced marriage are extremely difficult to compile, for few families will confess the true story behind a daughter's ending up in a clinic unconscious from an overdose of sleeping pills. Still fewer will spread the news about their runaway daughter among conservative neighbors who would automatically label her dishonored because she has spent a night away from parental supervision. Campaigns against forced marriage conducted by enlightened political leaders and feminists draw attention to the few dramatic cases that come to public attention, but hardly discourage a particularly determined father from hinting to his daughter that she would not be welcomed back home should the man of her choice divorce her one day. Unlike Yasmin, very few women have the wealth and education to stand on their own feet. Fathers in some countries impose their will through the laws requiring women to be married with their male guardians' consent. They can simply refuse to perform their office when they disapprove of their daughters' choice.

Nevertheless, optimistic stories about arranged marriage are perennially popular throughout the Middle East. The plot is standard: a beautiful girl resigns herself to marrying a man of her parents' choice even though she is secretly in love with another, only to discover on her wedding night that her parents have indeed married her to her beloved. Such blatant propaganda for obedience to parental wisdom may well help to reinforce faith in the only type of marriage that is practical for many women in sexually segregated societies.

Some gifted writers counter this rosy picture by caricaturing the darker side of arranged marriage to absurd extremes of black comedy that leave no room for cathartic tears and masochistically satisfying comments about how hard an honorable woman's life is. Raouf Kamil, a modern Egyptian writer, takes such an approach in his collection of short stories translated into French, under the title *Le Limon Rouge* (1975), for the benefit of French-educated Tunisians. In "The Beautiful Nurse," a village girl named Ratiba pours gasoline on herself and lights a match in order to evade a forced marriage with a detested cousin. Her father hesitates to put out the fire. Since she will be too disfigured to be marriageable, he reasons as she burns, he will be stuck forever with a daughter who has dishonored him by a public display of disobedience. On the other hand, the state will condemn him as a murderer if he lets her burn on. He finally allows the neighbors to extinguish the fire and takes her to the doctor. Fully aware that the father's prudence may yet be overruled by his distorted sense of honor, the kindly doctor sends Ratiba away to a nursing school to train for an independent professional life. Too poor to resist the handsome bribe the doctor offers him, the father signs his authorization for his daughter's registration at the school and the boardinghouse. When he returns home, he is roundly castigated by his entire clan for selling away the family honor.

With characteristic slyness Hoja (Teacher, Master) Nasreddin, the most beloved folk hero of the Middle East, attacked strictly arranged marriages many centuries ago by taking a more unusual point of view—the man's. In accordance with the code of sexual apartheid prevailing in his day, the young hoja was married to a veiled figure he had never met before. After the ceremony the bride removed her veil, showing her face for the first time. She was incredibly ugly. Mistaking his stunned expression for admiration, she coyly asked him: "What is your command, my lord? In front of whom shall I veil myself and to whom will I be permitted to show my face?" "You can show your face to anyone you like," the hoja groaned, "as long as you don't show it to me."[16]

One example of a successful rebellion against forced marriage is bridenapping, which is practiced in many Turkish villages. It is actually an elopement, since the woman is usually a willing accomplice, but it is carried out with the drama of a true kidnapping—the young man snatches his beloved away under cover of night to a horse or car held ready by his best friend. After she spends a night with her man, she is considered used material and nonreturnable—a case of using one tradition (honor) to fight another (arranged marriage). When a bridenapping occurred during my recent visit to the village of Sidé in southern Turkey, a few old women clucked about the bride's not choosing someone better, but everyone else talked excitedly about the clever way in which the couple outwitted the elders. The groom's adventures and prowess grew more herculean with each retelling at the coffeehouses. By the time the bride's parents gave the customary wedding party to legitimize the affair, I was almost disappointed to see an ordinary mortal claim the bride. Luckily, this bride had not been engaged to anyone else, for a jilted fiancé might have taken the kidnapping as an affront to his manhood and resorted to a vendetta.

Bridenapping is also the poor Turkish peasant's way of avoiding the exorbitant dowry which the bride's parents sometimes demand. Once the daughter becomes secondhand merchandise, their bargaining power is considerably weakened. If the rules of the game in the suitor's community do not allow kidnapping, he must often slave for years to accumulate the dowry or be forced to give up his beloved to another who can meet her price. Realizing that young men dissipated the most precious years of their lives in amassing a dowry rather than educating themselves and improving their marketable skills, leaders of many Muslim countries have tried to equate reasonable dowries with patriotism, but without notable success. There are good reasons for their failure.

What critics of the dowry say is partly true: greed does motivate some parents in arriving at the price. It is also true that the dowry can serve as a mere tool of vanity, an advertisement for a woman's desirability and her family's prestige that speaks long after the glorious wedding has become ancient history. My well-educated mother, a staunch supporter of women's right to study and work, never tires of boasting how much my father had paid for her. "Don't you feel like a slave purchased at the market when you talk like that?" I asked her one day. "Nonsense," she shot back, "your father occasionally needs to be reminded of how much he valued me at one time."

However, the dowry is above all a cushion against divorce. It may be the only alimony a divorcée ever gets. Thus, refusing the dowry can make a woman look very stupid in some circles. When one of my cousins lived in Saudi Arabia, other women often told her that she must have received an impressive dowry. Before she realized that they were simply complimenting her on her good looks and intelligence, she used to admit that she had asked for nothing and received nothing. "What did you marry for, then?" asked the surprised women. "For love," she answered. "Of course," they tried again patiently, "but didn't he give you something to tell you what he thought of you and your family?" "Well, I got this as a token dowry," she said sheepishly. The women gathered around her extended left hand to examine the diamond in her ring, which looked like a speck of dust compared to their quail-egg-sized gems. No matter how polite the ladies tried to be, they could not hide their pity for the dimwitted young woman and her impractical parents. "They hovered around me like a flock of mother hens after that," my cousin said, "just to make sure that I would not be cheated out of my rights while I was in Saudi Arabia. They were always advising me to get my husband to buy me more jewels."

She was speaking from the perspective of a professional woman able to support a family on her own if necessary. An increasing number of women like her have begun to accept only token dowry or help in furnishing the conjugal apartment rather than gold, property, or other inflation-proof items. Most of the Saudi ladies in my cousin's circle, on the other hand, had grown up before the 1960s, when the first schools for girls opened in their country. They had had only some

liberal arts education and lessons in religion from private tutors. A few had studied abroad, but none had marketable
skills. Marrying without a sum that would support them in
case of divorce would have been as impractical for them as
refusing alimony would be for an American divorcée with five
children and no profession. Actually, in today's inflated economy no lump sum or gold jewelry that a man of ordinary
means can give his bride as dowry is enough to support her on
her own for many years. The Islamic law on the dowry was
formulated in the days when divorcées could count on their
fathers' or brothers' support and had a greater chance of remarrying because of more widespread polygamy.

Yet while the evils of excessive dowry are obvious and are
decried loudly, many countries have not yet passed realistic
alimony laws to supplement the Shariah. At the same time,
supply and demand in the marriage market can work against
women. In the Arabian peninsula, for instance, the astronomical cost of marriage has driven quite a few men to seek brides
among Palestinians and Egyptians, who demand much smaller
dowries. Far fewer women get to travel or study abroad and
thus equalize their marital opportunities with their countrymen's, and in any case they are strongly discouraged from
marrying foreigners. Worried about the growing surplus of
unmarried local women, Saudi Arabia now requires its citizens marrying foreigners abroad to obtain prior approval from
their embassies. Abu Dhabi officials are considering the feasi-
bility of giving each man marrying for the first time a loan of
$13,500 if he takes a local woman as his wife. The loan would
be written off at the birth of their first child. Government
employees in neighboring Qatar already receive such gifts if
their first marriage is to a local woman, and plans are under
way to extend help to all other male citizens.[17]

The changes that are taking place in marriage customs
today improve a woman's chances of choosing her own husband, by according her greater freedom to meet men and by
easing the burden of dowry. It is believed that this amply takes

care of the modern woman's sexual needs: as they may be fulfilled only within marriage, what could be better than allowing her to marry the man she desires? Brought up on tales and songs of princesses who lived happily ever after with their princes, most young women conform to the ideal of Sleeping Beauty awaiting her prince's kiss.[18] On their wedding night they may feel no more apprehension than any highly sheltered young woman anywhere. Village girls brought up witnessing not only barnyard life but also traditional defloration ceremonies at weddings may take their experience in stride, especially as many of them tend to marry relatives.

But the fact that many women survive the virginity test and come to terms with their society's attitude toward them does not cancel out the problems inherent in judging a woman's merit by the condition of her hymen. Must women born with irregular hymens risk rejection on their wedding night? Must they avoid invigorating physical exercise for fear of breaking the sacred membrane? Should every woman be constrained to explain her behavior because her virtue must not fall under the slightest of suspicions? What is the effect of such anxiety on their sexuality?

Few have confronted the issue publicly.[19] One of these bold few, and perhaps the best known, is Nawal al-Saadawi, an Egyptian physician who was among the first in recent Arab history to write popular books on the effect of traditions on woman's sexuality. Obsession with virginity is the most important cause of sexual problems among Middle Eastern women, she asserts in *Women and Sex* and other books. Parents who suppress the adolescent's natural sexual impulses and her sense of independence in order to keep her a marriageable virgin and expect her to blossom sexually on her wedding night are unrealistic. Not everyone is a Sleeping Beauty. Unable to release the sexual impulses that they have for so long denied, some married women become frigid. Even those who escape clitoridectomy may thus end up psychologically mutilated.

They may not even realize that they are supposed to enjoy sex in marriage, Dr. Saadawi notes, because they are often brought up to think of sex purely as one of their duties to their husband, along with raising children and keeping house. These women consider themselves amply rewarded if their husband provides them with the material essentials of life and doesn't scold them or go off with other women. A wife who defines her happiness in terms of such an exchange is no better than a slave, the doctor points out. Sooner or later unfulfilled sexual desires take their toll on women, in the form of migraine headaches, nervousness, and other vague ailments for which tranquilizers are so indiscriminately prescribed. "Women must understand that physical and mental health are not possible without sexual enjoyment," Dr. Saadawi writes, and urges them to ask their husband's cooperation in reaching orgasm. A woman must speak frankly of her needs even at the risk of being scolded as shameless by a prudish husband, she insists, for taking sex as a mere duty will only intensify her frustration and anger. When *Women and Sex* was published, in 1972, Dr. Saadawi's message was a bold one even by American standards.

Yet the doctor has done nothing more iconoclastic than reiterate the teachings of the most respected Muslim scholars of the Arab caliphate. If her psychosomatic approach to human sexuality represents the latest in modern Western medicine, it also echoes the views of the physician Ibn Sina (Avicenna), who claimed in the eleventh century that good health depended on harmonious interrelationship of the body and the psyche.[20] Accordingly, sexual needs were not "weaknesses of the flesh" to be defeated by the soul. They were natural needs which had to be satisfied in order to maintain psychological and physical health. The theologian Imam Ghazali agreed that sexual fulfillment was essential for a woman's health as well as for her virtue, and instructed husbands on the proper techniques to satisfy their wives. Men were not to be preoccupied exclusively with their own pleasure, for example; they were to wait for their wives to reach orgasm. "A woman's ejaculation is often delayed, which excites her sexual desire even further," the imam explained.[21]

No creature merited greater disdain than a sexually egotistic man. A sixteenth-century Tunisian scholar named Shaykh Nefzawi described such a man in his *kama sutra* entitled *Perfumed Garden for the Soul's Recreation*: "He does not do his business with vigor and in a manner to give her enjoyment. He lays himself down upon her without previous toying, he does not kiss her, nor twine himself round her; he does not bite her, nor suck her lips, nor tickle her. He gets upon her before she has begun to long for pleasure. . . . Scarcely has he commenced when he is already done for. . . . Qualities like these are no recommendation with women."

The ideas of respected old Muslim scholars were too daring for twentieth-century Muslims. Dr. Saadawi never claimed to have written a Kinsey or Hite type of report, and stressed that she based her books on her limited private surveys and her own patients—casualties of honor whose problems were serious enough to merit professional help. But her books stirred up furious controversy, mainly because she attacked honor as it is understood today. Moreover, she exposed to the public the total unreliability of the traditional criterion for measuring honor. Since ruptured hymens could be repaired, with one turn of the surgeon's needle patriarchal safeguards nurtured over centuries had crumbled.

"What you are suggesting is sexual freedom for girls," many people accused her. "This does not mean that there should be no restrictions," she protested, "there should be, but restrictions coming from the individual herself and not ones which have been imposed on her." Social pressures that teach a girl to fear sex while allowing her brother full freedom can set the stage for an unequal and unhealthy relationship in marriage, she explained, adding reassuringly that "in the life of liberated and intelligent women sex does not occupy a disproportionate position, but rather tends to maintain itself within normal limits. . . . Ignorance, suppression, fear and all sorts of limitations exaggerate the role of sex in the life of girls and women. . . ."

Not everyone was convinced—not even the husbands of patients whom the doctor cured instead of keeping them on tranquilizers. Declaring that he was a good Muslim, one husband scolded her for preaching corrupt Western mores. Woman was not created to enjoy sex but to serve her husband and devote herself to her children, he insisted. Enough politicians and theologians agreed with such a man that Dr. Saadawi was dismissed from her post as Egypt's Director of Public Health.

Because of strong patriarchal prejudice and laws condemning women to second-class citizenship, Dr. Saadawi and many others argue that doing away with restrictive sexual mores alone is useless.[22] Legal and social inferiority in any sphere of life can harm sexual relationship and impede the development of love based on the spouses' respect for each other as equals. Some young women point out that these laws will remain in effect until society ceases to make their virtue its business. It is a chicken-or-the-egg? dilemma. No one has specific answers, but the feminists' main focus is on the ecological approach— that is, to reform not just one but all aspects of man-woman relationship.

According to this view, contemporary Western ideas on sexual freedom are only the other side of the same patriarchal coin, for sexual freedom will play into the hands of the patriarchy unless sexual inequality in law and social custom is eradicated. Furugh Farrukhzad, a young Iranian poetess, proved the point dramatically by breaking all sexual taboos without waiting for her society to change its attitude toward women.[23] Though she moved in upper-middle-class circles, among those who were no strangers to extramarital liaisons, Furugh paid heavily for violating traditions publicly and without apology.

In her late teens and early twenties she scandalized her

compatriots by writing frankly and defiantly about her sexual desires:

> I sinned a sin full of pleasure
> In an embrace which was warm and fiery[24]

> May the thought of reputation never be in my head
> This is I who seeks you for satisfaction in this way[25]

No Iranian woman writer had ever made men the object of her passions so explicitly without veiling her feelings in classical metaphors. She had desecrated the highest form of Persian art by speaking out as vulgarly as a whore. And she had added to the injury by taking lovers openly after her divorce, as if the sacred traditions were mere scarecrows. She was branded a whore and figuratively stoned by critics who focused on the immorality of her life and the topic of her writing, rather than judging her poems on their literary merit. Her ex-husband never allowed her to see their son, perhaps because of a personal grudge against her, but her notoriety inspired many women as well as men to condone his cruelty.

Refusing to be destroyed, Furugh continued to live a full life usually denied women. Nothing seemed wasted on her. When she fell in love with a cinematographer, she took up filmmaking seriously enough to win an award in Germany for her documentary on a leper colony (*The Black House*). She also matured so much in her poetic talents that by the time she died in an automobile accident in 1967, at the age of thirty-two, she was acclaimed as one of the greatest of Iranian poetesses.

Furugh transcended social censure through her art. Women in other occupations are usually constrained to at least keep up a respectable front. Even if they are discreet, they may be diminished on a spiritual level. "Before Khomeini," says an Iranian woman now living in the U.S., "Teheran had everything from free love and swinging parties to wife swapping.

Some women of the Teheran society were rebelling all the way against traditions. They weren't punished physically for it, of course—this was a liberal Westernized circle. But they did not correct their legal and socioeconomic handicaps, either. So they just went from being sex objects Oriental style to being sex objects Occidental style. They only won greater freedom to choose their masters, and were denied their human dignity in both cases."

Some uphold Islam as the answer, but in many societies today it is practiced selectively, to the patriarch's advantage. Yasmin could indeed have worked within the Shariah. She could have married her first lover on written condition that she could divorce him at will, thus sparing herself the indignity of masquerading under a false hymen. She could also have protected her interests in case of pregnancy. However, only educated and financially independent women know their rights and have enough bargaining power on the marriage market to impose conditions. Others must usually submit to their fathers' and husbands' standards according to the ancient bargain of honor.

The bargain is not easily broken even where there is no practical need for it, because it has defined femininity and masculinity for centuries. This has limited women's determination to pursue their rights or change the relationship between the sexes. For all her iconoclastic ideas and financial independence, Yasmin would not have married a man who had less schooling or a lower income than she. Each of them has enough income to support a family singlehanded, but she would never agree to have him stay at home to mind the babies while she worked. She wanted to pursue her career, but not as the family's only breadwinner, for her husband's ability to protect her was closely linked in her mind with his masculinity and his love for her.

Advertisements which women in some cities place in newspapers to seek husbands highlight the tenacity of traditional notions of masculinity and femininity which may have no survival value today. These women may want husbands with occupations which pay better than theirs for practical reasons, but they also insist on their being taller and older. Men invariably advertise for women who are younger, shorter, and less educated than they. They may force their wives into a traditional mold not necessarily because they want to but to prove their manhood to their society.[26] The cult of virginity, harems and veils, and even crimes of honor are simply extensions of such a mentality.

Because men and women are locked into time-honored reverse images of each other, woman's sexual liberation cannot be completed without a corresponding liberation in her man. Between them, however, stands the tradition-bound mother, who shapes their vision of womanhood.

9

⌐⌐⌐⌐⌐⌐⌐⌐⌐⌐⌐

Motherhood, Polygamy, and Divorce

Paradise lies at mothers' feet.
—The Prophet Muhammad

It is not enough to win rights. One must be able to keep them.
                    —A. Afetinan (Turkish historian and
                    adopted daughter of Ataturk)

The mother has been the central figure in the Middle Eastern woman's emancipation. Islam secured her rights in the seventh century in order to strengthen the family against urban problems. Feminists of the early twentieth century first justified modern education for women as a means of improving the quality of future mothers of men. Today the mother is the main subject of controversial attempts to clear Islam of misinterpretations accumulated over the centuries. At stake are her rights in family planning, polygamy, and divorce, which heavily influence her relationship with her husband and shape her children's image of womanhood.

Her rights had been distorted as she lost the political clout she enjoyed during the Prophet Muhammad's time and sank into the myopia of harem life or the ignorance of poverty. She had become little more than a sexual object and childbearing machine, whose main purpose in life was to produce sons for her husband's family. The penalty for failure to do so could be divorce or demotion to the status of wife number two. Though married women are beginning to escape this fate through education and work, the masses in many parts of the Middle East are still condemned to measure their worth in terms of their reproductive capacity.

Dr. Samira al-Mallah, a gynecologist at Al-Azhar University's Faculty of Medicine in Cairo, reported several years ago[1] that her practice included many recently married young women who begged her to cure them of sterility. There was usually nothing wrong with them medically, but the doctor found it hard to convince their in-laws that the brides were not sterile or diseased just because they failed to conceive after several months of marriage. Under such pressure, many a young wife is happy enough to give birth to a girl, for she at least proves herself fertile. No wonder the Arab mother's greatest pride is to be called Umm (mother of) Ahmed (or whatever her eldest son's name is), rather than by her own name, and to submerge her life in her son's, leading him to believe that women are created solely to serve his pleasure. In turn, the boy grows up to protect his mother against the vicissitudes of divorce and widowhood.

The work of a less educated nonprofessional and rural woman does not end there, however. Infant mortality is high: out of every 1,000 babies born in 1975, 117 to 128 died before reaching their first birthday, compared to only 20 in Europe and 15 in North America.[2] In order to ensure the survival of at least one son, the Middle Eastern mother goes on to bear an average of six children, making the birthrate in the area among the highest in the world.

Her plight is often justified by or blamed on Islam, but the Prophet Muhammad never sent a wife away or replaced her with another for failing to produce a son, even though all of his surviving children were girls. Nor did he forbid birth control. Parenthood was a godly duty, he said, but advised his followers against having more children than they could feed adequately. Instead of ordering abstinence, which would contradict his insistence on every individual's right to sexual pleasure, he recommended coitus interruptus—with the wife's permission, since withdrawal was believed to diminish her pleasure.

Early Muslim jurists followed the same line of reasoning to permit women to use other modes of birth control known in their day, and physicians were always on the lookout for more effective methods.[3] Their writings show that Islamic medicine of the Middle Ages knew about and recommended both the condom and forerunners of modern vaginal suppositories and the diaphragm. Abu Bakr al-Razi of Persia, the greatest Muslim physician of the ninth century, advised women "to place some medicaments at the opening of the uterus. . . . These medicaments either close up the opening or expel the semen and so prevent pregnancy. Examples of this are tablets or suppositories of cabbage, hanzal, kar, bull's gall, the wax secreted by animals' ears, the droppings of elephants and calcium water."[4] In the eleventh century Ibn Sina (Avicenna) described twenty different methods of contraception, including the condom ("the skin sack of the male," "the preventive retainer") made out of animal gut.

Modern birth control services have been approved in light of these earlier interpretations of the Shariah, but their availability to the general public depends much on each government's political and economic needs.[5] Linking poverty to overpopulation, Egypt and Tunisia have sponsored large networks of free family planning clinics. Turkey, Morocco, and Pakistan are also among those officially committed to reducing their populations. Iran, which used to send young women college graduates to teach family planning as a part of their post-college domestic peace corps service, closed its family planning clinics and removed contraceptives from the pharmacy shelves when the Islamic Revolutionary Government came to power. It was politically necessary to "reexamine" birth control in the light of Islam in order to placate the ultra-conservatives who feared it might lead to promiscuity. Women protested. The government revised its verdict: birth control is acceptable if both spouses agree to practice it and if it does not harm the spouses' health or, if it fails, abort the fetus at any time after conception.

Islam's basically liberal attitude toward birth control survives even in countries that encourage population growth and those that take no official stand in order to avoid offending the conservatives. If these countries do not sponsor clinics, neither do they ban private doctors and pharmacists from dispensing contraceptives. Kuwait, Oman, and the United Arab Emirates are among these. In cosmopolitan Lebanon, where family planning is actually prohibited by an antiquated law that nobody has bothered to abolish, the pill and other contraceptives are openly sold over the counter in pharmacies and distributed at the Family Planning Association clinics. Apparently everyone understands the game of getting around the law.

The game started back in 1969, when the International Planned Parenthood Federation, supposedly unaware of the pill's illegality, donated twenty-five thousand boxes of them to the Lebanese Family Planning Association. Customs officials confiscated the shipment, and the Family Planning Association complained to the Minister of Health. Someone had kindly donated tons of medicine for regularizing the menstrual cycle, the association informed the minister, and it begged him to save the drugs from going to waste at the bottom of the sea. The minister charitably complied.[6] Since then the association has submitted the same letter of request to the ministry each time a new shipment of pills arrives, and five successive ministers have sent back the same notice of approval. Pharmacists have successfully followed suit by asking permission to import the medicine. Today Lebanese women are among the heaviest users of contraceptives in the Middle East. Their case is a

perfect example of how Middle Easterners often choose a cir-
cular way to resolve a conflict without anyone—especially a
high-level official—losing face.

Abortion has been more controversial, mainly because neither the Quran nor the Prophet Muhammad mentioned it
specifically. Some Muslim jurists regard it as a sinful destruc-
tion of life, while others claim that it is permissible within the
first 120 days of gestation, before the fetus is infused with a
soul. When the woman's life is threatened by the continuation
of pregnancy, both camps unequivocally sanction abortion,
justifying their verdict by the Quranic statement "No mother
shall be treated unfairly on account of her child" (ii:233).
Therapeutic abortion is, therefore, legal in many of the Middle Eastern and North African countries, while elective abortion is allowed only in Tunisia and only in the first three
months of pregnancy.

Since abortion is usually performed only for a fee in most
countries, it remains the privilege of the middle and upper
classes. Unfortunately, so does contraception, even where free
clinics make it unnecessary for a woman to deprive herself of
bread in order to buy the pill. The middle-class woman is not
only educated enough to know of modern birth control techniques, she is also likely to have a profession or other outside
interests which motivate her to limit the number of her children. Turkish women with university degrees, for example,
averaged 1.4 children each in the 1960s, compared to 2.0 per
high school graduate, 3.8 per primary school graduate, and
4.2 per illiterate woman. Although the birthrate is somewhat
higher in other Middle Eastern countries (except Lebanon), it
also tends to decrease with the increasing education of the
woman,[7] rather than of her husband. The estimated female
illiteracy rate of 85 percent in this part of the world thus
explains its high birthrate.

Illiterate and semiliterate women have several strikes
against them if they do not want to be perennially pregnant.
They have to depend on radio programs or visiting social

workers to learn about modern contraception. For lack of funds and trained personnel, few countries have reached everyone. Only Tunisia claims that the majority of its women have at least heard about birth control. The distance between hearing about it and taking effective action is full of pitfalls. The maid of one Istanbul woman confessed her fear of having yet another child. Her employer told her about the pill and advised her to go to a free clinic. After some months the maid announced her pregnancy. "I took the pill but it didn't work," she said glumly. Instead of seeking counsel at the clinic, she had headed straight for the nearest pharmacy to get the magic pill, and had not paid close attention to the oral instructions that most druggists considerately give to any customer who speaks like a semiliterate. Her sense of economy had militated against swallowing the pill every day, and she had taken it as if it were aspirin, only on the days when "the need arose."

Dr. Malka al-Saati, who has analyzed obstacles to family planning in Baghdad in the early 1970s,[8] says that barely literate women do not take advantage of facilities even when they are right under their noses. Family planning clinics are ill equipped to handle these women's special problems. Unable to refresh their memory from instruction pamphlets, patients forget the details of the social worker's lecture on the pill and the diaphragm and use them incorrectly. The IUD works best for them, but clinics do not have enough women trained to insert it, obliging patients to wait many days for an appointment. Not being in the habit of keeping track of dates and hours, many of them forget their appointment.

The greatest problem is getting them to come at all. A midwife-abortionist without modern medical training who is afraid of losing business can turn an entire neighborhood against family planning with well-timed rumors about Mrs. So-and-so who had serious complications with the IUD. Whether or not these problems are less frequent than problems resulting from back-alley abortions is academic and beside the point at this level. The main obstacle is the cultural gap between the businesslike Westernized technocrats and the tradition-bound poor who value personal relationships in any transaction, so much so that they often visit a midwife for a small fee rather than go to a free clinic. As a longtime neighbor and mother confessor to her clients, the midwife has far greater influence on these women than the clinics' experts, who are regarded as outsiders.

In fact, anti–birth control propaganda from any source is effective among these women, not only because they have long been conditioned to accept "God's will" but also because they live in underdeveloped societies that require many sons in order to ensure the survival of at least one to support his parents in their old age. So economically vital are sons that Arab fathers are also happy to be called Abu (Father of) Ahmed (or whatever the eldest son's name is). Understandably, the worst curse one can pronounce on their wives is "May your womb shrivel up!" To counter this, some countries have shifted the emphasis from reducing births to spacing them better. The Algerian government's clinics are called "Birth Spacing Centers." Posters in rural Turkey proclaim that family planning means better spacing of births, not preventing them.[9]

Infant mortality, though still comparatively high, is declining steadily due to the advent of free medical care, but the mentality of underdevelopment lingers on, bolstered by women's willingness to bear many children for personal reasons. For many women the pregnant belly is as much a mark of youth and femininity as it is a proof of virility for her husband. Moreover, children define the very raison d'être of a woman who receives no pay and little social recognition for her work at home or on the farm.[10] Indeed, the only time that a woman from the poorer classes receives special attention is during pregnancy. At the birth of her child, the midwife makes her the star of a ritual that puts the entire family at her service and the best food on her table—another reason she prefers the traditional midwife to the efficient but sterile modern nurse,

who is not given to holding the new mother's hands throughout the labor.

Underlying the seeming vanity of the perennially pregnant
mother are the old twin bogeys of her marriage—divorce and
polygamy—which may continue to haunt her long after she
has delivered a son, and sometimes despite the husband's
exemplary devotion. *The Bride's Mother,* a famous Egyptian
film of the 1960s based on a novel by Abdel Halim Abdallah,
dramatizes a housewife's reluctance to give up her role as
victim. Overwhelmed by the pandemonium that his numerous
children unavoidably raise in a small house, a man begs his
wife to be excused from fathering more. "I'm yours forever.
I'll never leave you and our children," he pleads. When the
youngest baby wants to crawl into her parents' bed at night, he
eagerly welcomes her to avoid sex. But the wife has her way in
the end and does not give up proving her "youth and useful-
ness" even as she begins to nag her newly married oldest
daughter to have a child. "That's the only way to keep a man,"
the mother tells her. Indeed, recent statistics from Egypt link
large numbers of children to lower divorce rates.[11]

In the same manner polygamy, although now very rare,
clings to the Muslim woman's psyche as a shadow over her
dream of living happily ever after. Ask any woman and she
will mention at least one older woman in her family who lived
with co-wives. Or she may have heard of someone else who
did. Reports on polygamous unions are not all unfavorable.
My own grandmother was the fourth of four wives. Our men
love to tell the story of how number three got wind of the
rumor that her husband was planning to take a fourth wife to
complete his bliss. Reasoning very intelligently that she would
rather live with a woman she liked than take a chance on a
stranger, she pulled strings to bring a young friend of hers—
Grandmother—into the harem. And of course, the men add,
the co-wives lived in perfect harmony ever after. "Was it really
that good?" I asked my grandmother. "There are advantages
and disadvantages," she replied. She appreciated her friend's

companionship and help in caring for the children and surviving harem politics. "But we had our moments of jealousy, too," Grandmother added delicately, without going into detail.

While vehemently condemning twenty-five-year-old men with two wives, seven children, and no job, Algerian feminist Fadela M'Rabet admits that polygamy had its place in traditional society. If a woman lives cloistered with no one but a grouchy mother-in-law for company, she may welcome a younger co-wife with whom to share gossip and homemaking chores. Fadela remembers a pregnant young peasant woman who arrived at a maternity clinic with an older co-wife, to whom she clung for reassurance during the delivery of her first child. The young woman referred to her co-wife as someone like her own mother, who would take care of her baby while she recuperated. Jealous? Heavens, no, she replied. In fact, she was happy that the husband would leave her alone for a while, turning to the other wife. As my grandmother said, "Possessively romantic marriage between one man and one woman is new in the West, too. Didn't European wives accept their husbands' mistresses as a matter of course in the old days even if they did not like it one hundred percent?"

Despite such an attitude toward marriage, jealousy did often get the upper hand. Halidé Edib, the Turkish freedom fighter and feminist, recalled that the polygamous household in which she grew up at the close of the Ottoman era was constantly racked by undercurrents of tension, amounting almost to physical pain for the children. "The wives never quarrelled," she wrote, "and they were always externally polite, but one felt a deep and mutual hatred accumulating in their hearts, to which they gave vent only when each was alone with father. . . . Finally he took to having a separate room, where he usually sat alone."[12]

Another story about folk hero Hoja Nasreddin sums up the problems inherent in a polygamous relationship. As the hoja prospered, he took a second wife. Soon after, neighbors noticed that he was getting bald. "My older wife pulls out all my black hairs so that I will look as old as she does," the hoja explained with resignation, "and the younger one pulls out all my white hairs to make me look as young as *she* does. Between them I am losing all my hair."

Today, with the communal support of the extended family on the wane under the pressure of industrialization and inflation, children of polygamy stand to lose considerably even if brought up under more harmonious conditions. According to Moroccan sociologist Fatima Mernissi, whose grandmother was a concubine, the average polygamous man in her country is fifty years old and takes as his second and third wives women who are a generation or two younger.[13] Seldom does he survive long enough to support his younger children to adulthood, and he may not leave enough wealth to allow his wives to educate them adequately after his death. The older wives' children suffer especially, for a fifth of all divorces in urban areas are initiated by women who prefer not to live with co-wives[14] and either leave the offspring with their father or take them out into a life of poverty.

If left with the father, children can suffer more than just the pain of separation from their mother. Given the age profile of polygamous unions, the first wife's son may be older than his father's second wife—a situation which has stirred many a novelist's imagination. One of the bitterest treatments of this theme appears in *La Répudiation* (1969) by Algerian writer Rachid Boudjedra. The mother in the novel is in an impossible situation, divorced but forced to live on in the large compound of her husband's clan, stoically witnessing her middle-aged husband's senile attempts to charm his fifteen-year-old bride. Denied his sexual favors, the older woman is worse off than a co-wife. Hating his father for inflicting such cruelty on his mother, one of the sons turns to alcohol; the other seduces his beautiful young stepmother. In the end the pity that the sons feel for their mother overpowers their respect and love for her and alienates them altogether from their family.

Yet so strong a hold does polygamy exercise on the imagination that men who take one wife after another are looked on with bemused tolerance bordering on admiration, regardless of the financial and human consequences. In Cairo a friend pointed out to me a tiny, shriveled-up sixty-year-old janitor in her office building who had a reputation for great virility. He had married twenty times and was currently living with four wives, rumor had it. "Actually," my friend explained, "he married only a total of seven or eight times and is now living with only two wives. He just kept on repudiating wives who did not bear sons until he recently married a sixteen-year-old who gave birth to a boy. People love to blow up stories like that." He tacitly encouraged the gossip, which made him feel virile. Only a few remembered that he had more than a dozen living children, many discarded wives, and precious little money to support them.

So far only Turkey and Tunisia have banned polygamy altogether. Turkey replaced religious law with a civil code. Tunisia, which is committed to reform within the framework of the Shariah, claimed that the new law merely spells out what the Quran implied in the first place. The Prophet Muhammad had allowed polygamy under exceptional circumstances, when he had to find permanent homes for war widows, but he had virtually forbidden it by demanding that all co-wives be treated with absolute equality. Since it is humanly impossible to fulfill such a condition, the reformers maintained, the new Tunisian family law was in perfect accordance with Islam.

Thus began an intense ongoing debate between the conservatives, who claim to represent the letter of the Shariah, and the reformers, who favor what might be termed the annotated Islam, the one that translates into specific clauses the spirit of compassion that lies behind the general Quranic tenets. In other words, the state takes over the role of the extended family in watching over the woman's interests.

Not every country could take as free a hand in such reforms as Tunisia. Others have had to stick closer to the letter of the

Shariah for political reasons. Although Egyptian feminists campaigned for many years for a ban on polygamy, politicians had refused to cooperate, claiming that polygamy affected too small a percentage of older women to risk antagonizing devout Muslims by tampering with the Shariah. In July 1979 President Anwar Sadat finally issued an executive order requiring the husband to ask his wife's permission before taking a second wife. If he overrides her objection, she can get a divorce. With the new law, Egypt joined Syria, Iraq, and several other countries which solved the polygamy headache in a typically Middle Eastern fashion. Egypt formally bowed to the Shariah in order to placate the sizable population of conservative Muslims, but legislated around it to win over the equally significant and vocal group of liberals.

The law has made of the husband a donkey chasing a carrot at the end of a stick. He merely thinks he has the right to polygamy, since younger women would generally choose to divorce rather than live with a co-wife. "Since the alimony laws were also liberalized in our favor, we are basically no worse off than American women, who have to leave when the husband wants another woman," an Egyptian woman studying in the U.S. said, pointing out that the law was especially considerate of traditionally raised older women, who might not be able to face life alone if their husband brought home another wife. At least they have the option of staying on. The student's husband, also a student, protested, "Nothing has changed, really. When we got married, our contract said what the law says now. My wife's father made me sign a statement that she could divorce me if I took another wife." Countries which insist on governing strictly by the letter of the Shariah follow his line of argument that women have always had the right to restrict polygamy by inserting a rider in the marriage contract. Such a tactic did not raise eyebrows when marriage was a contract uniting two families for mutual interest rather than a romantic liaison between a man and a woman. The catch was that the bride's getting her way in the contract was contingent on her value in the marriage market. Also, today's romantic notions tend to interfere with her bargaining power. The biggest catch is that those who are most vulnerable to polygamy—uneducated women who marry the likes of our Cairo janitor—do not know their full rights.

Divorce is a particularly painful alternative to polygamy. By the standards of his day the Prophet Muhammad's divorce laws were kind to women. A man could not throw out his wife on a whim. He had to have a valid reason for telling her to get out. He also had to pronounce his intention to divorce her on three occasions, which presumably gave him time to simmer down and change his mind. In order to discourage men from turning the repudiation formula into a Damocletian sword over their wives' heads, Muhammad further ordained that no one could remarry his divorced wife before she had been married and divorced by another man; he could not divorce her as a warning or a punishment and then remarry her when he had gotten his way.

Unfortunately, the only tribunal for divorce cases was the husband's conscience, which has not served women well. In a fit of anger or meanness men do dismiss their wives by merely pronouncing the magic formula "I repudiate thee" three times in succession. In a stock scene from popular domestic comedies, a scrawny husband answers his fat, broom-wielding wife's tirades with a timid "I repudiate thee." When she keeps on screaming, he becomes annoyed enough to raise his voice for the second "I repudiate thee." At this point, she stops short in her tracks and retreats, grumbling and considerably shrunk in stature, for the third pronouncement would be fatal. Alone on the stage, the little man grows taller as he beats his chest in male pride, to everyone's laughter.

But in real life it is no joke. Some women live in ulcerous insecurity with husbands who use the repudiation formula on the slightest provocation. The terror lies in the fact that if the husband is spiteful, the divorcée is left virtually without support unless she has a profession or received a substantial amount of gold, income-generating land, or sheep as dowry. The wife's father or brother is expected to take her back, but this causes inordinate hardship in poor families. Although the Quran calls for "maintenance on a reasonable scale" for divorced women (ii:241), it is customary among those who claim to adhere to the letter of the Shariah to pay her the balance of the dowry agreed upon and support her only during the three months of chastity that she must observe after the divorce in order to see if she is pregnant by her husband. If she is, the child must be turned over to her ex-husband when it is born, along with her older children. The Quran left the mother's visiting rights after the nursing stage to be worked out amicably with the children's father, but rancor often leads to abuse, which explains why even financially independent women often put up with a hopeless marriage. An uneducated woman may even try to produce more children at this point, in order to revive her husband's interest and thus hang on to her older children and her bread. Usually the mother's pitiful efforts succeed only in eroding her children's sense of security and their image of women in general. Whether she stays or leaves, they are diminished.[15]

These tragedies are not isolated cases. The divorce rate is quite high in countries where unilateral divorce has not been curbed, according to Fatima Mernissi. The divorce rate in Morocco, she says, is about four times that of the U.S. for married women aged twenty to twenty-four, and five times that of Syria, the first Arab country to require the husband to justify his divorce in court. Tunisia and Turkey, which have abolished unilateral divorce, report only one-third to one-fourth Morocco's divorce rate. The chances of a Moroccan woman's being repudiated double after the age of twenty-nine, when her prospects for remarriage also diminish considerably. Under these circumstances a wife without a profession has no choice but to charm as many gold bracelets out of her husband as possible. Jewelry is her "salary" for domestic work and her nest egg for a rainy day.

Very few women are yet economically equipped to sue their husbands for divorce, but their numbers are likely to increase among professional women, especially where child custody laws are liberalized. The Quran (ii:229) gives this right to women provided that they return the dowry to their husband. The widespread consensus in countries that govern by the Shariah, however, is that a woman cannot sue for divorce unless she has stipulated this option in her marriage contract. The consequences of failure to take this precaution are described in a controversial Egyptian film entitled *I Need a Solution (Uridu Hallan)*, produced in the mid-1970s. Based on a real-life story by Hosen Shah, a prominent woman journalist with *Al-Akbar*, and with the lead played by Faten Hammama, one of the biggest stars of the Arab cinema (and, incidentally, formerly Mrs. Omar Sharif), the film drew more attention than the many articles and demonstrations on the un-Islamic spirit pervading current application of Islamic divorce laws.

The story starts with the heroine's decision to leave her unfaithful and mean husband. Now that she has raised their offspring to adulthood, she feels it her right to return to school and realize her own potential. But she must ask her husband to repudiate her, for she failed to insert in her marriage contract the clause giving her the right to sue. Her husband refuses to oblige, condemning her instead to a life of celibacy by withdrawing his sexual attention from her. He can always get another wife legally, and society does not prevent him from consorting with mistresses. Although he breaks Islamic law on these matters, the heroine remains obediently chaste, out of her own sense of honor and perhaps also because her husband could punish her for adultery if she did not comply with the law. Just when she has resigned herself to finding satisfaction exclusively through her study and career, she meets a man with whom she wants to rebuild her life. Since her husband is more determined than ever to punish her, she takes her case to court.

During a futile seven-year battle in the bureaucratic maze

of the courts she meets less fortunate sisters-in-arms who represent some typical Egyptian divorce problems. One is a penniless, childless sixty-year-old woman who was repudiated by her husband in favor of a young girl. She was awarded only a year's alimony. This might have tided over a much younger divorcée with prospects for remarrying, but the old woman is condemned to pauperism as a result of an abusive interpretation of the law, unless the courts will make an exception for her. Another who attracts the heroine's attention is the young mother of several children, whom the husband simply abandoned in order to escape paying the modest alimony and the dowry to which she would have been entitled had he divorced her. In desperation she turns to prostitution to feed her children, and appears in court one day in the provocative outfit of her new occupation to draw attention to the injustice perpetrated on her. Though the film's educated heroine is economically more fortunate, the divorce court leaves her with only two alternatives: she must either remain chaste or commit adultery with her new suitor and face the consequences.

In tribal communities where extended families watch out for one another's interests and keep their members in line, Islamic law may function in the spirit of mutual understanding and generosity the Prophet intended. A good example is a small Bedouin settlement in Wadi Fatima, Saudi Arabia. Motoko Katakura, a Japanese anthropologist who taught Arabic to children in the village between 1968 and 1970, reports that divorce among her pupils' parents was usually arranged quite amicably, with one of the spouses simply moving out of the conjugal home.[16] Here Islamic law was evidently interpreted to give the wife the right to leave on her own initiative by returning the dowry to her husband. The breakup was not as traumatic as it might be in larger villages and cities, especially because the wife's place in the tribal "job market" did not change. She continued to tend the herd and process the milk as usual, rendering her services to her father's household rather than her husband's until she remarried. She found a new husband fairly easily, since men did not insist on having younger wives and occasionally took those as many as twenty years older than themselves; kinship was more important than age. Child custody was also flexible. A divorced woman often sent her pubescent daughter to live with her father when she remarried, in order to minimize the possibility of an incestuous triangle; her ex-husband sent her their adolescent son, for the same reason. Since the extended family raised the children collectively anyway, the offspring of divorced parents moved from one home to another without feeling as uprooted as their urban cousins.

Without throwing out the Shariah altogether, as Turkey did, many countries have passed supplementary laws to spell out the spirit of fairness with which the Prophet had initially established the divorce guidelines. Basically this has meant curtailing the husband's right to repudiate his wife on a whim and assuring her of fairer alimony and child custody provisions. According to the Personal Status Law which President Anwar Sadat passed by executive decree in 1979 after years of opposition from the conservatives, the divorced wife is entitled to the house which she occupied while married and to 40 percent of the husband's salary for three years. If married to the same man for more than fifteen years, she draws alimony for life or until she remarries. Unless the mother is proved unfit, daughters stay with her until their marriage, and sons until fifteen years of age.

Many countries have granted women the right to sue for divorce for a limited number of causes, such as physical abuse, the husband's impotence or failure to support his family, his being afflicted with an incurable contagious disease, and his taking a second wife. In some countries—Tunisia, for instance—grounds on which women may sue for divorce have been expanded further to include mental incompatibility. With child custody usually awarded to the mother unless she is proved totally unfit, the Tunisian divorce law may well be among the most favorable to women—yet it does not grant alimony to all women who initiate divorce proceedings. In Pakistan a woman may also obtain divorce on grounds of mental incompatibility, but only if she returns the dowry to her husband. The years of unpaid labor that she has contributed to her husband's family is not taken into account. Thus, the only winner in these reforms is the financially independent professional woman. The law is specifically on her side in Iraq, where she may get a divorce if her husband forces her to live too far away from her place of work to enable her to commute.[17]

Many of the poor and illiterate women, on the other hand, do not even know their full rights against husbands who divorce them. Half a century after her country improved her legal status, many a rural Turkish woman fails to get even her minimal rights in divorce because she is too ignorant to register her religious marriage with the civil authorities—the only ones who can enforce the new divorce laws. (This ignorance is so widespread in rural areas that periodically the government passes special decrees to legitimize the children born of unregistered marriages.)

Nor do male-dominated courts always protect women's rights. Those which punish men's crimes of honor lightly are also prone to interpret the law in the husband's favor. The women independence fighters of the People's Democratic Republic of Yemen scored a feat of poetic justice on this point in 1974 when the Ministry of Justice ordered divorce cases to be heard by the Social Committees of the Women's Union before being judged by the courts. This resulted in extraordinary de facto trials of husbands by all-women courts packed with women spectators.[18] The reversal of the usual courtroom scene garnered so much publicity for the divorcées' cause that the predominantly male courts which were legally empowered to pass the final verdict could not ignore the judgment reached by the women's courts. However, such support systems for poor women are rare. Therefore, as women from more privileged families secure their rights through study and professions, the sad story of the Middle Eastern mother—the perennial pregnancies, the fear of divorce and polygamy—remains the story of Third World poverty and ignorance.[19]

But she has remarkable coping techniques which work around the system and redeem her dignity no matter what laws govern her.[20] Perhaps her greatest strength lies in her ability to cooperate with other women of the extended family and the neighborhood. These semiliterate women may not know the law or have the power to change it, but they do not take everything lying down, as is generally believed. They can be a most effective Greek chorus of gossipers who arouse neighborhood opinion against an abusive husband and plague his conscience. They drop in constantly on each other to make sure that they are reasonably well, to exchange cathartic tales of woe, to check out prospective brides and grooms for their households from among their friends' children. They share gadgets and utensils and help one another at births, weddings, and funerals.

In managing on an extremely tight budget these uneducated woman can show admirable organizational skills. In many of Cairo's old lower- and lower-middle-class neighborhoods, for example, women run co-ops, where a few of their members go to the market to buy and sell for the whole group, thus saving one another considerable time and money. Their most interesting money-saving project is their informal bank. Its operation varies slightly from group to group, but a typical one works something like this: the group decides to save so much per week or month and give the entire sum to each member in turn. The bank tries to time the cash gift according to each woman's needs. One may appreciate the money when her child is sick, while another may prefer waiting until she has to buy a wedding gift for a relative. Since their husbands generally work far away from the neighborhood and have no opportunity to organize among themselves, they depend heavily on their wives' subculture to stretch their wages and for support in times of crisis.

When a woman of this class feels particularly helpless in her frustration, she may resort to voodoo-like rituals in lieu of tranquilizers for temporary relief. In the village of Fateha, on the Nile between Cairo and Alexandria, for example, the *uzr* is popular. A para-Islamic ritual for airing discontent, the *uzr* allows the rebel to engage in basically harmless antisocial behavior, such as uttering nonsense, showing disrespect for superiors, neglecting housework and children, losing consciousness, getting depressed, weeping for no apparent reason, trembling, complaining of dizziness, stomachache, or headache. Since such a person is considered to be possessed by a spirit, she is not held responsible for any of her bizarre actions. When the husband has had enough, he organizes a *zar* ceremony[21] to exorcise the spirit. The priest tries to establish communication with the spirit while music and dance stimulate the possessed. She finally speaks in a strange voice, and everyone strains to listen. It is the spirit talking. It will leave the patient's body only on certain conditions, all of which happen to be favorable to the afflicted. When the spirit's wishes are granted and it leaves, a lamb is sacrificed for a thanksgiving party, with the patient, in fancy clothes and jewelry, the guest of honor. The malcontent wins her case—at least temporarily—without having to fly in the face of the patriarch and perhaps risk repudiation. Everyone's pride is thus saved.

The effectiveness of such rituals depends not only on the husband's low tolerance for his wife's annoying behavior but also on the attention and moral support lavished on her by women relatives and neighbors. Without this Greek chorus, the drama may end differently. He may simply repudiate her, for example.

With urbanization and migration disrupting extended families and neighborhoods where everyone's grandmother knew everyone else's, the old-girl network is crumbling. Younger couples consider it a step up on the social ladder to move into one of the modern matchbox apartments that are encircling and overrunning cities throughout the Middle East. No noisy and nosy neighbors dropping in all the time. No in-laws. Just the two of them in a love nest. He works. She looks after the baby, cleans, cooks, and waits in her best dress for her husband every evening. But the romance does not last long. Raja al-Almi, a reporter for the Tunisian magazine *Dialogue pour le progrès,* interviewed one of the inmates of the feminine mystique. "I'm not his slave. He spends all his free time with his friends and leaves everything up to me," she complained.[22]

The interview reminded me of lonely lower-middle-class Istanbul housewives who complain that their husbands never take them to the theater or restaurants or parties but spend all their leisure time with their men friends at the coffee shop. Aside from visits to Mother, these women say, they have little social life of their own in transient neighborhoods. Each is trapped inside her own apartment with her husband, children, television, and pulp romances. The best of the harem tradition —the companionship and support of other women—has disappeared, and the worst lingers on even where laws are extremely liberal.

It is not that the husband is always jealous of exposing his wife to other men; she is as exposed on her solo shopping expeditions as she is at a theater or a restaurant. The problem lies mainly in the fact that after centuries of harem tradition, which kept the sexes apart during most of the day even within the extended family, men and women have to relate intensely with each other for the first time in their history. Young couples in small urban apartments find that they have to be more than sexual partners and draw almost all of their daily emotional nourishment from each other. This is utterly new to them. There are no local models to follow, and the image of their tradition-bound old mothers blurs their vague ideals. The period of transition from a segregated to a desegregated society will be "loaded with tensions and fears" for both men and women, says Fatima Mernissi, warning that the legal and traditional privileges to which men cling at women's expense destroy the possibility of forging a better relationship. Not surprisingly, she points out, the divorce rate in the transitional group is very high.

Some women from this group have actually benefited from the vacuum created by the crumbling of the old ways before the new have set in. Out of the rubble they have built more equitable marital relationships to suit their particular needs. The story of Amina's mother, Rabia Laribi of Algiers (see Chapter 7), is a good example because she took advantage of both the remnants of the old order and the scant opportunities available to her in the new postwar society. Her first years as a bride in old Algeria had been particularly difficult. Unlike her village cousins who married their relatives and stayed close to home, at age twelve Rabia was married up the social ladder to a salaried clerk fifteen years her senior. Old Mother Laribi presumably liked her, since she recommended her to her son after carefully appraising her beauty, needlework, and cooking, as well as the dowry which her parents demanded. Yet she was not inclined to treat the young bride as indulgently as an aunt would treat her niece–daughter-in-law. In fact, she regarded Rabia as a peasant upstart who had to be groomed extensively to fit her dignified new position. If the child bride put too much salt in the stew or inadvertently left one corner of the floor unwashed, the queen mother lashed out: "What kind of a mother do you have that didn't teach you!" When Rabia bore two daughters in succession, her mother-in-law knew that the young woman was "no good" and hinted loudly to her son that he should divorce her. He never contradicted his mother's criticism of his bride, but in this matter he insisted on giving Rabia one more chance. The third child turned out to be a boy, Ahmed.

Rabia was assured of the housewife's traditional mode of rising to power in her husband's family. Adored and spoiled as a savior by his mother, Ahmed grew up to champion her cause far better than other sons. Because he is the family's first college student, he commands more than the usual respect from his father. Zohra, her eldest daughter, is like another faithful son in that she sends home a hefty contribution from Paris, which entitles her to vote in family conferences on important matters ranging from big purchases to little sister's schooling.

Rabia took advantage of the postwar hardships to bend her husband's pride enough to allow her to sew for others. Now that her venture has grown enough to keep her out of the kitchen most of the time, it is the mother-in-law who is the unpaid housewife. She is respected for her age but is not taken as the supreme authority on important matters. Shrewd head of the family that he is, the father prefers to join the powerful mother-son-daughter cartel, although he formally agrees with his mother at first, as tradition requires, and then allows himself to be courted away from his stand.

Even if she did not add to the family coffers Rabia might have been influential. As the understanding confidante who was not much older than her children, she knew the new generation as the much older, authoritarian father and grandmother did not. When the youngsters took on manners which were strange to their elders, it was Rabia who successfully mediated between them on matters ranging from Ahmed's long hair to Amina's schooling. So confused by the new generation was the aging Mr. Laribi that he depended heavily on his wife to communicate with his offspring and preserve peace in the family. Contrary to first impressions, he was thus nothing more than a constitutional monarch to whom everyone paid his token respects, while the real power was exercised by Mother, the prime minister—another illustration of how people in this part of the world can operate on several levels of reality. Few things in the East are solely as they appear.

The growth of public education has added another level of reality to family relationships. Educated sons and daughters sometimes become their mother's parents, helping her secure her rights and guiding her into the twentieth century. In novels which mirror his personal experiences, prominent Moroccan writer Driss Chraibi explores the significance of this new filial role in man's coming to terms with the image of womanhood. In *Le Passé simple* (1954) Driss, the adolescent son of a well-to-do family, impotently watches his illiterate mother tremble before her husband and suffer one pregnancy after another in order to keep herself in his precarious good graces. The boy's pity for her turns to scorn as he begins to view her as a mindless egg-laying machine submitting blindly to the worst of the old order. His own efforts to reach out to the new are so poisoned by her subhuman status that he leaves home. His mother's image haunts him, however. Years later, in *La Civilisation, ma mère* (1972), he understands that neither protecting her gallantly nor running away is the answer. He returns home to help her gain her rights.

He takes her out of the house, into a world which literally she has never seen since stepping into her husband's home as a thirteen-year-old bride. She hugs the trees in the park, talks to the actors on the movie screen, and learns to shape the letters of the alphabet. In middle age she is a child led through her first steps. But she grows fast. As soon as she learns to write she embroiders the word *Him* on one table napkin and *Me* on another. "Who's this Him?" asks the husband at dinner. "You, of course, not Me," she replies, unfurling her napkin on her lap as if it were a banner. Having discovered herself, she goes on to work for her nation's independence from France and leaves for Europe to widen her horizons further. Though furious and bewildered at first, the husband eventually admits that he likes his doll's metamorphosis into a woman, and that through her he has become a new man. The son, in turn, finds that his mother's liberation has given him a new identity. He had merely been a security blanket for her before. Now he is a man with a clear vision of new womanhood.

The neatly fictionalized reality has a feminine counterpart in the real-life story of Fatima Mernissi, one of Morocco's first "new women," who brought out an important dimension of reversing the mother-daughter relationship. Her cloistered mother had been cheated out of her widow's inheritance because she could neither read nor count. When Fatima grew up to be a widely traveled multilingual writer and professor, she not only helped her mother win back her inheritance but also taught her to read and count so that she could fight for her own rights. Fatima has remolded her mother on the intellectual plane, as many other young women have coaxed theirs into Western clothes and cosmetics, thus transforming the image of old age for themselves. But Fatima has gone further. Bridging the cultural gap that separated her from her mother inspired her to champion in her writings the cause of all older women and divorcées who have to fend for themselves in the Middle East.

10

᠁᠁᠁᠁᠁᠁᠁᠁᠁᠁

Spinsters, Divorcées, Widows, and Old Women

It is better to have a husband of wood than to remain an old maid.

—Middle Eastern proverb

Shall I tell you the greatest of virtues? It is taking back your daughter or sister when she has been repudiated by her husband.

—The Prophet Muhammad

A giver of maintenance to widows and the poor is like a bestower in the way of God, an utterer of prayers all the night, and a keeper of constant fast.

—Muhammad

"In a minuscule room almost black with the smoke of incense . . . the toothless old 'azzam' sat on a bed, staring at me. He asked my neighbor to step out and told me to come very close to him. . . . Then he began to mumble incantations and all the while he ran his bony hands over my body. As he worked himself up into an apparent trance he mumbled and caressed more insistently, lingering over my intimate parts. Horrified despite my eagerness to believe in miracles, I ran to the door and escaped."[1] The speaker is a twenty-eight-year-old Tunisian woman who had gone to an exorcist to rid herself of the evil spirits that her neighbors said kept her an old maid.

In spite of the well-understood pitfalls and burdens of marriage, women in the Middle East and North Africa still are so anxious to wed that they occasionally resort to such un-Islamic magic to reach their goal. Their ardent desire reflects more than a romantic dream of finding the ultimate Prince Charming, for to be a woman alone in today's patriarchal Muslim society is to be squeezed more than anyone else between the worst of the vanishing old order and the incoming new one—even though in some respects the traditional Islamic way of life is perhaps kinder than others to the spinster, divorcée, widow, especially the aging woman.

Remaining single over a long period of time is new to this part of the world. In early Islam, though wars reduced the male population, polygamy ensured that a healthy woman of childbearing age would not go for long without a husband unless she absolutely insisted on remaining single. Even an older woman often found some man who would marry her for her wealth or family connections, or in some cases out of pure obedience to the Prophet's command to protect widows and other women without family. If a man had the means to support a large harem, he obeyed all the more willingly, because he could look to his younger wives for sexual pleasure and heirs. Such an arrangement kept the number of single women to a minimum. Divorcées and widows returned to their paternal home without feeling that they would be a burden for very long.

Now that life in small urban apartments has all but banished polygamy to history, divorcées and widows have a slimmer chance of remarrying, and more women must face the possibility of lifelong spinsterhood. The prospect is alarming enough to fatten the purses of card readers, exorcists, and psychiatrists; the forces of modern enlightenment which swept away polygamy have as yet dislodged neither the prejudices against the unmarried nor the exigencies of honor.

Islamic society has remained strictly marriage-oriented and conspires relentlessly to round up every bachelor into the matrimonial fold. To begin with, there is Muhammad's decree that marriage is the only road to virtue. Even an irreligious bachelor usually feels compelled to marry by his need for sons as security against old age, since most countries did not provide pensions until very recently. Add to that the Islamic laws which allow a man to repudiate his wife with relative ease and therefore make him more willing to marry, and a spinster is regarded as an abysmal failure, an exceptionally undesirable leftover. Supplemental laws which many countries have recently passed to make divorce as well as polygamy more difficult for the husband encourage men to take a much longer time to choose wives, thus making it more difficult for women to "catch" them. Ironically, laws benefiting married women have turned out to be somewhat disadvantageous for their single sisters. But this new turn of events has not taken the sting out of spinsterhood.

There are very few respectable lifelong niches for a single woman. So as far as society is concerned, she is always a future wife until she is clearly too old to be marriageable. If she is a widow too old for remarriage, she is consecrated to her dead husband's memory and to her children's happiness. Her status is valid only when hooked to a man's, but there are rare exceptions—she can become a saint or a holy woman, for instance. The most colorful example of this existed among the Mzab Berbers living in the environs of Ghardaia in the Algerian Sahara, where their ancestors sought refuge a thousand years ago to practice in tranquility a puritanical brand of Islam to which other Algerians did not conform. There virgins, divorcées, and widows formed an association of holy women who taught religion, recited prayers on special occasions, and, most importantly, had a monopoly on the ritual cleansing of dead women at funerals. Since the Mzabs believed that no one could enter heaven unwashed, the holy ladies exerted considerable influence over women, while male religious leaders disciplined men not only by refusing them funerary cleansing but also by barring them from congregational prayers at the mosque and thus from one of the main meeting grounds for men. In the 1920s the holy women's power extended well beyond the harem under the leadership of Mama Sliman, who joined them after her fourth divorce. At a time when male teachers of religion in the Ghardaia area did no more than have their pupils memorize the Quran, the remarkable, self-taught Mama Sliman built a school for girls, where she encouraged intellectual discussions on Islam. When she finished her voluminous writings aimed at reconciling the traditional law of the Mzabs with the Shariah, she organized conferences in various oasis towns in the region and eventually assembled a civil and moral code, which she and her sister saints imposed on men and women alike.[2] The severest punishment meted out by the women judges to transgressors of the puritanical code was the denial of proper funeral services. So deeply did Mama Sliman's people fear that penalty and so greatly did they respect her that during her lifetime her code superseded the national law in importance in the Ghardaia area. After her death the saints lost much of their clout, although they maintained their respected status.

As Islamic institutions requiring women to be single are rare, and in any case attract only a devout few, most single women live in a social limbo, swallowing their family's "looks of despair" and "silent reproaches," as the Tunisian woman who visited the exorcist put it. "When I was twenty-two, the old ladies wished me a good husband as breezily as they would wish me a good day," a secretary in an Istanbul bank said, "but when I hit thirty, the good wishes became overcast with gloom, as if the person didn't quite believe that the wish would come true." The ladies blushed in confusion when they scolded their children or grandchildren for calling her "auntie" instead of "big sister," as younger unmarried women are affectionately called by Turkish children. The secretary's relatives began to criticize her more pointedly for dressing plainly. "Young ladies show off their prettiness these days," an elderly aunt whispered in her ear as she pressed upon her niece a frilly pink dress more suitable for a fifteen-year-old.

In a sense the aunt's gift symbolized the unmarried woman's eternal status as a chaste minor, theoretically dependent on paternal support and unable to protect her own virtue. Nevertheless, working women in big cities throughout the Middle East are beginning to seek a more independent life in their own apartments, though their lifestyle is so new to their society that it presents many problems. In Istanbul a few have dared to share their quarters with their lovers, although the end of a relationship invariably forced the woman to move to another neighborhood, especially if she ever intended to invite another man into her home. The secretary did not intend to go that far perhaps, but wanted to live alone at least for a year, to taste what she called true adulthood, to be accountable only to herself for the hours and the company she kept. When she went apartment hunting, she wondered where those few women were whom people always talked about as signs of the changing times, and how they managed to carry on their sexually liberated lifestyle. As soon as a prospective landlord found out she was single, he remembered another tenant who had already put down a deposit. Sometimes he simply raised the rent: "With the cost of oil these days . . ." one told her, although the apartment in question had no heat.[3] Istanbul's posh districts, far more tolerant, were beyond her financial reach.

Friends finally convinced her that in a country where honor ruled women, it was preferable to live with one's parents. Nosy neighbors and concierges aside, even sophisticated men were not above assuming that a woman who lived alone was promiscuous. The secretary decided to save her money for traveling. She continues to be a highly respected working woman at the office and a protected child at home.

Despite this schizophrenic lifestyle, a woman may be better off living with her family in the Middle East if her eventual goal is to marry rather than follow in the footsteps of a sexually free Simone de Beauvoir or a George Sand. The extended family that limits a woman's freedom also spares her the need to scour the singles bars and cocktail parties or plan strategies to meet eligible men. The old ladies who shower a single woman with embarrassingly loud prayers for a husband and the aunts bearing gifts of frilly pink dresses sincerely mean well and actually help in husband hunting, as tradition requires them to do. True, a few old ladies may propose a visit to an exorcist, but the majority are more practical and as systematic as any computer matchmaking service. Finally released from the tyranny of honor at menopause, older women can circulate more freely and have more time to visit friends and neighbors to look over their sons and daughters of marriageable age. Young women dreaded these creatures in the old days, when they were often married off without being consulted, but now many of them unexpectedly find themselves in an alliance with the old matchmakers.

With an army of elderly relatives scouting for her, a woman who is determined to marry usually finds a husband sooner or later. Although older men tend to look to a younger generation for wives, matchmakers can advertise their maturer candidates with admirable cleverness. At a ladies-only Pakistani dinner party near New York City I overheard an elderly woman ask another to be on the lookout for a husband for her niece, who was sitting across the table from me. Uncharitably, I marveled to myself at their optimism, for the candidate was very plain and shy and at least forty. She was brilliantly matched in Pakistan soon afterward. According to the party's hostess, the old aunt had convinced a widower in his fifties that a younger wife would plant a seed of jealousy between him and his growing sons and break asunder a family which still had small children to raise. Moreover, not only was the bride a qualified teacher, able to help support the family when the man became too old to do so, but she also had many relatives living in the United States—a fact of considerable importance to a man who wanted to send his sons to study and work here. In exchange, the bride won a kindly husband who gave her freedom to work or not, as she wished, so long as he could support the family. "She made an excellent match," the hostess said. Unlike many women of her age, the niece did not have to face the possibility of marrying a senile man or an impoverished one below her social rank, thanks to her aunt's skills in working out the matrimonial equation. No one was bothered by the businesslike nature of the union, for traditionally it has been believed that blind love interferes with the coolheadedness needed to make a sensible choice which will eventually inspire lasting affection between the spouses.

If a woman resists the pressure to marry "just anybody" and remains single, she may lack a definite status of her own, and a sex life, but she is not socially ostracized. Honor requires her menfolk to protect her. In social life this translates into family-centered or all-women functions. No hostess agonizes over pairing off her guests at parties, because most traditional weddings and other big celebrations segregate the sexes. Nor do most modern mixed parties try to recreate Noah's ark, with guests invited only in pairs. Whereas Western wives might regard unattached women as possible competitors, quite the opposite is true in the Middle East. Single women, alone or with their families, are welcomed more readily into private homes than are unaccompanied bachelors, who are held in deep suspicion. In other words, the harem mentality prevails. Men fear each other's intentions regarding their wives, sisters, and daughters, but women carry on the long tradition of sharing a man's company, if not his bed.

In fact, men beyond the love-struck adolescent stage seem to enjoy escorting large groups of women, not only on picnics but also to theaters and nightclubs. The respectable "casinos" along the European side of the Bosphorus in Istanbul seem to have very few tables for two. These nightclubs (music and dance halls without gambling facilities) are filled with banquet-sized tables to accommodate families and their guests, for a family in Turkey often means the whole clan, including grandmothers and maiden aunts. When discos hit Istanbul, everyone said that the age of Noah's ark had arrived. Indeed, young people do go out as couples, but the rules posted at the doors of many discos are still very Middle Eastern: no man may enter unless accompanied by *at least* one woman. Some families regard these new establishments as a modern version of the casino, for one of the invitations I accepted at a Turkish Mediterranean resort came from a family large enough to occupy a good half of the dance floor. The grandmother watched our purses while we danced.

The family-centered social life may thus make old age less lonely in the Middle East than in the highly industrialized West, but it cannot entirely erase the pain, especially for the aging spinster. What perhaps worries her more than the missed joys of love and companionship is the lack of a son who would assure her the highest rank in his household, according to tradition. Eventually passing from her father's protection to her brother's, the spinster may have to defer to her mother and sister-in-law for life. If she is fortunate, she may be "adopted" by a niece or a nephew. "My aunt had no children and borrowed me so often from my mother that I feel I have two mothers," an Egyptian journalist said, adding matter-of-factly that she expected to look after both of them when they grew old.

Although mothers of sons look forward to a more secure future, they do not find it any easier to cope with menopause, which they see as the end of their womanhood. Most have defined themselves solely as wives and mothers, and see their entire purpose in life coming to a close. Out of panic, they sometimes try to have just one more child, who will rejuvenate them in their husbands' eyes more effectively than a face lift.

When the periods stop altogether, they may at first convince themselves that they are pregnant. The Algerian folklore which whitewashes illegitimate births also explains the baby who never arrives: he is sleeping in the womb and will develop late. The midwife charitably goes along with the idea until her client bows to the inevitable.

With the submission comes the need to deal with a set of cruel stereotypes of the older woman. Though menopause restores to her the freedom to come and go unchaperoned and unveiled and see anyone she pleases, it can do so only by robbing her of her womanhood. Although in actuality she may continue to enjoy a good sexual relationship with her husband, according to the traditions of many Middle Eastern societies any sign of sexuality on her part is considered revoltingly unnatural.[4] North African folklore features a shriveled-up female demon named Aysha Kandisha, who seduces young men with her toothless grin and pendulous breasts, destroying them in the end with her insatiable sexual appetite. Such lust in a man of comparable age is not only tolerated but often admired as proof of virility.

Even if the older woman accepts her desexualization, she still gets a bad press, especially in relation to younger women. Folklore and the media love to portray old women as witches and procurers as well as wicked stepmothers and mothers-in-law exploiting beautiful younger women out of jealousy and greed. Of these ogres, the most ubiquitous in the life of the average young woman is the mother-in-law, regarded as a necessary evil since she comes with almost every marriage. What makes her particularly feared is that she is full of contradictions. After choosing a bride for her son, she turns around and abuses the wretched young thing, working her to the bone, finding fault with her every move, and rigidly imposing the tyranny of honor. Freed from a lifetime of constraints, the old lady might be expected to sympathize with the young bride, but she seems bent on justifying her own life by tormenting the young wife in the name of her son's interests. In fact, she is believed to be competing subconsciously for his love in order to secure her own future. "February's sun is for my daughter-in-law; that of March, for my daughter; and April's is for me," she cries triumphantly, according to a Lebanese proverb. So full of treachery is she supposed to be that a Moroccan proverb claims: "What takes Satan a year to do is done by the old hag within the hour." The most considerate old woman proverbially disguises her constant criticism against the bride as deliberately loud warnings to her own daughter: "I'm telling you, my daughter—but you listen, daughter-in-law." Not surprisingly, all these horror tales conclude that the mother-in-law is the number one marriage wrecker, kicking out the bride at will, sometimes against her son's wishes.

Highly sensitive to these stereotypes, many older women bend over backwards to befriend their daughter-in-law, if only to ensure harmony in the home where they spend so much time together. Such kindness has been reported by American-born brides, who were not chosen by their mother-in-law and were less than ideal members of the household before adjusting to the local culture. When a California woman returned to the U.S. from Morocco after her divorce, she missed her mother-in-law more than anyone else. "She was my bridge to the Moroccan culture and people," she said, "but more than that, she was an understanding big sister and mother—better than my own. If she weren't there, I'd have split sooner." Her sentiment is echoed by another California woman, Marianna Alireza, who married a Saudi Arabian in the 1940s and lived in his country for many years. In her book *At the Drop of a Veil* (1971), which depicts her life in Arabia before the oil boom, she describes the saintly patience of her mother-in-law, who helped her not only to care for her many children but also to find a comfortable niche for herself in the large extended family. By the end of her marriage it appeared that the person closest to her was her mother-in-law, who remained Marianna's friend despite her success in kidnapping the children from her ex-husband.

Though heard of rather frequently, such cases are always greeted with surprise, as if they were exceptional. The nasty image persists, fed by particularly sensational stories of bride abuse. The high position of the mother in her son's house and the relatively low status of the bride until she produces heirs tend to set the stage for fear, distrust, and sometimes animosity between the two female protagonists of the harem triangle. In fact, mother-in-law trouble ranks among the top causes for divorce in most countries. Indeed, matchmakers feel that they have a big ace up their sleeves when they can claim, "And he has no mother."

Yet the older woman is not obsolete just because her childbearing years are over. She is actually quite indispensable in a sexually segregated society. Not only does her asexual status allow her to move about more freely as a matchmaker than a man of her age can, but her experience makes her an invaluable teacher and adviser. A woman who marries young must depend on her mother-in-law to teach her the finer points of housewifery, including the secrets of concocting rouge and aphrodisiacs. The most naive young woman knows what the calculating beauties of the caliphs' harems knew: the best way to a man's heart is through his mother—a fact which keeps aging women from being ignored, if not always in everyone's affections.

The most despised old woman can find solace in her own daughter's love. Turks say that a mother-daughter relationship is like halvah with chunks of walnut in it—inseparable and complementary. In a sense, the old mother could be the young married woman's free alter ego, a link to her natal family and the outside world, enabling her even to overstep the bounds of honor if necessary in order to achieve happiness. Once the daughter has passed the virginity test in marriage, many a mother seems willing to relate to her as a woman rather than a mere vessel of honor. This usually means lending a sympathetic ear to tales of marital woes and thus serving as a safety valve in marriage, or giving money for such secret personal expenditures as abortion.

In his soul-wrenching novel *La Répudiation* Rachid Boud-jedra presents a mother who goes further. Obliged to marry off her beautiful fifteen-year-old daughter to an aging man for his money, the mother feels so guilty of having aborted her daughter's youth that she tacitly encourages her to carry on a clandestine love affair with the old groom's virile young son— an act exemplifying the complexities behind the black image of the old woman. Unable to give up her role as mother, she often does the dirty work to help her grown children.

Her only unequivocally beloved image is that of the grand-mother, the patient babysitter who passes on cultural tradi-tions. To those of us brought up in modern cities and abroad by Westernized parents, Grandmother represents our strong-est link to our cultural and religious heritage. My Turkish grandmother had a large repertoire of songs, dances, and em-broidery stitches to keep us busy on rainy afternoons before the advent of television. Other traditions that she passed on are still taught to youngsters despite competition from tele-vision. She took her grandchildren to the mosque in the eve-nings during the holy month of Ramadan, when the minarets were starred with lamps as if they were pencil-thin Christmas trees. The hauntingly beautiful recitation of the Quran which I heard then mingles in my memory with Grandmother's serene face and the sweets she bought for us on the way home.

More important than sweet memories and songs, perhaps, is the old philosophy of life that she transmitted when she would take us to the village of Anatolu Kavagi to eat fresh fish in an outdoor restaurant. We would do it in the old-fashioned man-ner, traveling in a boat that zigzagged slowly between the ports on the European and Asiatic shores along the Bosphorus toward the Black Sea. It took a whole morning to reach our destination, but Grandmother scorned those modern folk who zipped up in their cars in half an hour in the name of effi-ciency. They missed the whole point, she said, which was to sip tea on the sunny deck while contemplating the lacy spun-sugar palaces of the sultans alongside fishermen's humble wooden cottages. Each building in its own beauty attested to the dignity of its occupants, who joined hands to build the sacred mosques. And those tiny cemeteries wedged incongruously between shops and residences were to remind us of the transience of this magnificence. "Not in a gloomy sort of way," Grandmother stressed, "and not like the people who sit on the prayer rug all day long as if to accumulate as many points for holiness as possible before death. No, that's not the idea at all. When you know you're not going to live forever you enjoy the beauty of life every day and do not put it off because you're always in a rush or because you haven't yet gotten the most beautiful dress or boat that you want."

She never lectured; she merely commented dreamily now and again, her voice harmonizing with the waves lapping against the boat as if each village along the way were whispering its story as we passed by. Her homespun philosophy was derived from the best of Islam's: that every experience, every creation, every idea revealed its deeper beauty and meaning when viewed as an integral part of the whole universe—a sort of a spiritual and esthetic ecology. As a child I could see it best at work on the return journey, when the palaces and mosques and cottages that had proudly displayed their splendor in every detail faded into silhouettes in response to the setting sun, the better to set off its symphony of purples and crimsons. Everything in nature was taking turns, so to speak, to show off its beauty and to strike a harmonious note together. Everything in the universe had its place, and every age had its beauty and significance. Ecology is tipping off balance these days, and highways have proliferated along with modern folk in a hurry, but the slow boat ride along the Bosphorus remains a favorite pastime. For this, grandmothers must be largely responsible.

The story of the Muslim woman of the Middle East and North Africa would have ended right here, with her returning to the freedom she once knew as a child and reaping the fruits

of a tradition that honors old age, but her homeland is changing. The industrial and urban developments that discouraged
polygamy are also breaking apart the extended family, which
protected old and single women. The sad consequences have
begun to show. Such newcomers to the industrial age as Saudi
Arabia and Libya have just built old-age homes—hitherto
unheard-of institutions in the Middle East—although their
numbers are comparatively small and include institutions for
those who are too senile or ill to be properly cared for at home
by poorer people. In Tunisia the Ministry of Social Affairs has
launched publicity campaigns aimed at stemming the acceler-
ating social isolation of the old. The emphasis is on sensitizing
the young who grew up in nuclear families within the last
decade or so. In schools and youth clubs the plight of the
elderly is discussed and mother-in-law horror tales are reexamined. Some of the programs have students visit and shop for
the elderly without families. It is not that the young respect the
old much less than they used to, said Suad Chater, director of
Social Development at the ministry. Better medical care, she
pointed out, has increased the aging population, thus overburdening the young in inflationary times. "That is why we
are also thinking in terms of financial aid that would allow
some families to move to larger quarters where several generations can live together with a minimum of friction," Mrs.
Chater said.

The isolation of the elderly has reached nowhere near the
level that it has in the highly industrialized countries. Family
ties and the neighborhood network are still strong enough to
support the elderly, but many wonder how long this will hold
true. Their bleak future is reflected today in the plight of the
divorcée, who is perhaps the first beneficiary and victim of
modernization in the Islamic world.

In the old days of the extended family and man's un-
hampered right to divorce his wife unilaterally and keep her
children, women were often sent back to the paternal home at
a fairly young age. Unburdened by children, they had a far

better chance of remarrying than did widows, who not only tended to be older and associated with "the bad omen of death" in some countries but also had many offspring in tow. Today, thanks to many countries' liberalized laws granting women the custody of their young children, divorcées are, ironically, as disadvantaged as older widows in finding new mates, especially when they are stranded in their homes with little children and no relative to help care for them. Justifiably envious of their ex-husbands' freedom, some women leave their children in their mother's or aunt's home in order to return to school or build a career, sometimes living on their own. The Tunisian family courts were recently stunned to see some divorced women actually refuse custody of their children, the very right feminists had fought for.[5]

To make matters worse, the divorce rate is highest among the most helpless—the urban poor and migrants from rural areas. Even if they want to, unemployed or barely employed fathers and brothers cannot always take back the divorcée and her children, as honor requires them to do. A migrant divorcée may in fact be living too far away from her own family to consider returning home. With her ex-husband paying minimal alimony or none at all, such a mother is forced to look for work. Poorly educated and tied to young children, the average divorcée on her own qualifies only for the lowest-paying dead-end jobs—hand laundering, housecleaning, sewing. If she is lucky enough to find a babysitter who does not swallow her entire income, she may hire herself out to a factory or a sweatshop for below the minimum wage. In fact, divorcées, and to some extent widows, constitute the majority of the female labor force in the unregulated low-level jobs. They are the newest proletarian underdogs, and their numbers are growing at a phenomenal rate in some countries. In Morocco, for instance, the number of households headed by women increased by 33 percent between 1960 and 1971, while those headed by men remained fairly constant. Significantly, 83 percent of the female heads of households were divorced or widowed.[6]

At the white-collar and professional levels, however, work is the single woman's sturdiest pillar of support in a changing society, partially replacing the patriarch. Many a modern spinster finds through her career her raison d'être and the respect of her community. A financially independent wife finds it easier to escape an impossible marriage. And, as in the West, a good job is the divorcée's best hedge against destitution or child abandonment, since few countries grant adequate alimony or punish nonpaying ex-husbands severely enough.

To old women, who have never been totally obsolete in this part of the world, young working women offer a new lease on life. As the extended family of aunts and sisters crumbles, and as the patriarch finds it increasingly difficult to fulfill his end in the bargain of honor, the old mother or mother-in-law is more indispensable than ever as a babysitter, for she is rarely very far away from her grandchildren. The three main characters of the old harem—the mother, the daughter, and the daughter-in-law—are thus as firmly linked together in the uncertainties of social transition as they were in traditional times.

PART III

꒫꒩꒫꒩꒫꒩꒫꒩꒫꒩꒫꒩꒫꒩

11

॥॥॥॥॥॥॥॥॥॥

Working Women

Work is the liberator of women.
—Slogan of Algerian feminists

Women can maintain their dignity only by doing
paid work.
                    —President Habib Bourguiba of Tunisia,
                    December 26, 1962

To men is allotted what they earn, and to women
what they earn.
                    —Quran iv:32

Khadija is a highly successful Saudi Arabian entrepreneur,
although she has not yet reached her thirtieth birthday. A few
years ago she decided to invest her substantial dowry and inheritance in a boutique, but she did not want it to be just
another enterprise financed by a woman and run by men.
Strict sexual segregation in her country made it difficult
enough for women to get along outside the home without having to deal with male shopkeepers, she reasoned. She wanted
her customers to be able to shed their veils in her shop as if
they were at home and try on the dresses without feeling em-
barrassed. Accordingly, she hired an all-female staff for her
comfortably furnished boutique and nailed a "for women
only" sign on her door. Friends and family who warned her

that women liked to be taken shopping by their husbands and brothers and therefore would shun her place are criticizing no more, for her venture has done so well that she is planning to expand it and branch out into garment manufacturing.

Khadija is not the only woman who, paradoxically, owes her successful career to Islamic law and her country's strict harem tradition. Ever since the Shariah granted them exclusive rights over their inheritance and dowry as a hedge against divorce and widowhood, Muslim women have had a keen sense of property and a good nose for making their assets grow. It is not surprising, therefore, that many have followed in the footsteps of the other Khadija, who married the Prophet Muhammad fourteen centuries ago. Sexual apartheid forced women to run their import-export, real estate, contracting, and retail ventures through male representatives, but an increasing number of young women have begun to see the advantage of excluding men altogether and dealing directly with women clients. "Our loose-fitting traditional costume could be easily bought by our husbands and fathers," Khadija explained, "but now that many of us also wear European clothes, we want to get away from the one-size-fits-all approach and have our own shops where we can look around and try on things at ease."

Stressing that Saudi Arabia was not ready for a large-scale demolition of its harem tradition, Khadija excitedly pointed out the enormous advantages for women in entering a business or a profession while they are still segregated from men. "Look at Bahrain," she continued, "where television programs are produced and filmed entirely by women. And in Sharjah* a Palestinian woman lawyer was welcomed with open arms by the ruler himself because he needed a woman to take care of woman's legal problems."[1] In Saudi Arabia the popularity of the country's first all-women bank, set up in Riyadh in early 1980, has launched a race to capture a promising market.[2]

* One of the United Arab Emirates.

Saudi and foreign banks, including the U.S.'s Citibank, have started training women to run the branches they plan to open this year for women customers. "With a separate all-female economy," Khadija pointed out, "women directors will not be just tokens who are used to keep their sisters from advancing. When the top posts must be filled by women, no woman would be held back solely on the basis of her sex. In fact, we'll need all the qualified women we can get to serve the female half of our country."

Her optimism, colored though it is by her own dramatic success, may well be justified in light of these recent developments and her government's new five-year Development Plan, which calls for the gradual replacement of foreign workers by qualified Saudis. At present foreigners are believed to make up almost 70 percent of the country's work force. Petrodollars can easily pay for expensive foreign labor now, but there is a growing consensus that plans must be made for the future, when the oil reserves will run out. These plans invariably include recruiting more Saudi women into the labor force and perhaps training women engineers for the vast petroleum industry.

At present most Saudi women are shunted into fields which do not disturb the harem tradition. As they constitute less than one percent of wage earners, it is felt that there is still plenty of room for them in occupations which serve women and children, especially in education and medicine.[3] Girls who are attracted to medicine, for instance, almost automatically plan to be doctors rather than nurses.

Those who have no inclination for the grueling medical school studies generally drop out rather than settle for nursing, because it is considered degrading to serve people outside the family in a subordinate capacity. Such an attitude may keep many girls at home and their country dependent on foreign nurses for years to come. "But by starting at the top rather than with the servile occupations, which were for so long associated with femininity in the West, perhaps we won't have the problem of upgrading the image of the working woman in Saudi Arabia. When people think of an educated young working woman in our country, they don't think of a nurse or a secretary but a doctor or a professor or a businesswoman," said Khadija, who became fascinated with the importance of image while traveling in the United States.

It is too early to guess exactly how professional women will fare in Saudi Arabia, but in many other Middle Eastern countries harem traditions not only started women off in prestigious professions but also kept them there. Take the case of Turkey, which was among the first Muslim countries to open their professional ranks to women. Though Ataturk was resolutely committed to smashing the harem walls, the mentality which built them in the first place lingered on. Not surprisingly, teaching children was deemed the most appropriate occupation for women. Even the field of medicine was closed to women until 1922, when a heated debate on women's biological suitability for anatomical studies and the generally demanding work was resolved. Until then, women who did not want to see male physicians could call on only three or four Turkish women doctors educated in England and Germany.

Woman's Islamic right to manage her property was so well recognized, however, that it was considered desirable to have women lawyers who could defend her interests without compromising her virtue. Accordingly, the Istanbul University Faculty of Law put up little resistance in 1921 against Sureyya Agaoglu, its first woman applicant, insisting only that she round up two more women in order to make it worthwhile for the professors to lecture to them apart from the men.[4] Today, more than 15 percent of the lawyers and about 5 percent of the judges in Turkey are women. They take pride in the fact that one of their predecessors was the first woman in the world to be elected to her country's Supreme Court of Appeals.

Teaching, medicine, and law remained the most desirable feminine occupations, not only because they served women and children but also because they required many years of specialized training, which only the rich and the most determined could undertake. Aristocratic women, who were the first to work outside the home, went into these fields for personal fulfillment or to help develop their country, not because of financial need. Though Mufidé Kuley, one of the first women to enroll in a Turkish medical school, had to do odd jobs to support herself and her widowed mother before earning her degree, she was of a good family in extenuating circumstances after the fall of the Ottoman regime. So the aristocratic image stuck, and Mufidé's successors could practice medicine without violating the code of honor requiring their husbands and fathers to support them.

The same mentality helped Ataturk's efforts to integrate aviation[5] and other technical professions. Even if they put women in close contact with men, they were high-level occupations and therefore honorable and crucial for national development. Accordingly, women engineers were much admired as symbols of the new Turkey, and one of them was appointed controlling engineer for the construction of the Ataturk Mausoleum, the most visible and beautiful symbol of the republic in the capital city of Ankara.

Even though Turkey lacked trained manpower in all sorts of occupations, it was never considered patriotic to contribute a daughter or a wife to just any occupation, such as clerical work. While paying due homage to the women who worked in any job during the War of Independence, most Turks preferred to reconcile their patriotism to their sense of honor, which overruled Western sex stereotypes. Science and medicine were feminine in Turkey; secretarial work was not. Among the upper classes women either took up prestigious professions or stayed at home. The poorer classes could not afford to send even their sons to college, and were usually too conservative to let their daughters work among men unrelated to the family. To this day clerical work remains a male stronghold, with women occupying less than a quarter of the posts in this field. Many of these women work in civil service or banks, which employ large numbers of women and often have them supervised by women.

Though Turkey is one of the few countries that had aggressively feminist political leaders who personally watched over the first women to enter various professions, working women in other parts of the Middle East also tend to congregate in elite occupations.[6] Four times as many women enter professional fields as they do other branches of paid nonagricultural employment in Syria; three times as many in Egypt; and twice as many in Libya as well as in Turkey. Over 90 percent of professional women are concentrated in teaching and nursing and other medical work; but the rest make up a hefty percentage of the total number of workers in their particular specialties. For instance, women comprise about 24 percent of engineers, physicists, and other technical experts and 31 percent of physicians and 15 percent of accountants in Iraq, and 25 percent of doctors in Algeria. In the field of communications, women comprise about 22 percent of the work force in Lebanon, and almost 50 percent of it in Egypt.[7]

Such a large representation in the professions is unique to the Middle East. In the developing countries of Latin America, for instance, educated women are fairly evenly distributed between professional and nonprofessional white-collar jobs. Moreover, many less well educated women are active in sales as well as service-type and factory work, which the honor-conscious Muslim women tend to shun because of the opportunities for contact with the opposite sex. The only exceptions may be in the food processing, textile, tobacco, and garment industries, where large numbers of women are hired regularly or seasonally. The less arduous public-contact jobs in shops, hotels, and restaurants remain masculine domains. Even Egyptian women, who are among the most active in these fields, did not comprise more than 5 percent of the personnel in 1977. The need for a larger work force in developing their nations thus opened Muslim women's way to paid work, but harem traditions as well as the lack of highly trained male specialists have determined the nature of her work and so far spared the educated from being asked, "But can you type?"

As the educational base broadens to include girls who do not have the will or the means to commit themselves to long professional training, and as an increasing number of families find it necessary to depend on more than one paycheck, prejudice against clerical-secretarial and even sales work fades in the Middle East, too. Resistance against women in sales is breaking down fast in the largest Turkish cities. If Kuwaiti women are still discouraged from becoming private secretaries, their Lebanese and Jordanian sisters already occupy at least half of the posts in this field. In fact, Libya and Saudi Arabia are thinking of alleviating their worker shortage by feminizing their clerical pools in order to free men for more physically arduous tasks.[8]

These countries may have to provide special incentives to encourage women to stay in the field, however. Clerical workers, along with women in other nonprofessional categories, often quit when they get married, because they prefer to stay at home rather than toil in dead-end jobs that bring no special prestige to themselves or their husbands. Moreover, these less educated women also bear children earlier and more frequently. Labor laws provide good maternity leaves: the fifty days at half pay plus special breast-feeding breaks and nurseries on the premises which Libya offers are fairly typical of the benefits that other countries have instituted for working mothers. But such benefits evidently have not yet offset the social disadvantages of continuing to work after marriage unless the economic situation demands it. As a result, the percentage of women in the total nonagricultural labor force in Muslim countries has remained among the lowest in the world: roughly 11 to 12 percent for the region as a whole in 1980, compared to 23 percent in Latin America, 37 to 38 percent in Europe and the U.S., and 49 percent in the U.S.S.R.[9]

The highly committed and respected professional women,

on the other hand, tend to remain in the work force after marriage. They are the main beneficiaries of circumstances which left the Middle East without an adequate number of professionally qualified men on the eve of their national independence and industrialization programs. Because educated women were needed, at least in certain professions, they were readily granted generous maternity leaves and equal pay for equal work. Although these laws have not always been fully respected by employers, professional women have enjoyed fairly good chances for advancement on the job compared to their Western counterparts. They have not yet become presidents or prime ministers, and a few who won ministerial rank have been called upon to look after the needs of women and children in health, education, and social welfare. Far fewer women than men are employers or senior managers. But an encouraging number have climbed quite high in "masculine" fields in such countries as Egypt and Turkey, where women have been in the professions for over half a century. In Egypt, for instance, the influential national radio and television networks are headed by women—Safia al-Muhandis and Hemat Mustapha, respectively. And the number of bank managers in Turkey is growing so rapidly that banking is on the way to becoming a "feminine" occupation. Akbank, one of the biggest financial institutions in the country, reported in 1979 that 78 of its 571 branches were directed by women.[10] Arriving a generation later to the feminist camp, Tunisia has already put a woman engineer, Zubeida Lattiri, at the head of the nation's electricity and gas services. She is one of the first in the Middle East to introduce solar energy to a village.

Women bosses, while not yet legion, are now numerous enough to be taken apparently in stride by men in these countries—at least in big cities.[11] Their success in being accepted may be due not only to men's liberalism but also to these women's attitude, shaped by the legacy of the harem, where both the chiefs and the braves were women. Since the first professionals were from wealthy households, where they had grown up exercising authority, they merely carried their experience to the outside world without having to suffer conflicts over their feminine identity or apologize to men or court their approval. Authority was never the antithesis of femininity for these women.

The only catch to this is that it was mostly the chiefs of the harem who went on to become chiefs in modern professions. To this day one's social status and connections, rather than sex, remains the single most important factor in getting plum jobs in the professions. The image set by the harem princesses in professional posts, however, does benefit any woman fortunate or talented enough to crash the barrier of nepotism and poverty. American sociologists have admiringly noted that no matter how humble her origins, the Turkish woman has well absorbed the harem traditions which give her a sense of independence from men and enable her to behave strictly as a skilled professional on the job.

In Egypt, where many of the large enterprises are government-run, the explicit civil service type of criteria, based on seniority, school grades, and sometimes qualifying exams, that are used for hiring and promotions may also deflect the issue of sex and take some of the sting out of being "passed by" for a woman in the promotional shuffle. Ironically, any resentment that may be directed against women bosses tends to come mostly from other women, according to Dr. Moursi Saad al-Deen. In an informal survey that he conducted among women working in government institutions while he was head of the State Information Department of Egypt, Dr. Saad al-Deen was astonished to find that 80 percent of his respondents preferred a male boss. "I do not understand why,"[12] concluded the man who was the first in his nation's history to appoint women to work abroad as press attachés.

Writing recently in *Al-Akbar*, one of Egypt's leading newspapers, about the obstacles which women themselves place against their own professional advancement, Dr. Saad al-Deen, who is now adviser to the Egyptian National Council, the equivalent of an American think tank, pointed out that some women bring to their job the worst of the harem traditions instead of the best. A few women took the assignments he gave them as press attachés, for example, and started worrying about compromising their reputation once they arrived at their posts abroad, where they had to meet men. The same problem was reported from a woman consul stationed in Europe. "This is ridiculous, for meeting men is a basic requirement of [these] jobs . . ."[13] Dr. Saad al-Deen wrote, emphasizing that such incidents put the men who promoted these women in a very difficult situation. Given the traditions of the country, he explained, he could not explicitly order women to meet men.

As the job market for an increasing number of university graduates shrinks, however, such real or imagined feminine complexes work into the hands of men who do not have Dr. Saad al-Deen's ideals and hamper women's professional advancement despite progressive labor laws. Jaouida Guigua, a judge in a Tunisian juvenile court, explains how insidiously this can happen. Her country is one of the few in the Muslim world which allow women to be judges even though the Quran rules a woman to be worth only half a man on the witness stand. The pay for all judges is determined mainly by seniority, regardless of which court they serve. On the surface, therefore, everything appears to be perfectly equitable for women judges in Tunisia. But women are shunted into the juvenile section rather than the criminal court in order to spare them the pain of sentencing people to hard labor and death. The catch in this seeming kindness is that the juvenile court has a smaller number of posts available, thus forcing qualified women to wait for many years in subordinate positions while their male colleagues walk into the criminal court and advance to more powerful posts at an earlier age.[14]

Worse yet, some of the antifeminist prejudices are incorporated into law. For instance, some countries require adult women to obtain their husbands' or male guardians' written permission to work or to travel abroad.[15] Not even a woman minister or ambassador is exempt from the law. If, in the course of handling important matters, she forgets to get the permission before going abroad to represent her government, her husband can have her arrested.

The most universal obstacle against a career woman's progress, however, is found right in her own home. Juggling a profession and marriage has grown more difficult in recent years as the extended family with its built-in babysitting service disintegrates in city after city. Even younger men who are happy to see their wives bring home a paycheck usually consider it beneath their dignity to share in the housework.[16] Frozen foods and labor-saving gadgets are a luxury. Although maid service is cheaper than in the U.S., it is not within everyone's budget. To judge from drawing-room gossip and numerous magazine articles, women who can afford help cannot always devote themselves wholly to their professions because they cannot always find the right maid. The number of nurseries falls far short of need in many countries despite laws requiring employers to provide them.

Husbands who sprawl out in front of the television set after dinner while their wives do the entire day's household chores have become the liberal press's favorite rogue in the past decade. Saida Mokni, a Tunisian journalist, recently asked a man whether he did not pity his wife, who was overburdened with two full-time jobs as career woman and homemaker. He replied without hesitation: "I am liberal enough to let her go out to work as she wished to; and now it is up to her to assume full responsibility for her choice."[17] A long anonymous letter from a Turkish professional woman to the editor of the popular weekly *Hayat* tried to play on her compatriots' pride in being as liberal as the West. "The Western woman works outside the home, but her husband shares household chores with her. . . . Our men, on the other hand, call this being henpecked. Is this an enlightened person's way of thinking?"[18] she wrote more than a decade ago. But all to no avail. Things have not changed much since then. A young Turkish physics professor recently noted with cynical resignation that her father refused to fetch even a glass of water for himself, but her young husband manages at least to get his own water.

Most women expect the Middle Eastern husband to take a long time to learn to take his glass back to the kitchen and wash it himself. In the meantime he resolutely buries his nose in papers which carry an inordinate number of cartoons that feature Amazons on their way to board meetings telling their little apron-wearing husbands what to cook for dinner. Less flattering cartoons depict fat social butterflies gorging themselves on baklava in the living room while the husband slaves in the kitchen. If he lives in Egypt, the husband may catch a movie entitled *My Wife's Pride,* in which the heroine is her husband's boss at the office. At home, however, she is his servant, forced to do menial domestic chores in front of visitors while he lounges on the sofa in macho splendor.

In a marriage-versus-career dilemma the career generally loses, laments Egyptian feminist Dr. Nawal al-Saadawi, for society considers a woman's career tangential to her primary role as wife and mother. The educated woman pays a high psychological price for giving in to such a view, the doctor writes in her controversial best-sellers *Women and Sex* and *Women and Neurosis.* Yet if she persists in carrying on both the job and the housework without help, she is too overburdened to reach her creative peak and thus remains bitterly dissatisfied. Insisting that an educated woman has no choice but to seek fulfillment in her career outside the home, Dr. Saadawi calls for a redefinition of roles in marriage. In the meantime, if she must choose between marriage and career, the doctor concludes, she is better off choosing her career.

Few women are so bravely committed to a profession in a society that regards marriage as their ultimate goal. And few try to modify their role within marriage, mainly because the problem has hit them so suddenly and so recently that they are stunned. There are Turkish women whose grandmothers combined careers with marriage, but this caused no difficulty in the old days, when the extended family lived together and maids were easily available. The career woman did not have to redefine her domestic role then. For all practical purposes, she simply relegated it to a surrogate. Today, with more than 70 percent of the families reduced to nuclear size in Turkey's metropolitan areas, the professional woman is the first to assume two burdens. Brought up to view housework as a feminine domain and a career as a privilege, she is ill equipped to escape the stereotyped sex role. She is doubly handicapped by her adroitness in leading a schizophrenic life, which American sociologists admired so much. While she functions professionally at work, she readily resumes her traditional feminine role at home to serve her husband. Not to do so might be a blow to her concept of femininity as much as to his masculinity. Women as well as men believe in the modern Middle Eastern adage that "the best wife is one who takes care of you at home like a mother, works in the office like a man, and makes love to you like a courtesan."[19]

The professional women of Saudi Arabia may be next in line for this sort of a dilemma, if one can judge by recent estimates that almost 70 percent of those who are now working live in nuclear families.[20] "We won't have to worry for a long while to come," Khadija, the young entrepreneur, said. Nuclear families keep close ties with their kin, but wealth is also a saving grace for her and many of her working friends. They hire nursemaids for their children and have a chauffeur or a male member of their family drive them to work, since no woman is allowed to drive in their country. But, contrary to popular opinion abroad, not every Saudi is a Rockefeller. If the trend toward breaking up of the extended families continues in big cities, childcare and transportation could pose a problem when more women outside the elite families are recruited into the work force. Khadija insists that the paternalistic government will do something about it, since it needs women's labor and is at the same time committed to preserving the mother's nurturing role in the Muslim family.

Indeed, the Saudi Arabian Public Transport Company has already established a bus network in Jeddah with a harem section provided in each vehicle. A few pilot day-care programs have also been launched. The General Presidency of Girls Education, for instance, has more than five nurseries and kindergartens for its employees' children. The emerging need for nurseries has opened to women further opportunities not only for gainful employment but also for business. A few of them are planning to build and run private nurseries.

Other innovative solutions have surfaced. A few enterprises which hire women have feminized their work schedules to conform to the staff's childcare and homemaking duties. Women's banks and a garment factory, for instance, allow their employees to work only in the morning, or a few hours in the morning and another few in the evening, with the long lunch break customary in hot countries, which allows women ample time to go home to be with their children. Khadija summed up the exciting ideas about working women that this approach has engendered among her friends: "It is very rigid antifeminist thinking to say that everyone must remain at his desk from nine to five or eight to six or else let her diploma gather dust during her childrearing years. There is no magic in such a schedule made for men. Why should we live by it and apologize for our womanhood? Why shouldn't working mothers get special breaks to nurse their babies? They do in China and it hasn't cut down on efficiency. Why can't two women share one full-time job?" Though admitting that there were inconveniences to sexual segregation, Khadija stressed that such work rules catering to women would have little chance of getting off the ground in a desegregated society.

Few women in Egypt or Turkey or Tunisia would consider a harem economy as a solution to their problems of running a home and a career, but Khadija's thoughts underscore the vulnerable foundation on which these women have built their career and emancipation. In order to be equal to their male colleagues they have become "like men," and failed to bring about deeper social changes to reconcile the woman's natural role with her career in the outside world. They have in effect failed to break down the harem, since their womanhood is still trapped in it. The few who succeed in becoming both super-moms and super-engineers do so on the shoulders of countless unpaid or ill-paid maids, old aunts, mothers, laundresses, seamstresses, and cooks. Add to these the remaining 60 to 70 percent of the Middle East's female population who cultivate the land for little or no pay or migrate to the city to offer cheap labor, and the professional woman has 90 percent or more of her countrywomen at her service, making it possible for her to continue her juggling act between the home and the office.

This is not to denigrate her accomplishments. Someone had to break out of the traditional mold, and doing so entailed personal sacrifice and risk. The first Ottoman Muslim actress, Afifa, was arrested by the police when she appeared on the stage. The lovely Mufidé Kuley might have married into luxury instead of working her way through medical school to graduate as one of the first women doctors in Turkey. Amina al-Said, one of Egypt's first women journalists, had to work without pay at first. Today journalism and medicine rank among the most popular fields of work for Egyptian and Turkish women. And acting in the legitimate theater is considered quite respectable, too. No man could have achieved so much without help, either.

But there remain the other 90 percent or more of women who cannot follow the path paved by pioneer professional women because they are poor, illiterate, or bound to children or long hours of menial labor outside the home. Many of them do not benefit from their countries' liberal labor laws because they work in the unregulated sector, such as sweatshops, farms, and other people's homes. In February 1976 the Egyptian journal *At-Talia* published an interview with Umm Muhammad of Cairo,[21] who epitomizes the very poor working woman in many Middle Eastern cities. The wife of an ironer and mother of eight children, all living in one room, Umm Muhammad is forced to leave the care of her children to her sixteen-year-old daughter and work eight to twelve hours a day as a hospital attendant's assistant in order to help her husband keep the family from total starvation. She enjoys no employee benefits, not even maternity leave, because she is considered temporary help. Yet she has resigned herself to accepting as many children as God will give her, since the contraceptive pill made her too weak to work. Barely literate, she has little hope of finding a regular job which would at least entitle her to employee benefits. In any case, she cannot afford to take time off to search for another job.[22]

In agriculture women who receive any wage at all are lucky, since most of them are supposed to be merely tangential family helpers lending a hand when necessary, as children do. In reality, women are full-time workers on the land. In many areas of Turkey, for instance, men plow the land and thereafter sit in coffee shops until the crops are harvested, at which time they make another social occasion out of going to the market to sell their crops and pocket the money. All of the long months of work in between is relegated to women, who are thus the actual producers of wheat, tobacco, sugar, and tea—the nation's main cash crops. As if this were not enough, these women also care for animals, process olives, pickle vegetables, make yogurt and cheese, and weave cloth. Obedient housewives go to paradise, they say. A similar picture prevails throughout the Middle East, where 50 to 70 percent of the rural workers are women. Almost everywhere women's participation in farm work is growing as men emigrate to the cities or abroad in search of better-paying jobs.

Yet this is hardly reflected in agrarian reform laws, which usually recognize men as the owners or tillers of the land and therefore the only ones eligible for membership in various cooperatives that disseminate information on improved farming methods. Even in Iraqi collective farms women who toil alongside their husbands have often been barred from membership in these farms.[23]

Granted, these problems of the other 90 percent are complex and are properly the government's duty to solve. However, educated women are indispensable to this process where the harem mentality lingers. In fact, women teachers, doctors, and social workers do serve their governments' projects in remote rural areas—sometimes as a part of their obligatory peace-corps-like assignment in return for the free education they receive. But, like their male colleagues, most prefer to work in lucrative posts close to their city homes, especially where the euphoria of national liberation has subsided. The problems of living alone in conservative villages make women especially reluctant to go where they are most needed. When they are married, their husbands' work determines the site of their residence, which is usually in metropolitan areas. Few retain their missionary zeal, while the rest become increasingly alienated from the tradition-bound illiterate masses as the years remove them from the idealistic atmosphere of the college campus and trap them in the cares of their highly Westernized existence.

This breast-beating, however, seems to have spurred the growth of a new phase in feminist consciousness which does include the other 90 percent in an unexpectedly unpatronizing way. Although its ideals embraced everyone, the first phase of feminism was basically elitist, devoted mainly to smashing harem walls and opening university doors for upper-class women who were to help develop their nations by becoming doctors and lawyers. The only way for a woman to emancipate herself was to succeed these pioneers in the professions. The second phase promises to be much more democratic. While continuing to advocate mass education, for obvious reasons, it also seeks to "professionalize" agricultural labor and homemaking, which will inevitably occupy an overwhelming majority of the silent 90 percent for many years to come.

Some of the most promising innovations have taken place on the farm. About a decade ago the Union of Iraqi Women convinced their Minister of Agriculture that women were important agents of agricultural improvements since they constituted at least half of the work force. The result was the Thatilsalasil Collective Farm, for women only.[24] For the past eight years approximately fifty women have lived with their families in the collective's housing project and reported every morning to the vast fields in the north of Baghdad to work under the instruction of university-trained women experts in agriculture and animal husbandry. Until 6 P.M. their day has been organized to give them time to learn the three R's and the basics of health and nutrition, which they would never have been able to do if they had had to pull themselves away from their families' constant demands in order to attend school far from their place of work. Women have also shared in the farm's ever-growing profits, and take home a basket of produce every day. So successful has the farm been that Iraq recently established a few more collective farms for women. But not every country is wealthy enough to invest in such projects.

It is not surprising, therefore, that homemakers' wish to be officially recognized as economically active contributors to their nations' GNP has been largely ignored. But they have champions for their cause.[25] One of the most vocal is Dr. Julinda Abu Nasr, who gives courses on Arab women at Beirut University College and publishes an English-language journal on women entitled *Al-Raida*. Nobody is demanding salaries for housewives, which would be enormous given the countless services they perform, the professor emphasizes. She points instead to the health and social security allocations that employed husbands receive for each dependent in many countries. "The wife should get her share of the sum," suggests Dr. Abu Nasr. Better yet, she continues, the homemaker should be recognized as her husband's full partner in the family and therefore co-owner of his property.[26]

This becomes imperative where men migrate to the city or to another country in search of work. Not being recognized as her husband's full economic partner in such cases puts a woman's entire family at a disadvantage. For example, the husband of a nomadic woman of Saudi Arabia may stay away for months at a time in the city to work as truck driver or laborer. She not only makes and looks after the family tent but also cares for the camels, milks them, and makes yogurt and cheese. It is only thanks to her full-time labor that the nomadic way of life in the desert is possible. Yet all the camels and other important property, except her dowry, are her husband's. If she ever needs a loan to buy more animals or tools, she is as disqualified as a minor because the assets are not registered in her name. Since only work that brings wages is counted, the woman's indispensable contribution to the economy and her needs in doing it better are ignored. Dr. Aisha al-Mana, director of the Women's Social Welfare Office in the Eastern Province of Saudi Arabia, is preparing a document asking her government to redefine work to include unpaid Bedouin homemakers and others in similar situations. Such efforts are a first step in reconciling the masculine world of work and the feminine world of homemaking and in ultimately blurring the traditional sex stereotypes which forced women doctors and engineers to be "like men" in order to survive in their professions.

Such reforms depend much more on a change of attitude than on great wealth, Fatima Mernissi contends.[27] The United States, she points out, is one of the richest nations in the world and yet condemns its working women to inordinate difficulties by failing to provide adequate childcare facilities, while economically struggling China offers both day-care centers and special nursing breaks. The Middle Eastern woman, she feels, is well placed to gain her rights because her society still needs her skills in its efforts to catch up with the industrialized world. Moreover, unlike American women, who have to claim their rights from a strong, well-organized male establishment, Dr. Mernissi continues, Muslim women are dealing with a society in transition, where seemingly rigid traditions are being challenged by both men and women. Such conditions can favor the emergence of innovative solutions for "the other 90 percent" of women now working for little or no pay.[28]

Today's professional women should also benefit from the second phase of feminism, because upgrading women's traditional occupations may eventually help blur sexual stereotypes at home. Reform on the domestic front may be left to the discretion of individual couples, for it does not tangibly serve any country's economic interests as improvements on the farm are likely to. However, Mernissi sees good chances of success for wage-earning women. They may provoke ambivalence and even resentment at first for upsetting the patriarchal order, but as an increasing number of young women join the work force and share similar responsibilities with men, she suggests, they will have a better potential to win men's cooperation in establishing full equality in all spheres of their lives.

12

᭡᭡᭡᭡᭡᭡᭡᭡᭡᭡᭡

Women and the Islamic Revival

You should not be extremists.
—The Prophet Muhammad

They tell you fairy tales, too, you women of the West—fairy tales which, like ours, have all the appearance of truth.
—Zeyneb Hanoum, 1908

Only a little over half a century has elapsed since the first Muslim woman stepped out of the harem, and already some of her successors are clamoring to go back. Calling for a return to "pure" Islam, a visible minority of university students have donned the veil for the first time in their lives and demanded segregated classes even in such bastions of Muslim liberalism as Tunis and Cairo. Their reading habits have also changed, for books on religion compete with secular works on the best-seller lists.[1] To his utter dismay and astonishment, President Bourguiba of Tunisia found himself labeled a villain by some of those he had fought to emancipate for many years. Nor was President Sadat of Egypt spared protests by women when he recently liberalized marriage and divorce laws in their favor. "Just a youthful rebellion against adults and the establishment," a few laughed indulgently, while others dismissed the events as eccentric footnotes to the steady process of modernization in the Middle East—until Iran exploded in Islamic revivalism.

The whole world watched in disbelief as masses of Iranian women proudly put on the chador, fought against the Westernized shah Muhammad Reza Pahlavi, and played a decisive role in bringing to power the Ayatollah Ruhollah Khomeini. The old religious leader vowed to build an ideal society modeled after the one which was believed to have existed under the Prophet Muhammad's rule. However, what the ayatollah has established so far since he returned from exile on February 1, 1979, is not the world of Khadija and Aysha but a puritanical theocracy, which put a heavier-than-ever premium on women's chastity and modesty. Anything that could possibly lead to promiscuity was forbidden—no discos, no pop music, no alcohol, no magazines or posters showing the shape of the female body, no unveiled women on television, no swimming in mixed company, and no coeducational schools. In short, the sexes were not to socialize anywhere in public. A Center for Campaign Against Sin was established to monitor violations,[2] and in order to discourage temptation further women were strongly urged to hide their charms at least in demure Western attire and head scarves, or, preferably, in the figure-concealing piece of cloth called the chador (literally, "the tent").

As if this were not enough, some of the women were apparently prepared to go to even more conservative extremes than the old ayatollah intended them to do. "The man works because he is stronger. It's best for us women to use our power within the family," they told Western journalists. Khomeini had banned women only from such "immodest" jobs as acting and secretarial work and had announced his intention of welcoming them in respectable lines of work, the notable exception being that they could not be judges because they were deemed too emotional and sensitive to mete out severe punishment—despite the fact that women had shown enough competence in the immediate past to have been promoted to senior judgeships. All of them were removed to less visible posts under the new regime.

Muslim women elsewhere who equated their emancipation with Westernization felt profoundly betrayed by this turn of events. Most Iranians are of the Shiite sect of Islam, which split off from the Sunni majority over quarrels of succession to the caliphate shortly after the Prophet's death. Although Shiites have since introduced minor variations to the interpretation of the Shariah, the women of both sects share basically similar problems. More important, Iranian women were the first to fight for their country and their rights. In 1905, when their Egyptian and Turkish sisters still languished in their harems, Iranian women organized mass demonstrations in protest against their shah, who bled his country dry with the help of British businessmen and Russian cossack troops. "It is not too much to say that without the powerful moral force of those so-called chattels of the oriental lords of creation . . . the revolutionary movement, however well conducted by the Persian men, would have early paled into a mere disorganized protest," wrote Morgan Shuster, an American who supported the anti-shah faction battling for a constitutional government.[3]

The shah, Muhammad Ali, was finally deposed in 1909, but the war did not end for the women. The new leaders thanked the good ladies for their self-sacrifice and devotion to the cause of freedom and asked them to please return to their harems. Bitterly disappointed, women continued to fight on for their emancipation, taking time out to help the men fight their battles whenever necessary. Since the clergy condemned education for girls as anti-Islamic and laymen agreed only too willingly, aristocratic women sold their jewelry to build schools and taught at them. Undaunted by the obscene jeers which greeted them and their pupils on the way to school, they marched along the main streets of Teheran unveiled in broad daylight. They did not win the official right to unveil until 1935, however. With the right to vote granted in 1963 and the right to ask for divorce in 1975, Iranian women have undergone what is perhaps the longest struggle for feminism in Islamic history. Why then are they running away from their hard-earned emancipation?

"We are not escaping. We are just redefining our freedom. The Western model didn't work for us," said Peri, a young Iranian woman who fought for Khomeini during her student days in Teheran. Peri left her country in the late seventies, during the shah's reign, partly to escape the dreaded SAVAK (secret police), who murdered her brother, and partly to earn her Ph.D. in the U.S. She had had time to recover somewhat from the fever of the revolution, which she says makes people speak in hyperbole and embrace those whom they never would in more sober times. "It is not fashionable to admit this, but the West did offer a lot of good things to us women," she continued, citing education as the best example. Schooling for women, which was a sacred Islamic duty at one time, had fallen into disuse until liberal Western ideas came to Iran. Unfortunately, neither side maintained high standards in the trade of ideas and goods. Iran exchanged its oil not only for factory equipment but also for weapons, whiskey, more fancy cars than there were streets for, and pop culture of questionable value. The exchange grew more frantic and bizarre as the great wealth that flooded into Iran in the wake of the quadrupling oil prices in 1973 inspired the shah to catch up with the U.S. and West Germany in two decades.[4]

Predictably, rapid industrialization and the avalanche of mass-produced imports unhinged the old economy and caused cultural disorientation. Even the young professionals were alienated from their own heritage without finding roots in the new, which often led to confused notions of what it meant to be modern. To the average mind, free sex and alcohol, along with a suit with the most fashionable European labels, often epitomized the progressive West. "But, of course, you cannot package Shakespeare profitably," Peri noted, adding that Western businessmen were not to blame entirely. "We were fools for importing indiscriminately. We embraced the West, realistically willing to accept its thorns along with its roses. But it seems that we've ended up with more thorns than we bargained for."

The commercialized Occidental "culture" was particularly brutalizing to women because it exploited their bodies to sell modern merchandise and false dreams while it appeared to promise liberation from traditional shackles. "Because we didn't tackle the real feminist issues, we just went from being sex objects Oriental style to being sex objects Occidental style. Worse yet, we often got squeezed in between," Peri said. "Under such circumstances the chador could be a tool for reasserting a woman's human dignity by forcing people to respond to her talents and personality rather than to her body alone."

That is what she discovered accidentally when she wore the chador, for the first time in her life, during an anti-shah demonstration in order to escape SAVAK photographers and to declare her solidarity with the religious leaders against a monarch widely regarded as a puppet of the Western powers. The chadors of village and servant women she had previously viewed as a sign of slavery, but at the same time she failed to recognize the antifeminist aspects of the skin-tight jeans that she once coveted as a symbol of emancipated chic. She was not alone in her patronizing attitude. Films and posters invariably depicted the intelligent successful person in a Western suit or dress, surrounded by ultramodern gadgets and furniture.[5] The illiterate poor wore traditional costumes and ate off the grubby floor, overrun by scores of unkempt children.[6] Somehow the successful man was never shown enjoying the finer Persian lifestyle. "It just goes to show you," she noted, "how alienated we were from our own traditions and culture. The veil is also a national costume, after all, just like the Japanese kimono, and not half as uncomfortable."[7] Although it exposes the face, the beautiful kimono may indeed be one of the most misogynistic garments created. It forces the female curves into a sexless tubular silhouette by literally strangling the shameful breast and the assertive diaphragm. The long narrow skirt forces well-bred ladies to keep their thighs tight together when walking or sitting. And yet the kimono is never condemned as harshly as the chador.

Peri harbored no illusions that the chador itself would eradicate the sexual double standard prevailing in both Oriental and Occidental attitudes toward women. She did believe that it might be a useful first aid in undoing some of the damage done to woman's dignity when the veil was removed from her body without also being stripped from society's mind. It would also symbolize a fresh start in her people's attempts to reform their society.

Peri's was a line of thinking that led to the "roots" movement among college students in the late sixties and early seventies.[8] The young suddenly discovered Sufism and Persian literature and searched in them for solutions to their spiritual anguish that Western technology and culture had failed to provide. Everything Iranian was beautiful then. For some this enthusiasm was merely a fad and a way of being different from their Westernized parents, as the hippie lifestyle was in the United States, but for others it became a spiritual mission to scrape away the debris that had settled over their civilization when it grew stagnant and to unearth the viable layers underneath which would serve as a foundation for a better society. The most important discovery in this "dig" was Islam, which the intellectuals and professionals had for so long dismissed as anachronistic superstition in favor of Marxism and other modern political isms.

It was a young Sorbonne-educated professor of sociology named Ali Shariati who led them to Islam. The son of a theologian, and a long-time opponent of the shah, Dr. Shariati called, in his lectures and some eighty books and pamphlets, for a cleansing of Islam.[9] When stripped of misinterpretations which had twisted it for centuries, Islam could help solve the problems plaguing modern Iranian society, he argued. Banned from working in universities because of his anti-shah activities, he earned his living as a village teacher and devoted himself to lecturing in mosques, drawing large crowds of students who had rarely frequented those religious establishments before. His particular appeal to women was his fervent belief that complete equality of the sexes was possible only within the Islamic moral framework. By the time he died, in 1976, reportedly of a heart attack* at the age of forty-five, he had made Islam the new hope of Westernized young intellectuals.

But the intelligentsia did not embrace the religion merely out of a dreamy quest for cultural identity. In the clergy they found powerful allies in their opposition to the shah's suppression of civil and intellectual liberties. Though motivated by their own grievances against the monarch for confiscating the mosque lands and for liberalizing marriage and divorce laws, religious leaders sincerely tried to help the many victims of the regime and won great moral authority over the people.[10] The ayatollahs, the top men in the Shiite religious hierarchy, often had such clout that they could help a poor ignorant soul caught up in the baksheesh-hungry web of government bureaucracy. Even the famous clerics whose coffers bulged with handsome contributions from the faithful lived humbly and distributed their income to rural migrants and others most cruelly struck by the mismanaged, overly rapid industrialization, which made the rich richer and the poor desperate. A penniless man who had to visit a sick mother in his village could knock at the local ayatollah's door with reasonable assurance that he wouldn't be turned away. As a way of redistributing wealth Islam seemed better than communism, especially since it also managed to fight for the small bazaar merchants whose profits were squeezed by modern multinational corporations and corrupt government officials.

* Some say assassination.

What even the most irreligious of the young admired in these old clerics was their courage in opposing the shah. They not only helped finance and organize demonstrations but actually marched with the crowd against armed soldiers. In some cases they served as a shield for the demonstrators. The ayatollah Mahmoud Taleghani, one of the most eminent of Teheran's religious leaders, led a crowd of students to reopen Teheran University after it had been closed down by the shah. The soldiers guarding the campus hesitated to fire on unarmed young students led by a holy man, and withdrew. The same ayatollah, along with such colleagues as Khomeini, also spent decades in prison and in exile. No matter what the risk to themselves, they could be trusted to help the anti-shah factions. When Peri's brother failed to come home one day, her frantic parents visited an ayatollah as well as a lawyer after making the rounds of the SAVAK cemeteries and jails. His grapevine helped locate the corpse, and his followers translated the mourning over such tragedies into powerful protests which finally brought down the shah. "The choice between an Iranian Hitler who did not like the chador and the ayatollahs who liked it was not difficult, as you can see," noted Peri, who had left the country in deference to her parents' fear of losing their one surviving child to the shah's SAVAK. Women were not immune from SAVAK's wrath, for their political influence has been feared and respected for generations in Iran. In fact, an old Persian saying claims that "when women take part in a riot, the situation becomes serious."

It was not hard to understand Peri's rallying around the ayatollahs in order to oust a hated despot, but what was not clear was exactly how she and her friends could ever build their "new non-Western type of emancipation" in a theocracy which sought eventually not only to enforce the veil but also to ban birth control and repeal the Family Protection Law of 1975, which had liberalized marriage and divorce laws in women's favor. Hardly had they put down their guns and protest placards when thousands of women decided that living in constant fear of pregnancy, unilateral divorce, and polygamy spelled oppression in any culture and marched in the streets again to shout: "In the dawn of freedom, we have no freedom." "I'd have joined them, too," admitted Peri, who intends nevertheless to wear the chador or a head scarf when she returns to Iran, at least for a while. "Compulsory chador is tyranny and does not make the political and feminist statement I want to make by wearing it voluntarily," she explained. The fact that Khomeini modified his position and announced that he only wanted women to dress "modestly" indicated to Peri the possibility of carrying on a dialogue with the religious leaders of the new Islamic republic. She was upset to hear that more than a hundred civil servants who refused to wear the chador to work had been fired.[11] But her confidence was strengthened when thousands of women marched in protest against the ruling and were shielded by the police from counterdemonstrators and stone throwers. More important, Khomeini approved birth control methods which did not harm the health or abort the fetus, provided the methods were acceptable to both spouses. "We have to keep vigilant," Peri concluded, "so that Islam does not lose its true spirit and degenerate into totalitarianism."

However, it takes literacy and a knowledge of the scriptures to be able to argue that the Quran neither demanded veiling nor forbade birth control. With female illiteracy running well over 50 percent, the conservative local mullahs, or ministers, and other militant fundamentalists have had a fairly free hand in imposing their antifeminist views. It is not surprising, therefore, that thousands of chador-clad women poured into the streets to shout against their uncovered sisters when the director of national radio and television called for such a demonstration of support.[12] And when female revolutionary guards flogged two brothel madams in the city of Kermanshah, the veiled ladies marched again—to demand severer punishment.[13] They apparently did not lack a certain sense of sexual equality (or humor), for they also forced one customer to marry the prostitute he had visited the night before.[14] But by their sheer numbers and blind obedience to authority, these women—and their men—could drown out the moderate voices and usher in a reign of religious fanaticism in Iran.

The prospect was disquieting for Muslim women in other countries, too. Since the Shiites constitute only about 10 percent of all Muslims, the ayatollahs could not easily export their revolution to the Sunni majority. But the lopsided socio-economic conditions favoring the growth of fundamentalist revival in Iran exist in many other parts of the Islamic world, in countries that have tried to catch up with the West by introducing sophisticated heavy industries despite the fact that semiliterate peasants constitute the majority of the populace. This has brought material benefits to only a small minority of the educated elite while dispossessing peasants, artisans, and unskilled workers. In at least thirteen of the twenty-nine officially Muslim countries the annual per capita income is below $800,[15] which means that the poor majority must subsist on beans while the privileged fly off to Paris for shopping sprees.

These are unnatural times by traditional Islamic standards, which extoll communal sharing and solidarity of the patriarchal family. The problem is so vast that even the best-intentioned national leaders cannot help the masses fast enough to make the leap from the Middle Ages to the twenty-first century. In fact, the educated are themselves often trapped schizophrenically between the traditional and the new. As people of other countries in similarly unsettling situations seek solutions in political isms and religious cults, an increasing number of the discontented in the Middle East have turned to Islam, which satisfies their search for cultural identity as it promises remedies for their secular problems.

Given the circumstances under which revivalism tends to flourish, it is not surprising that the adherents are usually the culturally disoriented young and the unemployed. The most fervent born-again Turkish Muslims, for instance, are found among the unemployed youth and rural migrants in city slums as well as the culturally disoriented "guest workers" in Germany. Muslim Brotherhood, one of the most important politico-religious movements in Egypt, also draws its following from among the economically impotent—the unemployed professionals and university students with dismal prospects for employment in a poor overcrowded country. Islamic revivalism is thus a refuge for the patriarch shorn of his power, and may increasingly attract those who are in peril of losing control over their destiny in an uncertain age dominated by industrial rather than human needs.

Since revivalism gathers strength from debilitating economic uncertainties as well as cultural identity crisis, it often goes beyond prayer meetings and ascetic practices to bid for political power. Indeed, political action seems a logical step in a religion that has legislated not only on spiritual but also on sociopolitical matters. The Muslim Brotherhood has been a political force to contend with for a long time.[16] In Turkey a revivalist group led by an engineer named Necmettin Erbakan attracted support, especially among villagers, by promising to reinstitute the Shariah as the law of the land.[17] Although such a move would be clearly unconstitutional in a country which separates church and state, Erbakan's group had grown into the National Salvation Party, holding 27 out of 450 seats in the National Assembly in 1980 until the military coup in September suspended all political activity. Some revivalist groups have resorted to terrorism. Members of Takfir wa al-Hejira (Penance and Retreat Society) in Egypt assassinated a cabinet minister in 1977[18] and planted bombs in movie theaters in order to restore their brand of morality. Almost any religious group can claim legitimacy, because Islam does not have a central supreme authority, as the Vatican is to Roman Catholicism. Anyone—an engineer as well as a theologian—can interpret the Shariah. If enough people follow him, he has a movement. This state of affairs has prevented revivalism from growing into a monolithic tidal wave.[19]

Though constituting a minority in most countries and representing many different approaches to Islam and politics, revivalists very often agree on one policy: women's morality is the remedy for social and economic evils. Granted, this is a way of reemphasizing the importance of the traditional code of honor to the family's unity and may be a reassertion of patriarchal power. But because the issue of honor is also exploited as a panacea for totally unrelated problems, it can degenerate into a mere political banner. One of the first acts of faith that Turkish "guest workers" perform in Germany when they see the Islamic light is to withdraw their daughters from German schools in order to protect them from the strange foreign ways they had always feared. The uneducated cloistered daughter comes to symbolize the Turkish village from which the father was uprooted for economic reasons.

Such a mentality has proved a boon for secular politicians. Whenever President Muhammad Siyad Barre of Somalia wanted to placate the uneducated Muslims in the poverty-stricken countryside, who periodically flared up in anger against the rich, Westernized city folk, he flogged a few prostitutes and ordered women to be "decent."[20] Not a penny changed hands in the process, but a sense of social justice was satisfied by the president's paying lip service to Somalia's "Islamic" values.

General Zia ul-Haq of Pakistan, on the other hand, appears to have waved a similar political flag in order to legitimize his power over a multiethnic nation unified only by Islam so that he could go on to impose his plans for the country. These included enforcing the payment of the *zakat*, an annual social welfare tax which constitutes one of the five pillars of Islam. Apparently it was not visible and dramatic enough to rally the illiterate masses, although they stood to gain from the zakat, so the general introduced public flogging or death for adultery and alcohol consumption.[21] The punishment has not eradicated these sins, which have merely gone underground,[22] but the Islamic whitewash has given the government time to work out the practical and political aspects of translating its programs into action.

Like American women crusading against the Equal Rights Amendment, many Islamic women appear to be willing victims in the cause of revivalism. By protesting militantly on the streets, Egyptian women affiliated with the Muslim Brotherhood or other groups blocked the passage of liberal divorce laws for five years. A disconcerting number of these opponents were literate. As unemployment and inflation worsened in Tunisia during the past decade, women fundamentalists began to call out more loudly to their sisters to rediscover their true vocation in motherhood instead of competing against men.

One young high school teacher went right up to President Habib Bourguiba himself to complain about the feminist laws he had enacted over the years. In 1975 a Miss Hend Chalbi raised eyebrows by appearing in a splendid gold-embroidered red kaftan and a white head veil instead of the usual business suit at a conference that the president traditionally gave on the twenty-seventh day of Ramadan to discuss his various reforms in Islamic light. Taking the microphone from the dumbstruck politicians and religious scholars, Miss Chalbi lamented her compatriots' futile search for freedom and happiness outside the pale of Islam. Free abortion, an outright ban on polygamy, and all the other daringly liberal laws for which Tunisia was famous in the Arab world came under attack.[23] As if waiting on cue, veiled young heads began to appear on the streets of Tunis soon afterward. Glorification of homemaking and motherhood turned into a defense of polygamy: "Better four legal wives than one legal and a hundred illicit unions."

In both Egypt and Tunisia economic conditions make polygamy so difficult that at best young women's defense of the practice remains an academic exercise, tinged perhaps with nostalgia for the good old days of the romantic sultans' harems which none of them have known. In Pakistan, however, an American woman who actually lives with a co-wife and veils herself has emerged as an experienced apologist for the polygamist way of life. Born in 1934 in New York of German Jewish parents, Margaret Marcus took the name of

Maryam Jameelah upon converting to Islam in the U.S. and migrated to Pakistan in 1962. There her religious mentor arranged to make her wife number two of a worker for Jamaat-e-Islami, Pakistan's largest Islamic party, which enjoys considerable influence among the educated classes. "It is better for a woman to share her husband's love with another woman who is also his legitimate wife and maintain her right to remain under the protection of his roof where her children can receive the love and care of both parents,"[24] she argues in one of the many pamphlets published by her husband and distributed as far away as Saudi Arabia. The alternative, she warns, is that a man will resort to illicit affairs and ultimately drive his old wife out of the house, thus causing much unnecessary suffering for the children. Polygamy is not so difficult to accept once the woman suppresses the "exaggerated individualism"[25] with which Western education afflicts her, she stresses.

With a similar shift in perspective Maryam reveals the justice behind unilateral divorce. It is far better for a woman to be divorced in the privacy of her home than have her husband publicize her faults in order to win a divorce from a judge, she maintains, adding that a man who arbitrarily threatens his wife with divorce is not worth keeping as a husband anyway. Nor should she fear being left alone, since in the ideal Muslim society the men of her family would take her back and find a worthier husband for her. No need to worry about earning her own bread or displaying her charms or making a thousand and one plans to ensnare a man. The foolish modern woman gives up all her Islamic privileges by going out to compete against men. She not only loses protection but can never wholly escape her sacred feminine destiny of motherhood and home-making, thus overburdening herself unjustly and botching up both tasks. "From the Islamic point of view," she concludes, "the question of the equality of men and women is meaningless. It is like discussing the equality of a rose and a jasmine.... Islam envisages their roles in society not as competing but as complementary. Each has certain duties and functions in accordance with his or her nature and constitution."[26]

Her arguments appeal especially to young women over-whelmed by the painful uncertainties and contradictions of the rights which they have won only recently. The euphoria of stepping out of the harem into schools and offices has given way to the anxiety of passing exams and choosing a career, not to mention finding a job and a husband and keeping them both. Unlike Peri, who plans to wear the chador without giv-ing up her goal of teaching at a university and "perhaps edit-ing a journal," some educated women want to turn their backs on everything and let the men work because they are "stronger and free from psychological changes that come over women once a month." "Holding a job could be anti-liberation for some of us," agreed a Tunisian woman in a letter to the editor of the liberal weekly *Dialogue pour le progrès* in 1979, explaining that those who had to slave both at home and in the office had no time to develop their spiritual life or deepen their relationship with their families. Unemployment and all the attendant social evils would be solved if women stayed at home, claims a young Egyptian economics student who veils herself (although her older sisters laugh at her). Thanks to President Sadat's reform of marriage and divorce laws, how-ever, she fears that fewer women will be able to stay at home, for men are thinking twice before getting married these days.

In the U.S. educated women who wanted to return to their traditional homemaking role might work for the anti-ERA movement or knead bread in a commune. In the Middle East they have recently found their raison d'être in Islamic revival-ism. Unlike their illiterate sisters, these women have seen the world outside the harem and have rejected it. Their numbers are small, but they have dealt a tremendous psychological blow to the feminist cause.

If Islamic revivalism is a vote of no confidence against the injustices and uncertainties of rapid industrialization, women's defection from the "modern life" is also a searing indictment of the Eastern feminists' equating their movement too rigidly with Westernization, without tempering it enough with the good things of the East. It was understandably necessary to rebel against tradition in order to break out of the harem, and in the 1920s, when Muslim women began to stir for the first time in appreciable numbers, the Westernized aristocrats leading the movement naturally looked to the suffragists for inspiration. Not that Islam was rejected outright. Huda Sharawi of Egypt, as well as President Bourguiba and other feminist leaders, carefully justified their reforms by stripping away the dust of antifeminist scholarship that had accumulated over the scriptures in the course of centuries. But the main thrust of the liberation process was toward Western ideals. Generations of girls thus grew up with an either-or mentality, convinced that to be Western was to be free and to adhere to tradition and Islam was to remain enslaved. North Africans went so far as to adopt their former colonial master's jargon in describing this attitude, indiscriminately referring to everything French as "évolué" (evolved), as if their own traditions were a primitive state from which they had to rise up. Such a dictatorship of values exacted a heavy psychological toll among women who could not meet the standard.

So firmly entrenched was the belief in the superiority of Western values that Muslim women had to live in the West before they could appreciate their own heritage. To their surprise, many found that they did not want to live entirely by Western ideals. When Peri arrived in California as a wide-eyed undergraduate in the late sixties, she was eager to mimic her American friends, who she imagined were paragons of emancipated womenhood. It turned out that she was on a fairly equal footing with them except in one aspect—boyfriends. "How I envied those girls who seemed to have found their true love so early in life and did not even have to get married in order to consummate it," she said, "and I decided I wanted a boyfriend, too." She timidly began to accept invitations from her male classmates to theaters, pot parties, and protest marches. To her dismay, the young men wanted to sleep with her before they made the effort to know more of her personality. No matter how politely she pleaded with them to wait until they became better friends, some of them went away offended. "Who would want to take you to a party if you insist on sitting around as stiffly as a piece of driftwood?" her American roommate sniffed, advising her to let sex open the door to friendship and love. Try as she might, Peri could not reverse what her Muslim upbringing told her was the natural sequence of events. She did not want sexual relations to be as casual and meaningless as a handshake. Moreover, she wanted to reserve the right to say no to a man. Sexual liberation as practiced on her campus seemed to be nothing more than an increased license for men, with penalties for women who did not comply.

"Social life was limited without boyfriends because people were as paired as shoes, and virgins were stigmatized as surely as nonvirgins are in Iran," Peri noted. Deciding to forgo boyfriends until she met a man she truly liked, she tried to spend more time with women, as she had done back home in Teheran. But she was astonished to find that American women socialized with each other only as a last resort, when they were not invited out by men. And when they did chat among themselves, they invariably talked of men, defining themselves largely according to their relationships with men, instead of discussing politics and other important issues. Worse yet, they seemed to think too much intelligence was unfeminine, for they were afraid to major in engineering and other sciences—afraid that men would find them masculine. And so they went on defining themselves not as Mary, Jane, and Carol, but as Mary pining away for John, Jane breaking up with Dick, and so forth. It was no better than a harem, where women lived only for the day they would be singled out by the sultan and led away to his chambers. Like harem inmates, Peri's classmates seemed interested in a man not so much for his individuality as for his symbolic value. He was a tool to advertise a woman's desirability and to legitimize her presence at social functions. "A male escort is mainly a guarantee of safety and respectability for American woman, just as the chador is for the traditional Eastern woman," Peri added.

So desperately did her American classmates fear being left alone that many seemed to jeopardize their own interests by moving in with their boyfriends before getting married. Peri could think only of the disadvantages of such an arrangement. "A woman does the housework and worries about getting pregnant," she noted, "without any legal assurance that any child she might bear would be supported. If she loves and trusts a man that much, why not just marry him? She can always get a divorce if the relationship does not work out. It is so easy in California. In this way she would be protecting her child and sparing herself the indignity of begging for palimony, as they say in Hollywood."

Disillusioned with American women's version of liberation, which still seemed to make them nothing but sex objects, Peri began to miss her women friends back home, who did not use each other as social spare tires. The all-female company and the family-centered social life that the code of honor imposed in Iran had their advantages. No single or aged woman was ever shunned, for she was always invited as an individual or along with her parental family, without being considered only a half of a pair. So strengthening was the kinship support that Peri could pursue her career boldly, knowing that she could always return home to the circle of her family.

Nor did Iranian women need male escorts to ensure their physical safety on the streets. It was certainly more comfortable to be accompanied, for strange men called out gratuitous endearments and obscenities to women walking alone on the street. But the code of honor, which required women to be not only supervised but protected by family and neighbors, kept the streets relatively safe. Peri felt that Americans enjoyed much less equality on the streets than did chador-clad Iranian women. "Being able to parade down the street in your shorts," she pointed out, "does not mean you're free if you can get mugged and raped without anyone coming to your rescue. In big cities unchecked crime against women shuts American women up in a harem of their own fear." Peri did not like the Khomeini regime's reinstitution of flogging for adultery, but in view of the fact that the Shariah requires four witnesses to the offense before it can be punished, she could not help wondering whether the number of people affected by this decree in Iran would be much smaller than the victims of rape in the U.S. once the revolutionary anarchy is tamed.

She was beginning to understand Khomeini's accusation of the West for perpetrating cultural imperialism, which claimed a monopoly on truth. He had pointed to the inconsistency of condemning to death smugglers of ten grams of heroin while letting sellers and consumers of alcohol go scot free, when in fact they also wrecked homes and caused death on highways and violence at home and outside. Because Western enterprises have a stake in the liquor trade, Khomeini contended, they scream when Iran condemns drunkards and alcohol merchants to be flogged. Public flogging, they add, is barbaric. Khomeini answers that if punishment is to be a deterrent, why hide it hypocritically? By the same token, why should Westerners hold up Muslim polygamy as a sign of backwardness when they have serial polygamy affecting more than 50 percent of their population?[27] "Or this business of kept women. Might as well be frankly number two and be legally protected," Peri added.

It was the American women's liberation movement of the 1970s that confirmed her more favorable reassessment of Muslim women's status. When Peri came back to the U.S. in the late 1970s for graduate study, she was amused and gratified to see her American women classmates discovering the joys of friendship with other women[28] and the right to be intelligent and successful in such masculine professions as law and medicine. "They have found out the difference between sexual license and feminist emancipation. They are complaining more about being exploited as sex objects. They are catching up to Muslim women," Peri said gleefully.

Unlike some of her Iranian friends who turned completely

against Western mores in favor of strictly traditional Islam, Peri hoped to combine the best of both. "A cafeteria-style Islamic revivalist," she called herself jokingly. She did not agree entirely with the Iranian revolution's policies, but practiced Islam in her own way to find spiritual comfort: she prayed, set aside part of her allowance for charity, and tried to be good to those around her. "To me that is what being Muslim is about. It's not being obsessed about covering a few more inches of skin or staying at home and having a dozen children because I am afraid that my husband will divorce me arbitrarily or take a second wife," she explained.

Many revivalists find it hard to understand her, feeling that everyone has to take the entire package of being Muslim as they understand the concept. And this can include bizarre notions ranging from not being allowed to sing and dance to having to stay cloistered at home. In Tunisia a few young women who were attracted to the spiritual aspects of Islam admitted that they hesitated to commit themselves because they liked to wear jeans and did not fancy wearing the veil in summer. Such misconceptions about Islam are perpetuated because the moderate elements abandoned Islam to the ultra-conservatives and the illiterates and the politicians who exploit them. Peri plans to return to her country despite her apprehensions, precisely because she wants to contribute to the shaping of the new Islamic republic.

Only time will tell how the religiously liberal Peri and her more fundamentalist sisters will influence their country's destiny. But the young women's return to Islam has made a deep impact on the secular majority everywhere in the Middle East, challenging them to reassess their heritage and their society's mad rush to catch up with the West. They have ended with a world of steel, concrete, and nuclear wastes, which left the majority of women as vulnerable as ever, if not more so, given their persisting legal and socioeconomic disadvantages. In a society afflicted with crumbling extended family systems, urban isolation, unemployment, exploitation of the human body, devaluation of the aged and others bringing no immediate cash profit to the industrial cause, the ill effects strike women first. The majority of women do not seek remedies in a sanctuary of harems and veils, but they have lost their undiluted faith in the West, which did not, after all, have all the answers to their problems. The disillusionment, however, has broken the dictatorship of a single set of values and freed women to look into their own heritage with an open mind. It is impractical and unwise to try to recreate the past, but the early Islam of Khadija and Aysha and the best of Muslim scholarship which stressed the need for ecological balance in society as well as in nature could inspire fresh solutions for a world out of balance. The results may well launch a period of true sharing between the East and the West.[29]

$\mathcal{N}otes$

CHAPTER 1. WOMEN IN EARLY ISLAM

1. For a detailed historical account in English of Muhammad's life and teachings, see W. Montgomery Watt, *Muhammad at Mecca* (Oxford, England: Oxford University Press, Clarendon Press, 1953) and *Muhammad at Medina* (Oxford: Oxford University Press, Clarendon Press, 1962). In his *Islam in Focus* (Indianapolis: American Trust Publications, 1975), Dr. Hammudah Abdalati, who was a member of the Department of Islamic Culture at Al-Azhar University, one of the most prestigious universities for religious studies in the Islamic world, gives a thoughtful discussion of Islamic law.

2. Different types of marriage practiced among the Arabian tribes at the dawn of Islam are described in Watt, *Muhammad at Medina*, pp. 378–79, and in Gertrude H. Stern, *Marriage in Early Islam* (London: Royal Asiatic Society, 1939), p. 25. See also Diana Richmond, *Antar and Abla, a Bedouin Romance* (London: Quartet Books, 1978), for a romanticized portrayal of pre-Islamic tribal life. The book deals with one of the most celebrated love stories of Arabia.

3. The problems of transition from a tribal to an urban way of life which Meccans experienced when Muhammad was growing up are detailed in Watt, *Muhammad at Medina*, chapter 3.

4. The English translations of the Quran are from A. Yusuf Ali, trans., *The Holy Quran* (Washington, D.C.: American International Printing Co., 1946). *The Koran*, J. M. Rodwell, trans. (London: Everyman Library, Kent, 1974), is also a worthwhile reference because it presents the surahs in the order in which they are believed to have been revealed to Muhammad, rather than arranged by length.

Eventually different sects and schools formed around varying interpretations of the Quran and the Hadith. Muslim judges pronounced their own decisions on matters not covered by the Quran and the Hadith. Today the Shariah encompasses such decisions as well as the Quran and the Hadith, although the degree of importance accorded the decisions varies considerably from sect to sect. The Quran and the Hadith, however, remain the backbone of the Shariah in all sects. This book does not delve into sectarian nuances but focuses mainly on what the Quran says about women's rights. Some of Muhammad's pronouncements are quoted to supplement the Quran. Variations in the interpretation and application of the Shariah are discussed only where appropriate.

5. The independence that women enjoyed during Muhammad's time is documented by Nabia Abbott in *Aishah, the Beloved of Mohammed* (Chicago: University of Chicago Press, 1942). Pp. 110–11 describe Muhammad as a champion of women's right to choose their mates, even if this meant that he himself had to overrule the parents' choice.

6. The first year of Hegira, the Muslim era. Based on a lunar calendar, the hegira year is shorter than the solar year. A.H. 1401, for example, began on November 10, 1980, and will end on October 28, 1981. For a table converting A.H. to A.D. see Romeo Campani, *Calendario Arabo, Tabelle comparative delle Ere Araba e Christiano-Gregoriana mese per mese (Egira 1–1,318) e giorno per giorno (E.V. 1900–2000)* (Paris: Paul Geuthner, 1914).

7. The "affair of the slander" is described in greater detail in Abbott, p. 36.

8. Muhammad's sayings are excerpted from Muhammad ibn Muhammad al-Ghazali, "Le Livre des bons usages en matière de mariage," *Vivication des sciences de la foi*, Bibliothèque de la Faculté de Droit d'Alger, XVII, trans. L. Bercher and G. H. Bousquet (Paris: Maisonneuve, 1953), and Allama Sir Abdullah Al-Mamun al-Suhrawardy, *The Sayings of Muhammad* (New York: E. P. Dutton & Co., 1941).

9. Abbott, pp. 112–14.

10. For her life story and French translations of some of her poems, see Khansa bint Amr, *Le Diwan d'al Hansa, précédé d'une étude sur les femmes poètes de l'ancienne arabe per le P. de Coppier S.J.* (Beirut: Imprimerie catholique, 1889).

11. For a detailed account of the lives of Aysha and other wives of Muhammad, see Abbott.

12. Aysha's and Umm Salama's contributions to the Hadith are described in Abbott, p. 201. For an exhaustive bibliography of writ-

ings on the Quran and the Hadith, see Fuat Sezgin, *Geschichte des Arabischen Schrifttums*, Vol. I (Leiden: E. J. Brill, 1967).

13. Quoted in Abbott, p. 173.

CHAPTER 2. WOMEN IN THE ARAB CALIPHATE

1. Translated by Najib Ullah, *Islamic Literature: An Introductory History with Selections* (New York: Pocket Books, Washington Square Press, 1963). Reynold A. Nicholson has also done a well-known translation, quoted in *Translations of Eastern Poetry and Prose* (Cambridge: Cambridge University Press, 1922).

2. The origin and significance of the veil in both the Christian and the Muslim Mediterranean worlds are discussed very interestingly by Germaine Tillion in *Le Harem et les cousins* (Paris: Editions du Seuil, 1966) and by Jean-Francis Held in "Toutes voilées," *Le Nouvel Observateur*, April 2, 1979.

3. Caliph Walid I's story is told in Nabia Abbott, *Two Queens of Baghdad: Mother and Wife of Harun al Rashid* (Chicago: University of Chicago Press, 1946).

4. Mahbuba's story is told in Ullah, pp. 52–53.

5. Zubaydah's story is detailed in Abbott, *Two Queens of Baghdad*, and also Philip K. Hitti, *History of the Arabs from the Earliest Times to the Present* (New York: St. Martin's Press, 1968).

6. The Princess Abbassa's tragedy is described in Anthony Nutting, *The Arabs, a Narrative History from Muhammed to the Present* (New York: Clarkson N. Potter, 1964), p. 115.

7. Abbott, *Two Queens of Baghdad*, pp. 98–99.

8. Abbott, *Two Queens of Baghdad*.

9. According to documents cited in Boydena Wilson, "Medieval Women East and West, a Documentary History," preliminary edition (New York: Queensborough Community College, 1979), midwives in the Islamic world were often given far more detailed instructions on handling difficult deliveries by themselves than were their counterparts in Europe.

10. The account of women in Islamic medicine is derived mainly from Kate Campbell Hurd-Mead, *A History of Women in Medicine from the Earliest Times to the Beginning of the Nineteenth Century* (Haddam, Conn.: Haddam Press, 1938), and from suggestions by Dr. Ilza Veith of the Department of History of Health Sciences, University of California School of Medicine, San Francisco.

11. For a short discussion of medieval Muslim women scholars and their society see Maleeha Rahmat Allah, *The Women of Baghdad*

in the Ninth and Tenth Centuries as Revealed in History of Baghdad of al Hatib (Baghdad: Baghdad University, 1963).

12. Hitti, pp. 238–39.
13. A fascinating account of Al-Fadl's life and poems, as well as a description of salon life under the Abbassid caliphs, appears in M. C. Huart's article "La Poétesse Fadhl, scènes de mœurs sous les khalifes Abbasides," *Journal asiatique*, Vol. 17, January 1881, pp. 5–43. See also Louis di Giacomo, *Une Poétesse grenadine du temps des Almohades: Hafsa bint al-Hajj*, Collection Hespéris, No. X (Paris: Institut des Hautes Etudes Marocaines, LAROSE, 1949).
14. Free translation from the Arabic found in Huart, p. 39.
15. The story of Rabia is derived from Margaret Smith, *Rabia the Mystic and Her Fellow Saints in Islam* (Amsterdam: Philo Press, 1928).

CHAPTER 3. WOMEN IN THE OTTOMAN ERA

1. Abu Abd Allah Muhammad Ibn Battuta, *Travels in Asia and Africa 1325–1354*, trans. H. A. R. Gibb (New York: Robert M. McBride & Co., 1929), pp. 100–48.
2. Ronald Jenning, "Women in Early 17th Century Ottoman Records—The Shariah Court of Anatolian Kayseri," *Journal of Economic and Social History of the Orient*, Vol. 18, Part I, 1975, pp. 53 ff. discussing women litigants in a conservative Anatolian town between 1600 and 1625, suggests that women fought to protect their property rights, at least.
3. A. Afetinan, *The Emancipation of the Turkish Woman* (Paris: UNESCO, 1962), pp. 31–32.
4. *The Complete Letters of Lady Mary Wortley Montagu*, Vol. I (Oxford, England: Oxford University Press, Clarendon Press, 1965), p. 406.
   For a male European's impressions of Ottoman Turkey between 1554 and 1562, see Ogier Ghiselin de Busbecq, *The Turkish Letters of Ogier Ghiselin de Busbecq*, trans. Edward Seymour Forster (Oxford, England: Oxford University Press, Clarendon Press, 1928).
   N. M. Penzer, *The Harem: An Account of the Institution . . .* (Philadelphia: J. B. Lippincott Company, 1966), gives a very detailed description of life in the Turkish sultan's harems. See also Vedat Nedim Tor, editor of the magazine *Sanat Dunyamiz* (Istanbul), for articles on life in the Ottoman era, and Professor Suheyl Unver, *Levni* (Istanbul: Turkish Press Broadcasting and Tourist

Notes 251

Dept., Maarif Basimevi, 1957), for reproductions and discussion of miniatures recording palace women's life in the eighteenth century.

For stories about several European women who lived in Turkey or other parts of the Middle East in the nineteenth century see Lesley Blanch, *The Wilder Shores of Love* (New York: Simon & Schuster, 1954).

5. Montagu, p. 407.
6. Ibid., p. 388.
7. Lucy Mary Jane Garnett, *The Women of Turkey and their Folklore* (London: D. Watt, 1893).
8. The beginnings of modernization in Ottoman Turkey are described in Tezer Taskiran, *Women in Turkey* (Istanbul: Redhouse Yayinevi, 1976), and in William R. Polk and Richard L. Chambers, eds., *Beginnings of Modernization in the Middle East: The Nineteenth Century* (Chicago: University of Chicago Press, 1968).
9. Zia Gokalp, *Turkish Nationalism and Western Civilization*, trans. and ed. Niyazi Berkes (New York: Columbia University Press, 1959). See also Taskiran's notes and bibliography for references on pro-West and profeminist intellectuals.
10. Emine Foat Tugay, *Three Centuries: Family Chronicles of Turkey and Egypt* (Oxford, England: Oxford University Press, 1963), p. 240.
11. Zeyneb Hanoum, *A Turkish Woman's European Impressions* (London: J. B. Lippincott Co., 1933), p. 25.
12. Ibid., p. 81.
13. Ibid., p. 177.
14. Ibid., p. 39.
15. Ibid., p. 98.
16. Ibid., p. 120.
17. Ibid., p. 53.
18. Ibid., p. 215.
19. Ibid., p. 157.
20. Ibid., p. 204. Zeyneb's disappointment with London and with Europe in general is expressed in a series of letters dated November and December 1908.
21. Also see Selma Ekrem, *Unveiled: The Autobiography of a Turkish Girl* (New York: Ives Washburn Publishers, 1930), for an account of a young woman who leaves the Ottoman era behind to visit the eastern United States alone during the flapper era. The experience sharpens her analysis of her own culture.
22. Zeyneb, p. 95.
23. Fatma Aliye's life was reconstructed from personal recollections by

relatives and friends and from her biography by Ahmet Mithat, *Bir muharrire-i Osmaniyenin neseti* (Istanbul: Kirkambar Matbaasi, A.H. 1311 [A.D. 1893–94]). Excerpts from this book have been translated from the Ottoman to modern Turkish by Melahat Togar and Bedia Ermat in Ahmet Mithat, "Ilk Turk Kadin Yazari: Fatma Aliye Hanimin Hayat Hikayasi," serialized for thirteen weeks starting January 1, 1977, in *Hayat* (Istanbul). See also Melahat Togar, "Buyuk Teyzem Fatma Aliye Hanim," *Hayat Tarih Mecmua #11* (November 1976), pp. 48–49, and Taha Toros, "Fatma Aliye Hanimin Son Gunleri," *Hayat*, n.d.

24. *Kadinlar dunyasi* (*Woman's World*), May 15, 1914(? Some dates are not clear because papers were damaged.).
25. Ibid., January 25–February 7, 1914.
26. Ibid.
27. *Hanimlara mahsus gazete*, June 5, 18—.
28. *Kadinlar dunyasi*, January 25–February 7, 1914.
29. Ibid., January 11–24, 1914.
30. Ibid., January 25–February 7, 1914.
31. *Hanimlara mahsus gazete*, October 26, 1894 or 1895.
32. *Kadinlar dunyasi*, January 11–24, 1914.
33. Ibid.
34. See Irfan Orga, *Portrait of a Turkish Family* (New York: Macmillan, 1950), for the life of a young widow braving the transition.

CHAPTER 4. NATIONAL LIBERATION/WOMEN'S LIBERATION

1. For discussions of women's role in the Turkish Revolution see the works of three women writers: Afetinan, *The Emancipation of Turkish Women*; Halidé Edib, *The Turkish Ordeal* (New York: Century Co., 1928); and Taskiran, *Women in Turkey*. Taskiran's bibliography lists many worthwhile Turkish sources. Edib's contribution to the Revolution is also discussed in Patrick Balfour (Lord Kinross), *Ataturk: A Biography of Mustapha Kemal, Father of Modern Turkey* (New York: William Morrow & Co., 1965), which describes Ataturk's efforts to Westernize his nation.
2. Nawal el-Saadawi, *The Hidden Face of Eve: Women in the Arab World*, trans. Dr. Sherif Hetata (London: Zed Press, 1980), pp. 169 ff, stresses that not all women participating in the 1919 Egyptian revolution against the British were aristocrats. The women of the lower classes did the dangerous and dirty work. They even stormed jails to try to save their imprisoned compatriots. Some lost their lives in the attempt. Yet they remained the unsung hero-

ines of the Egyptian national and women's liberation movements, which concentrated on the problems of the aristocratic leaders. The lower-class women did not have to worry about harems and veils or university education. They hoped instead to improve their working conditions in factories and sweatshops, but their demands were not supported by their wealthy sisters, who knew how to deal with the poor more through charitable works than self-help projects.

See also Nada Tomiche's excellent discussion of lower-class women's first brush with industrialization, "The Situation of Egyptian Women in the First Half of the Nineteenth Century," in William R. Polk and Richard L. Chambers, eds., *Beginnings of Modernization in the Middle East: The Nineteenth Century.*

3. For Djamila Boupacha's story, see *Djamila Boupacha,* trans. Peter Green (New York: Macmillan, 1962), by Simone de Beauvoir and Gisele Halimi, both of whom defended her when she was captured by the French.

4. Ataturk's speeches are found in A. Afetinan, *Ataturk Hakkinda Hatiralar ve Belgeler* (Ankara: Turk Tarih Kurumu Basimevi, 1959). Many of the best-known passages are translated into English in Taskiran, *Women in Turkey.*

5. Taskiran, pp. 60–61.

6. Bedia's story is told in Refik Ahmet Sevengil, *Sahnede 50 yil, Bedia Muvahhit* (Istanbul: Hurriyet, Yoruk Matbaasi, 1973).

7. Resat Nuri Güntekin's classic novel *Calikusu* (*The Wren*), 11th ed. (Istanbul: Nurgok Matbaasi, 1962), depicts the painful clashes with tradition experienced by a young Turkish woman who goes out alone to teach in remote villages.

8. His speeches are excerpted by Fadela M'Rabet in *Les Algériennes* (Paris: Maspero, 1967), pp. 286 ff.

9. The aristocratic Egyptian feminists' activities and ideas are well detailed in the magazine *L'Egyptienne.* They are summarized in Bahiga Arafa, *The Social Activities of the Egyptian Feminist Union* (thesis, American University at Cairo, 1954), and in Lois Beck and Nikki Keddie, eds., *Women in the Muslim World* (Cambridge, Mass.: Harvard University Press, 1978).

10. *L'Egyptienne* VI, 1927.

11. Ibid. VI, 1925.

12. Ibid.

13. Well-known Egyptian male poets of the late nineteenth and early twentieth centuries also defended women's rights. Some of their verses are translated into English in Mounah A. Khouri, *Poetry and the Making of Modern Egypt* (1882–1922), Vol. I (Leiden: E. J. Brill, 1971).

See also Mona N. Mikhail, *Images of Arab Women: Fact and Fiction* (Washington, D. C.: Three Continents Press, 1979), for other intellectuals who shaped Egyptian feminism and for feminist poets from other lands.

14. Algerian women's role during and after the independence movement is summarized in David Gordon, *Women of Algeria,* Harvard Middle Eastern Monograph Series XIX (Cambridge, Mass.: Harvard University Press, 1968). His notes give many interesting leads. See also Juliet Minces, "Women in Algeria," in Beck and Keddie.

15. Fadela M'Rabet's personal recollections of pre- and post-independence Algeria appear in "Etre Femme en Algerie," *Nouvel Observateur,* July 10, 1978.

16. Described by Gordon.

17. Gisele Halimi, "La libération pour tous . . . sauf pour elles?" *Nouvel Observateur,* July 10, 1978.

18. Boumedienne's hopes for the new Algerian woman are quoted in *Le Monde,* August 22–23, 1965, and March 11, 1966.

19. By *West* Algerians usually meant French; former British colonies meant English. With American influence increasing in the Middle East, the West has now come to represent many things connoting "them" as opposed to "us," without necessarily implying antagonism between the two. It could be the Christian world as opposed to the Muslim camp (or the whole Third World). But it can also have fairly specific meanings when used in context. While an "Eastern" garment may be a kimono, a kaftan, or a sari, "Western" apparel usually means the modern garments first manufactured in Western countries, and does not refer to dirndls and embroidered aprons. In the Middle East a Western education means modern education, including the sciences and the liberal arts, which prepare the young for industrialized society. Indeed, *industrialization* may often be substituted for *Westernization*—as in "the evils of Westernization," for example. In the Middle Ages the most progressive schools were found in the Arab world, which was the center of civilization for Christians as well. When the Islamic world declined most of its schools were gradually reduced to teaching only religion. While a few are outstanding schools of theology today, the others are simple Quranic schools which stress rote memorization of the scriptures and are poorly qualified to prepare students for the demands of modern society.

20. In an attempt to define the modern Algerian woman Assia Djebar examined Muslim women's status in various countries in her photo-essay *Femmes d'Islam* (London: Andre Deutsch Ltd., 1961). Also see her novels for an Algerian woman's insight into her society in

painful transition. One of her books, *La Soif*, has been published in English as *The Mischief*, trans. Frances Frenaye (New York: Simon & Schuster, 1958).

21. Statistics on 1975 from *World's Children Data Sheet of the Population Reference Bureau* (1979) and *World's Women Data Sheet* by the Population Reference Bureau and UNICEF (1980). For a summary of the status of Arab women in general, see Debbie Gerner-Adam, "The Changing Status of Islamic Women in the Arab World," in *Arab Studies Quarterly*, Vol. I, #4 (1979), pp. 324–53.

22. In other oil-rich Arabian states which are less rigidly conservative than Saudi Arabia, Egyptian and Palestinian women professionals who came to serve women's needs have generally been allowed to live as they did back home, thus serving as Arab filters for the modernization of local women.

23. Sociologist Fatima Mernissi sees great advantages in pressing for women's rights in a transitional Third World society. See Fatima Mernissi, *Beyond the Veil: Male-Female Dynamics in a Modern Muslim Society* (New York: John Wiley & Sons, 1975), pp. 108–109.

Chapter 5. Childhood

1. In Ghazali, "Le livre des bons usages en matière de mariage."

2. Lawrence Van Gelder, "Despite Feminism Americans Still Prefer a Son to a Daughter," *New York Times*, January 29, 1978.

3. Daisy Hilse Dwyer, who analyzes the role of women in Moroccan folklore in *Images and Self-Images: Male and Female in Morocco* (New York: Columbia University Press, 1978), recounts the "Hansel and Gretel" tale on pp. 69–71.

4. Statistics on page 91 excerpted from Population Reference Bureau's *World's Children Data Sheet*, 1979, *Population Bulletin*, 1978, *Children in the World*, 1979, and World Bank's *World Atlas of the Child*.

5. See, for example: Halidé Edib, *Memoirs of Halidé Edib* (New York: Century Co., 1926); Zeyneb Hanoum, *A Turkish Woman's European Impressions*; Jelila Hafsia, *Cendre à l'aube* (Tunis: Maison Tunisienne de l'Edition, 1975).

6. Traditional childrearing methods in Gordes, Turkey, were described by Mahsoud Bey.

7. Genital mutilation of girls is described at length in the World Health Organization's *Khartoum Conference Report*, 1979, and

summarized by Claire Brisset in "Female Mutilation: Cautious Forum on Damaging Practices," *The Guardian*, London, March 18, 1979.

See also Robin Morgana and Gloria Steinem, "The International Crime of Genital Mutilation," *Ms.*, March 1980, pp. 65 ff.

8. In *For Yourself: The Fulfillment of Female Sexuality* (New York: Doubleday & Co., Anchor Press, 1976), pp. 18 ff, Dr. Lonnie Barbach, psychologist and sex therapist at the University of California Medical Center, San Francisco, summarizes the Western medical establishment's acceptance of clitoridectomy as treatment for masturbation and nymphomania, which sometimes was a euphemism for man's fear of woman's potential for unfaithfulness. Though clitoridectomy was most common in the late 1800s, it was performed in the U.S. as recently as the mid-twentieth century.

In *The Hidden Face of Eve* Dr. Saadawi stresses that the patriarchal exploitation of women's sexuality crosses cultural boundaries. She points out, for instance, that clitoridectomy is a physical counterpart to Freud's theory that the center of sexual response shifted from the clitoris to the vagina as the female matured. Barbach (p. 18) affirms that until quite recently physicians in the West subscribed to such theories and denied women the legitimate function of their clitoris. Saadawi calls this "psychological clitoridectomy."

9. Saadawi.
10. Ibid., Chapter 1.

Chapter 6. Growing Up in a Traditional Society

1. The word *harem* evokes visions of voluptous odalisques guarded by eunuchs. The caliphs of Baghdad and the sultans of the seraglio did keep opulent harems of concubines, but, generally speaking, the harem denotes private quarters for all women of the family and their female visitors and does not imply that the master of the house has more than one wife. Nor does it necessarily mean that the women are guarded by eunuchs, though their quarters are off limits to men unrelated to them. Needless to say, not everyone today wants nor can afford separate apartments for women. If a man of modest means or with a modern haremless house wishes to segregate his womenfolk, he usually leaves the house to them and meets his male friends in a local coffee shop. That man has the "harem mentality." Such a mentality lingers on in many disguises even in cosmopolitan cities, such as Beirut, where women may be

self-conscious about entering a café or a cinema alone. Western women who find it more comfortable to dine in the privacy of their hotel room rather than go out to a restaurant on their own while on a business trip will sympathize with this experience.

2. Books by "outsiders" on the feminine world of traditional Middle Eastern Muslim societies include: Elizabeth W. Fernea, *Guests of the Sheik: An Ethnography of an Iraqi Village* (New York: Doubleday & Co., 1965), the story of an American woman who lived veiled in an Iraqi village; Henny Harald Hansen, *Daughters of Allah: Among Moslem Women in Kurdistan* (London: George Allen & Unwin Ltd., Ruskin House, 1960), a Danish ethnologist's stay with a Kurdish family; Margaret Khan, *Children of the Jinn: In Search of the Kurds and Their Country* (New York: Seaview Books, 1980), an American woman among Kurds.

Not specifically about women but a novel which eloquently describes the desert is *Seeds of Corruption* (Boston: Houghton Mifflin Company, 1980) by Sabri Moussa, an Egyptian journalist who wandered by mistake into the eastern desert by the Red Sea and was so fascinated by it and its people that he lived there for a while.

Chapter 7. Growing Up in a Transitional Society

1. Translation from Mona Mikhail, *Images of Arab Women*, p. 58.
2. Population Reference Bureau, *World's Children Data Sheet*, 1979.
   Fayza Zayani, Bahrain's Superintendent of Social Development, who headed her country's delegation to the World Conference of the United Nations Decade of Women in Copenhagen (July 14–30, 1980), stressed education as the Arab woman's most important first step toward emancipation. "The biggest problem of Arab women," she declared, "is lack of adequate education. Our recommendations will include measures to prevent girls being taken out of school to be given in marriage and to provide education facilities for women who missed regular education." Reported in "Women to Take Stock of Their Progress," *Gulf Mirror* (Bahrain), June 27, 1980.
3. The United Arab Emirates recently began to pay each student $4.00 a month for attending primary school and $40.50 a month for attending high school. Parents receive $17 to $125 a month for keeping each child in school. The incentive has proved effective. When modern schools opened in 1975, fewer than 400 chil-

dren had enrolled. Their number had not exceeded 450 even when education was made compulsory in 1972. With monetary rewards, the total school enrollment climbed to 31,500 in 1979. This report by Pamela Swift in *Parade* magazine, *Washington Post*, August 10, 1980, does not break down the figures by sex or level of education.

4. Debbie Gerner-Adam, "The Changing Status of Islamic Women in the Arab World," *Arab Studies Quarterly*, Vol. 1, #4 (1979), p. 334.

5. University attendance figures from UNESCO, *Statistics of Education Attainment and Illiteracy 1954–1974*, No. 22 (Paris: 1977); Farida Allaghi and Zakiya el-Sahli, *On Libyan Women*, Libyan Papers No. 8 (New York: Mission of the Libyan Arab Jamahariya to the UN, n.d.); and Gerner-Adam.

6. Taskiran, *Women in Turkey*, pp. 39–40.

7. Gordon, *Women of Algeria*, p. 93.

8. "L'âge difficile," *Dialogue pour le progrès*, April 22, 1978.

9. Adel Malek, "An Attempt to Disseminate Sex Education Through Television," in Isam R. Nazer, ed., *Sex Education in Schools* (Carthage: International Planned Parenthood Federation MENA, 1976).

10. Sex education has proved volatile for the New Jersey State Board of Education, too. Though the board mandated only the teaching of the subject and not attendance in the classes, two state lawmakers are trying to annul the April 1980 decision. "N.J. To Teach Facts of Life," *New York Times*, April 13, 1980.

   See also "The Games Teen-agers Play," *Newsweek*, Sept. 1, 1980, pp. 48–53, which indicates that in the realm of teenage sex and sex education, problems surprisingly similar to the Middle East's linger in the U.S.

11. Nazer, p. 113.

12. News of its impending publication appeared in *Al-Raida* on May 1, 1980.

13. Her analysis was condensed and reviewed by *Al-Raida* in May 1979.

   The powerful influence of cinema on the young in a sexually segregated society is underlined by Laila Baalabaki in *I Live* (published in French as *Je vis*. Paris: Editions du Seuil, 1961.) A young student from a conservative town tries to learn the Western ways of Beirut. Since he lacks the courage to approach "decent women" and does not like to associate with prostitutes, he has only one avenue for learning about the opposite sex: "The only school which taught me of life, psychology, and women was the cinema," he confesses (p. 103).

   See also the review of "The Image of Women in the Egyptian

Mass Media," by M. Suwaif, et al., in *Al-Raida*, November 1979. The 1977 study analyzes fiction in women's magazines.

14. The press perpetuates this attitude, too. The November 1980 issue of *Al-Raida* reviewed a study of woman's image in the Lebanese press between 1935 and 1975. Both the Egyptian and the Lebanese press glorify woman's traditional roles and exclude her from the conventionally masculine areas outside the home.

15. According to Peter A. Iseman, "The Arabian Ethos," *Harper's*, February 1978, pp. 37–56, men in Saudi Arabia watch television about four hours a day, and women watch more than six hours. Though the programs are limited in scope, they are supplemented by videotapes and films from the U.S. and Europe as well as from the entertainment capitals of the Middle East. In fact, the Saudis are the world's best customers for videotapes, with parties to show and to swap tapes becoming a popular social activity in the big cities. Since the guardians of public morals do not invade private homes, the nature of video programs depends mostly on individual tastes. Foreign videotapes will thus influence the secluded women of Saudi Arabia and other conservative oil-rich states.

16. Considering the traditional view of honor to be an obstacle to effective fighting, some members of the General Union of Palestinian Women have suggested a more radical redefinition of honor which would exclude sexual behavior and concentrate on virtues of greater survival value today.

17. Some books about growing up in the Middle East: Souad Guellouz, *La Vie simple* (Tunis: Maison Tunisienne de l'Edition, 1975), about an illiterate village girl in Tunisia; Jelila Hafsia, *Cendre à l'aube*, about an upper-middle-class Tunisian girl's life; Gisele Halimi, *La Cause des femmes* (Paris: Editions Grasset & Fasquelle, 1973), which includes a good account of the feminist lawyer's frustrations when her freedom was abruptly curbed at adolescence; Tahar ben Jelloun, *Harrouda* (Paris: Editions de Noël, 1973), a fascinating story of a boy growing up in Morocco. Jelloun has also written about North African immigrants to Europe, in *La Plus Haute des Solitudes* (Paris: Editions du Seuil, 1977).

CHAPTER 8. LOVE, SEX, AND MARRIAGE

1. Ghazali, "Le Livre des bons usages en matière de mariage."
2. Saadawi, in *The Hidden Face of Eve*, and Mernissi, *Beyond the Veil*.

3. Ghazali, p. 64.
4. General references on sex in the Islamic world include G. H. Bousquet, *L'Ethique sexuelle de l'Islam* (Paris: Maisonneuve et Larose,
1966) and Abdelwahab Bouhdiba, *La Sexualité en Islam* (Paris:
Presses Universitaires de France, 1975).
5. The European art of courtly love is said to have been inspired at
least in part by the poets of the Arab caliphate. See Andreas Capellanus, "The Art of Courtly Love," trans. John Jay Parry (New
York: W. W. Norton & Co., 1941).
6. In *Images and Self-Images* Daisy Dwyer describes a defloration
ceremony in a Moroccan village. Tunisian author Jelila Hafsia
describes one in her novel *Cendre à l'aube*, as does Zoubeida Bittari, an Algerian woman, in her autobiography, *O Mes Sœurs
musulmanes, pleurez!* (Paris: Editions Gallimard, 1964). For a
discussion of this ceremony as it occurred in the 1940s and 1950s,
see Youssef el-Masry, *Le drame sexuel de la femme dans l'Orient
arabe* (Paris: Robert Laffont, 1961), pp. 129 ff.

Saadawi, *The Hidden Face of Eve*, p. 29, discusses an Egyptian
village wedding where the ritual defloration was carried out by a
midwife's fingers in front of witnesses in order to prove the bride
a virgin before she was finally accepted by the groom. Some Moroccan and Algerian families prove their daughter's virginity by ob-
taining a certificate of virginity from a doctor before her marriage.

Child marriages, though increasingly prohibited by law, still
exist partly because of some parents' and grooms' eagerness to assure themselves of the bride's virginity. The poor may also marry
off their daughters early in order to relieve themselves of an economic burden. Where the dowry is customarily handed to the
bride's parents rather than to the bride herself, the poor have an
added incentive for keeping child marriage alive.

For President Bourguiba's public criticism of such traditional
marriage customs as ritual defloration and excessive dowry, see
Fadela M'Rabet, *Les Algériennes*, pp. 286 ff.
7. English anthropologist Emrys L. Peters reports in "The Status of
Women in Four Middle East Communities" (in Beck and Keddie, *Women in the Muslim World*) that at a Bedouin wedding
he attended in Libya the bride failed the virginity test, which
caused a commotion among the guests. But she remained married,
and nothing was said about it later.
8. Saadawi, p. 26, summarizes data gathered by Baghdad's Institute
of Forensic Medicine between 1940 and 1970 and published in the
Iraqi Medical Journal, February 21, 1972. Fewer than half the
women examined (41.3 percent) were considered to have a "nor-

mal" hymen—that is, the type which tends to survive intact until first sexual intercourse and then bleeds noticeably.

9. Crimes of honor have been discussed by many. See Saadawi, pp. 25 ff. Nabeela Saab Barakat, a Lebanese woman lawyer, attacks the laws condoning it in "The Law Applied to 'Honor Crimes' Is a Disgrace to the Law," *Al-Raida*, February 1979.

   Nazik al-Malaika of Iraq, the Arab world's poetess laureate, wrote verses capturing the sense of vulnerability to which all women are condemned because crimes of honor are allowed in some areas of the Middle East. In "To Wash Their Shame Away" (1949) a man kills a young woman to save his honor and goes off to celebrate his victory with a cabaret girl. "And tomorrow who knows?" Nazik warns. "How can we ever guess how many of us will be thrown in the wilderness to wash their shame away?" (Translated by Rose Ghurayyib in *Al-Raida*, February 1979. Another translation is in Kamal Boullata, ed., *Women of the Fertile Crescent* [Washington, D.C.: Three Continents Press, 1978].)

   Married women continue to be responsible for their fathers' and brothers' honor, through fidelity to their husbands. Laws may be lenient toward a husband who kills his wife for real or suspected adultery, while a wife who kills her erring husband enjoys little tolerance in a court of law. In some parts of the Middle East, however, married and formerly married women have a few socially sanctioned (though not necessarily Islamic) loopholes that allow them greater sexual liberties. In *Les Algériennes* M'Rabet mentions the concept of the "sleeping baby" accepted in some parts of Algeria. Such a baby develops late in the womb; thus, it may be born more than nine months after a woman has last seen her husband.

10. Saadawi, Chapter 5, describes various forms of cheating at virginity tests. Masry, *Le drame sexuel*, p. 83, quotes from the Egyptian weekly *Rose el-Youssef* (July 15, 1958): "Crime statistics for the last five years show an appreciable drop in the number of crimes of honor. This decrease corresponds to the lowering of the fees for surgical reconstruction of the hymen."

11. Elizabeth W. Fernea and Basima Qattan Bezirgan, eds., *Middle Eastern Muslim Women Speak* (Austin: University of Texas Press, 1977), p. 128.

12. The Sociocultural Women's Association of Kuwait has called for the abolition of these laws, arguing that they are un-Islamic. "Studies about Women's Status in Kuwait and the Arab Gulf" (Kuwait: 1976) was reviewed in *Al-Raida*, May 1, 1980.

13. In one area of the Middle Atlas Mountains in Morocco, divorcées

and widows do not necessarily return to their natal families and a chaste way of life while awaiting remarriage. Some of them became "free women" (*hurya, huryin*), socializing freely with men, engaging in casual sexual relationships, and even living in common-law unions. Though the word *huryin* is also used for professional belly dancers and courtesans, who usually do not marry, many ex-housewives who become temporarily "free" eventually marry and are accepted back into society's respect. See Vanessa Maher's report on fieldwork done between 1969 and 1971, "Women and Social Change in Morocco," in Beck and Keddie, pp. 100–23.

14. Western brides also enter into legal contracts, although they may not know it at the time. See Susan Edminton, "How to Write Your Own Marriage Contract," in Francine Klagsbrun, ed., *The First Ms. Reader* (New York: Warner Books, 1973), pp. 91–107.

15. Though many Muslim authorities insist that a woman has the right to seek divorce only if she has so stipulated in her marriage contract, Dr. Hammudah Abdalati, who was a member of the Department of Islamic Culture at Al-Azhar University, contends in *Islam in Focus* that both men and women have the right to seek divorce (p. 181). Abdalati mentions some of the conditions under which a wife may be justified in initiating divorce proceedings: "If he [the husband] has no love or sympathy for her [the wife], she has the right to demand freedom from the marital bond, and no one may stand in her way to a new life" (p. 118). "If she (the wife) is harmed or her rights are violated, she can always refer to the law or obtain a divorce if it be in her best interest" (p. 174).

16. For more tales of the hoja, see Idries Shah, *The Exploits of the Incomparable Mulla Nasruddin* (London: Jonathan Cape, 1966).

17. Government help with dowries is reported in "Doha Talks of Marriage," *San Francisco Chronicle*, June 26, 1980.

18. The prince's kiss can be a rude awakening for young women who have had no chance to become acquainted with men as physical entities. In *Cendre à l'aube*, probably set in the Tunisia of about twenty-five years ago, Jelila Hafsia describes a highly sheltered upper-middle-class sixteen-year-old girl who marries a young man she had been allowed to see only under discreet supervision. On her wedding night she is so shocked to have the prince of her romantic dreams turn into a panting, sweating man that she resists his advances. The groom feels compelled to rape her in order to prove his virility and her virginity. Today Tunisian women of her class marry at a later age and are generally more sophisticated, but her experience may still apply to young brides from conservative circles. Remarkably similar problems of love, sex, and marriage in France

in the 1940s are described by Simone de Beauvoir in *The Second Sex*, trans. H. M. Parshley (New York: Alfred A. Knopf, Inc., 1953), Part V, Chapter 16.

19. One unusual critic of the sexual oppression of woman is Nizzar (or Nizar) Qabbani, Syrian diplomat and poet. Though he has gained considerable fame for his romantic poems about women, he also assumes the voice of a woman rebelling against her inferior status as sexual object. Some of these poems have been put to music and sung by well-known entertainers. For English translations of selected verses see Arich Loya, "Poetry as a Social Document: The Social Position of the Arab Woman as Reflected in the Poetry of Nizar Qabbani," *The Muslim World*, Vol. LXIII, #1 (January 1973), pp. 39–52. See also Mikhail, *Images of Arab Women*.

20. O. Cameron Gruner, *A Treatise on the Canon of Medicine of Avicenna, Incorporating a Translation of the First Book* (London: Luzac and Co., 1930).

21. Ghazali, "Le Livre des bons usages en matière de mariage."

22. The Syrian-born Ghada al-Samman is one of the most popular young Arab women writers who attack the social and legal handicaps imposed on women. She exposes various prejudices and social conventions which pass for love and form the basis for marriage. She also has a sensitive eye for the problems of her society in transition. An English translation of an interview she gave on her views on sex and marriage appears in Fernea and Bezirgan, pp. 398 ff. See also her book *Hubb* (*Love*) (Beirut: Dar al-Adab, 1973).

23. See Michael C. Hillmann, "Furugh Farrukhzad: Modern Iranian Poet," in Fernea and Bezirgan, pp. 291–317. For English translations of some of her poems, see Leo Hamalian and John D. Yohannan, eds., *New Writing from the Middle East* (New York: New American Library, Mentor Books, 1978).

24. Farrukhzad, "The Sin," *The Wall* (Hillmann, *op. cit.*).

25. Farrukhzad, "The Hidden Dream," *The Captive* (Hillmann, *op. cit.*).

26. In her poem "Dearest Love—III" Salma al-Jayyusi, a well-known contemporary writer of Lebanese-Palestinian parentage, eloquently dramatizes the paralyzing effect of social pressure on men who want a less traditional relationship with women. She describes a woman who wakes up to her potential and breaks out of her harem to conquer the world. Her husband is confused but fascinated. "I saw your beauteous face calling me," he says, ". . . but when I turned to follow / love was shouted down by voices / booming from my father's grave." The peers as well the elders finally force

him to stifle his personal inclinations and prove his manhood by taking a second wife, "who hears and obeys without a murmur / who knows how to put / the muttering grave to sleep." The poem appears in Boullata, *Women of the Fertile Crescent*, pp. 126–28.

Raymonda Hawa Tawil, *My Home, My Prison* (New York: Holt, Rinehart & Winston, 1980), describes how honor operated in day-to-day life in her marriage in Amman, Jordan, during the late 1950s and 1960s, and sensitively shows how peer-group pressure can force a liberal husband to prove his masculinity by restricting his wife.

CHAPTER 9. MOTHERHOOD, POLYGAMY, AND DIVORCE

1. Dr. Samira el-Mallah, "Current Problems in Gynecology and Their Effects on Patient Attitude," in Cynthia Nelson, ed., *Cairo Papers in Social Sciences: Women, Health, and Development*, Vol. I, Monograph 1 (Cairo: December 1977).

2. Population Reference Bureau, *World's Children Data Sheet*, (Washington D.C., 1979).

3. Islam's attitude toward birth control is discussed by Basim F. Musallam, "The Islamic Sanction of Contraception," in H. B. Parry, ed., *Population and Its Problems: A Plain Man's Guide* (New York: Oxford University Press, 1974), and also by Saadawi, *The Hidden Face of Eve*, Chapter 9.

4. Saadawi, p. 68.

5. The policies of various Middle Eastern governments are summarized in a table in a periodical published by International Planned Parenthood Federation, *People* magazine, 1979, devoted exclusively to family-planning problems in the Islamic world.

6. George Dib, *Law and Population in Lebanon*, Law and Population Monograph Series #29 (Medford, Mass.: Tufts University, 1975).

7. Nadia Youssef, "The Status and Fertility Patterns of Muslim Women," in Beck and Keddie, *Women in the Muslim World*, p. 90.

A 1975 study of the effects of Tunisia's liberal abortion law, reported in *Population Studies* No. 49, April–June 1979 (Cairo: Population and Family Planning Board Research Office), and summarized in *Al-Raida*, November 1980, indicates the importance of socioeconomic factors and illiteracy. Most of the Tunisian women seeking abortion were married and had more than three living children; about half of those who seek abortion in Denmark,

England, and Sweden had only one child. Most of the Tunisian women were poor and illiterate. The literate women took better advantage of extensive family planning services.

8. In "Family Planning: The Difficulties Facing Implementation in Iraq" (thesis, University of Baghdad, 1973).

9. International Planned Parenthood Federation, *People* magazine, 1979.

10. *The Mischief* by Assia Djebar examines a woman's thirst for children.

11. See Susan and Martin Tolchin, "Women in Egypt: From Queens to First Ladies," *San Francisco Chronicle*, March 25, 1980.

12. Edib, *Memoirs of Halidé Edib*, pp. 145–47.

13. Mernissi, "The Patriarch in the Moroccan Family: Myth or Reality?" in James Allman, ed., *Women's Status and Fertility in the Muslim World* (New York: Praeger Publishers, 1978).

14. Ibid.

15. In *Le Harem et les cousins*, p. 116, Germaine Tillion stresses the effect that the mother's precarious position in the family can have on the child where unilateral divorce prevails.

16. Motoko Katakura, *Bedouin Village: A Study of a Saudi Arabian People in Transition* (Tokyo: University of Tokyo Press, 1977).

17. Amendments to the Iraqi law are given in "Civil Statutes Law Amended: More Rights for Women Granted," *Baghdad Observer*, March 17, 1980.

18. Tabitha Petran, "South Yemen Ahead on Women's Rights," *Middle East International*, June 1975.

19. Poor women are not only ignorant of their rights but too burdened with the business of scraping together a living to think about legal rights. See R. Y. Ebied and M. J. L. Young, eds., *Arab Stories East and West* (Leeds, England: Leeds University Oriental Society, 1977), and Yusuf Idris, *The Cheapest Nights and Other Stories*, trans. Wadida Wassef (Washington, D.C.: Three Continents Press, 1978), which contains good short stories describing the lives of poor women.

20. See, for example, Sawsan el-Messiri, "Self-Images of Traditional Urban Women in Cairo," in Beck and Keddie, pp. 522–39.

21. Described in Soheir A. Morsy, "Sex Differences and Folk Illnesses in an Egyptian Village," in Beck and Keddie.

22. "Les Révoltées," *Dialogue pour le progrès*, March 25, 1978.

CHAPTER 10. SPINSTERS, DIVORCÉES, WIDOWS,
AND OLD WOMEN

1. *Dialogue pour le progrès*, April 2, 1979.
2. See Amélie Goichon, "La Vie féminine au Mzab," *Revue du monde musulmane*, 80, Vol. 62, 1925, pp. 27–138; A. M. Goichon, *La Vie féminine au Mzab: étude de sociologie musulmane* (Paris: P. Geuthner, 1927); and Attilio Gaudio, *La Révolution des femmes en Islam* (Paris: René Julliard, 1957).
3. Compare the Turkish woman's difficulties in living alone with those of her Italian counterpart. In "Portents of Real Change for Italian Women, *The Guardian*, June 6, 1976, Campbell Page writes from Milan: "In Italy, where the family is the best economic safety net, it takes nerve to break away and ignore the Catholic standards of female unobtrusiveness. When they have broken away, the women say it is almost impossible to rent a flat because landlords still think two or three women would only live together to set up as a brothel."
4. Mernissi, *Beyond the Veil*.
5. Raja el-Almi, "L'Abandon de l'enfant par la femme divorcée," *Dialogue pour le progrès*, March 25, 1978. *Elele* (p. 37 of supplement, December 1979) also says that young divorced couples tend to leave their children with their parents, which the editors note may be better for the children than subjecting them to life with young divorced people who are anxious to rebuild their own lives.
6. Fatima Mernissi, "The Patriarch in the Moroccan Family: Myth or Reality?" in Allman, *Women's Status and Fertility in the Muslim World*.

CHAPTER 11. WORKING WOMEN

1. The first woman lawyer of Sharjah is discussed by Margaret Pennar in *Status of Women in the Arab World*, International Almanac, Arab World #8 (New York: Broadcasting Foundation of America).
2. Women's banks are discussed in Elias Haddad, "Jeddah Is Talking About Banking for Women," *San Francisco Chronicle*, February 25, 1980; "Banking on Women's Business," *Finance 80* (Bahrain) *Gulf Mirror*, June 1980; Kathy Lund, "Women's Banking Booms," *Arab News*, May 26, 1980.

3. For a discussion of Saudi women in the work force, see Kay Hardy Campbell, "Women in the Workforce," *Saudi Business*, Rabi al-Thani 27, 1400 (1980), pp. 23–29.

4. For a discussion of Sureyya Agaoglu and other first professional women of Turkey, see Tezer Taskiran, *Women in Turkey*, pp. 82 ff.

5. A Libyan woman recently enrolled at the Oxford Air Training School in Britain.

6. Nadia H. Youssef, *Women and Work in Developing Societies* (Berkeley: Institute of International Studies, University of California, 1974).

7. International Labor Office, *Year Book of Labor Statistics* (Geneva: ILO, 1979).

8. *Al-Raida*, August 1979 (an issue devoted to women and work); Jordanian Information Bureau, *Al-Urdun*, October–November 1979.

9. Population Reference Bureau and UNICEF, *World's Women Data Sheet of the Population Reference Bureau* (Washington, D.C., 1980).

10. This information came from Dr. S. Kursunoglu and A. Sanatkar of Akbank, Istanbul.

11. Attitudes toward women bosses in some Turkish companies are explored in Beraet Zeki Ungor, "Women in the Middle East and North Africa and Universal Suffrage," *Annals of American Academy of Political and Social Science*, January 1968, pp. 72–81.

12. "Man . . . for Her Should Be a Supporter," *Al-Akbar*, April 9, 1980.

13. Ibid.

14. *Dialogue pour le progrès*, August 19, 1978.

15. In 1979 Egypt amended its laws to allow women to take jobs outside the home without their husbands' permission. In the past women who worked without such consent jeopardized their rights to be supported and to obtain a divorce.

16. Even in contemporary American society many men consider housework a woman's duty, regardless of whether she holds a job outside the home. According to a marketing survey conducted by advertising agency Batten, Barton, Durstine, and Osborn, 82 percent of the men interviewed in the eighteen-to-fifty age group said they approved of working mothers, but about 80 percent said that laundering, cleaning the house, and cooking were women's jobs. See Bernice Kannen, "She Brings Home the Bacon and Cooks It," *Ms.*, March 1980, p. 104.

The double work burden borne by women around the world and

the poor reward they reap were dramatized by the following slogans at the World Conference of the United Nations Decade of Women, Copenhagen, July 14–30, 1980: "Females are one-half of the world's population, do two-thirds of the world's working hours, receive one-tenth of the world's income, and own one-hundredth of the world's property." "Almost all the training and technology for improving agriculture is given to men . . . 50 percent of the agricultural production and all of the food processing is the responsibility of women."

A Beirut University College study of married women in three Lebanese cities, reported in *Al-Raida,* November 1980, suggested that the wife's employment outside the home tended to blur but not eliminate traditional sexual roles within the family. Although working couples shared more household responsibilities, men gravitated toward tasks requiring some technical skills or contacts outside the house, which usually remained "done" for some time, while women were stuck with such never-ending daily chores as washing, cleaning, ironing, cooking, and feeding babies. These chores were shared in less than 25 percent of the cases. The study stresses, however, that an employed woman tends to share in making major decisions and is far better educated and more conscious of her rights than is her homebound sister.

17. "Les Travailleuses," *Dialogue pour le progrès,* March 26, 1978.
18. Sevket Rado, "Calisan Kadinin Zorluklari," *Hayat,* April 13, 1967. Some of the young educated couples have begun to share housework, but many do not face the issue of division of labor because they can afford cleaning women.
19. For a discussion of the effect of the harem legacy on professional women, see Lloyd and Margaret C. Fallers, "Sex Roles in Edremit," in J. G. Peristany, ed., *Mediterranean Family Structures* (Cambridge: Cambridge University Press, 1976).
20. Campbell, "Women in the Workforce," p. 24.
21. The interview was excerpted and translated by Judith Tucker, "Interview: The Cares of Umm Muhammad," Middle East Research and Information Report No. 82 (Washington, D.C.: MERIP), and reproduced in *NAJDA Newsletter,* April–May 1980, pp. 3 ff.
22. See also Nada Tomiche's excellent discussion of lower-class Egyptian women's first brush with industrial work in "The Situation of Egyptian Women in the First Half of the Nineteenth Century," in Polk and Chambers, *Beginnings of Modernization in the Middle East: The Nineteenth Century*; Laverne Kuhnke, "The 'Doctoress' on a Donkey: Women Health Officers in Nineteenth Century Egypt," *Clio Medica,* Vol. 9, No. 3 (Amsterdam: B. M.

Israel, 1974), pp. 193–205; and Mona Mikhail, *Images of Arab Women*, pp. 47 ff.

23. *Al-Raida*, August 1979 (issue devoted to women and work).

24. Described in F. el-Manssoury, "A Model Farm Where No Men Are Admitted," *Iraq Today* magazine (n.d.).

25. An increasing number of articles have begun to appear in the press on the housewife's valuable contributions. See, for example, "Femme au foyer ou femme au travail," *Dialogue pour le progrès*, May 12, 1980. "A housewife also exercises a profession requiring certain aptitudes and will power. I am furious when I hear someone say that housewives stay at home all day and do nothing," commented one interviewee.

26. The demand for recognition of housewives is also made in *Al-Raida*, August 1979.

27. Mernissi, *Beyond the Veil*, pp. 99–109, and "The Patriarch in the Moroccan Family: Myth or Reality?" in Allman, *Women's Status and Fertility in the Muslim World*, pp. 312 ff.

28. The recent concern with "the other 90 percent" has opened up some interesting new jobs for educated women. A young woman named Rose Mary Ghannoun has recently become a loan officer and investment counselor to rural women—one of the first women in Lebanon to occupy such a post. A member of the International Development Agency's rural reconstruction project, she also acts as a personal counselor, encouraging her clients to persevere in their independent financial ventures even if family pressures and local traditions militate against them. See *Al-Raida*, November 1980.

Chapter 12. Women and the Islamic Revival

1. A best-seller in Egypt is *My Journey from Atheism to Faith* by Mustapha Mahmoud. In Tunisia books by the Muslim Brother Hassan el-Banna sell very well, as do works by his disciple Sayyid Qotb. Books on religion are also popularized through cassette tapes among the semiliterate.

2. Anthony Goodman, "Teheran Talks of Sin: A New Crackdown," *San Francisco Chronicle*, June 27, 1980.

3. For an excellent discussion of women's role in the Iranian revolution of 1905–11, see Mangol Bayat-Philipp, "Women and Revolution in Iran 1905–1911," in Beck and Keddie, *Women in the Muslim World*.

4. For a short discussion of the events leading up to Khomeini's take-over, see Nicholas Gage, "Iran: Making of a Revolution," *New York Times Magazine*, December 17, 1978.
5. Donné Raffat's novel *The Caspian Circle* (Boston: Houghton Mifflin Company, 1978) portrays the moneyed classes in Iran during the late shah's reign.
6. See Samad Behrangi (1939–68), *The Little Black Fish and Other Modern Persian Stories*, trans. Eric and Mary Hoogland (Washington, D.C.: Three Continents Press, 1976), for children's tales which poignantly dramatize the plight of the Iranian poor classes. The book was underground literature during the shah's time.
7. For a very good article on the origin and significance of the veil in the Mediterranean world, see Jean-Francis Held, "Toutes voilées," *Le Nouvel Observateur*, April 2, 1979.
8. Fashion has been a popular way to express the "roots" sentiment in secular terms. In Bahrain the art of making the intricately embroidered national costume had all but disappeared during the oil boom, until a thobe-making contest was established. It attracted a surprisingly large number of young participants. In Turkey modern fashion inspired by rural crafts has recently become popular. Some of the young Saudi Arabian women justify their modernization by using it to enhance their traditions. In the realm of fashion a few women have gone into business by designing modern garments inspired by their traditional costumes. Ferial Kelidar, an Iraqi woman, has made such an art out of adapting traditional designs to modern fashion that her House of Iraqi Fashion is now supported by the Ministry of Culture and Arts.

   Safeya Binzagr became a painter, though it was considered improper to express herself outside her home. She applies her talents to record an old way of life that is fast disappearing under pressures of industrialization and oil wealth. Her paintings have been reproduced in *Saudi Arabia: An Artist's View of the Past* (Lausanne: Three Continents Press).
9. Ali Shariati's books in English translation include *Marxism and Other Western Fallacies*, trans. Hamid Algar (Berkeley: Mizan Press, 1980), and *On the Sociology of Islam*, trans. Hamid Algar (Berkeley: Mizan Press, 1979).
10. For background information on the Iranian ayatollahs' power base, see Ray Vicker, "Allah's Agents: Iran's Moslem Leaders Wield Great Influence on Citizens' Lives," *Wall Street Journal*, February 1, 1979.
11. "Islamic" uniforms for women civil servants are discussed in "Wearing Veils: 5,000 women say no; 4,000 men say yes," *San*

Francisco Chronicle, July 6, 1980, and "Iran Fires Women who won't Wear Veil," *San Francisco Chronicle*, July 9, 1980.

12. "The Unfinished Revolution," *Time*, April 2, 1979, pp. 34–37.

13. *World* magazine, *San Francisco Sunday Examiner-Chronicle*, July 22, 1979, p. 20.

14. *Paris Match*, March 23, 1979.

15. R. Hrair Dekmejian, "The Anatomy of Islamic Revival: Legitimacy, Crisis, Ethnic Conflict and Search for Islamic Alternatives," *Middle East Journal*, Winter 1980, pp. 1–12. This has a good overall discussion of Islamic revivalism.

16. Eric Davis, "Islam and Politics: Some Neglected Dimensions," paper presented at the Alternative Middle Eastern Studies Conference, New York, 1979.

17. Doyle McManus, "In Turkey, a Comeback for Islamic Fundamentalism," *San Francisco Chronicle*, July 23, 1980; John Kifner, "The Turks Have a Word for It—Kemalism," *New York Times*, September 21, 1980.

18. Christopher Wren, "The Muslim World Rekindles its Militancy," *New York Times*, June 18, 1978.

19. Islamic revivalism has been going on for a long time. See Ralph Patai, "The Dynamics of Westernization in the Middle East," *The Middle East Journal*, Vol. 9, No. 1, Winter 1955; G. H. Jansen, *Militant Islam: The Historic Whirlwind* (New York: Harper & Row, 1980; condensed in the *New York Times Magazine*, January 6, 1980).

20. *Meed Arab Report*, July 18, 1979, p. 9.

21. Gerard Viratelle, "Islamization of Pakistan: Repressive Measures First," *The Guardian*, April 22, 1979; Tyler Marshal, "Pakistan's New Islamization Drive," *San Francisco Chronicle*, September 10, 1980.

22. Sin is said to have gone underground in Iran, too, with alcoholic beverages available on the black market at astronomical prices. See Doyle McManus, "Iran's Campaign Against Sin Is Brutal," *San Francisco Chronicle*, July 11, 1980.

23. Souhayr Belhassen, "Le Voile de la soumission," *Jeune Afrique*, April 25, 1979.

24. Maryam Jameelah, *Islam and the Muslim Women Today* (Lahore, Pakistan: Muhammad Yusuf Khan, 1976), p. 30.

25. Ibid., p. 6.

26. Ibid., p. 44. See also Jameelah's *Westernization versus Muslims* (Lahore: Muhammad Yusuf Khan, 1976).

27. Khomeini's ideas are detailed in Ayatollah Ruhollah Khomeini, *Islamic Government*, translated under the name of *Ayatollah*

Khomeini's Mein Kampf by Joint Publications Research Service
(New York: Manor Books, 1979), and *Islam and Revolution*,
trans. Hamid Algar (Berkeley: Mizan Press, in press).

28. See Gloria Steinem, "Sisterhood," in Francine Klagsbrun, ed., *The
First Ms. Reader* (New York: Warner Books, 1973). Steinem
underlines the need for cooperation and friendship among women.

29. For those wishing to read further on Middle Eastern Muslim
women, the following are useful references:

Meghdessian, Samira Rafidi, *The Status of the Arab Woman:
A Select Bibliography* (London: Mansell House, n.d.).

Qazzaz, Ayad al-, *Women in the Middle East and North Africa:
An Annotated Bibliography*, Middle East Monographs No.2 (Austin, Texas: Center for Middle Eastern Studies, University of Texas,
1977).

Raccagni, Michelle, *The Modern Arab Woman, a Bibliography*
(Metuchen, N.J.: Scarecrow Press, 1978).

In addition to listing some good references, Nikki Keddie also
stresses some of the important points to keep in mind in reading
about Middle Eastern women. See her article "Problems in the
Study of Middle Eastern Women" in *Journal of Middle East
Studies* 10 (1979), pp. 241–64.

For an illuminating discussion of the stereotypes harbored by
Westerners about the Middle East, see Edward W. Said, *Orientalism* (New York: Pantheon Books, 1978).

Bibliography

AVAILABLE IN ENGLISH

Abbott, Nabia. *Aishah, the Beloved of Mohammed*. Chicago: University of Chicago Press, 1942.
————. *Two Queens of Baghdad: Mother and Wife of Harun al Rashid*. Chicago: University of Chicago Press, 1946.
Afetinan, A. *The Emancipation of the Turkish Woman*. Paris: UNESCO, 1962.
Alireza, Marianna. *At the Drop of a Veil*. Boston: Houghton Mifflin Company, 1971.
Allman, James, ed. *Women's Status and Fertility in the Muslim World*. New York: Praeger Publishers, 1978.
Balfour, Patrick (Lord Kinross). *Ataturk: A Biography of Mustapha Kemal, Father of Modern Turkey*. New York: William Morrow & Co., 1965.
Battuta, Abu Abd Allah Muhammad Ibn. *Travels in Asia and Africa 1325–1354*, trans. H. A. R. Gibb. New York: Robert M. McBride & Co., 1929.
Beauvoir, Simone de. *Memoirs of a Dutiful Daughter*, trans. James Kirkup. New York: Harper & Row, 1958.
————, and Gisele Halimi. *Djamila Boupacha*, trans. Peter Green. New York: Macmillan, 1962.
Beck, Lois, and Nikki Keddie, eds. *Women in the Muslim World*. Cambridge, Mass.: Harvard University Press, 1978.
Behrangi, Samad. *The Little Black Fish and Other Modern Persian Stories*, trans. Eric and Mary Hooglund. Washington, D.C.: Three Continents Press, 1976.
Blanch, Lesley. *The Wilder Shores of Love*. New York: Simon & Schuster, 1954.
Boullata, Kamal, ed. *Women of the Fertile Crescent: Modern Poetry by Arab Women*. Washington, D.C.: Three Continents Press, 1978.
Busbecq, Ogier Ghiselin de. *The Turkish Letters of Ogier Ghiselin de Busbecq*, trans. Edward Seymour Forster. Oxford, England: Oxford University Press, Clarendon Press, 1928.

Capellanus, Andreas. *The Art of Courtly Love*, trans. John Jay Parry. New York: W. W. Norton & Co., 1941.

Djebar, Assia. *The Mischief*, trans. Frances Frenaye. New York: Simon & Schuster, 1958.

Dwyer, Daisy Hilse. *Images and Self-Images: Male and Female in Morocco*. New York: Columbia University Press, 1978.

Ebied, R. Y., and M. J. L. Young, eds. *Arab Stories East and West*, Monograph and Occasional Series No. 11. Leeds, England: Leeds University Oriental Society, 1977.

Edib, Halidé. *Memoirs of Halidé Edib*. New York: Century Co., 1926.

———. *The Turkish Ordeal*. New York: Century Co., 1928.

Ekrem, Selma. *Unveiled: The Autobiography of a Turkish Girl*. New York: Ives Washburn Publishers, 1930.

Fernea, Elizabeth W. *Guests of the Sheik: An Ethnography of an Iraqi Village*. New York: Doubleday & Co., 1965.

———, and Basima Qattan Bezirgan, eds. *Middle Eastern Muslim Women Speak*. Austin: University of Texas Press, 1977.

Garnett, Lucy Mary Jane. *The Women of Turkey and their Folklore*. London: D. Watt, 1893.

Gordon, David. *Women of Algeria*, Harvard Middle Eastern Monograph Series XIX. Cambridge, Mass.: Harvard University Press, 1968.

Gornick, Vivian. *In Search of Ali Mahmoud: An American Woman in Egypt*. New York: Saturday Review Press, 1973.

Hamalian, Leo, and John D. Yohannan, eds. *New Writing from the Middle East*. New York: New American Library, Mentor Books, 1978.

Hansen, Henny Harald. *Daughters of Allah: Among Moslem Women in Kurdistan*. London: George Allen & Unwin Ltd., Ruskin House, 1960.

Hitti, Philip K. *History of the Arabs from the Earliest Times to the Present*. New York: St. Martin's Press, 1968.

Hurd-Mead, Kate Campbell. *A History of Women in Medicine from the Earliest Times to the Beginning of the Nineteenth Century*. Haddam, Conn.: Haddam Press, 1938.

Idris, Yusuf. *The Cheapest Nights and Other Stories*, trans. Wadida Wassef. Washington, D.C.: Three Continents Press, 1978.

Jameelah, Maryam. *Islam and the Muslim Woman Today*. Lahore, Pakistan: Muhammad Yusuf Khan, 1976.

———. *Westernization versus Muslims*. Lahore, Pakistan: Muhammad Yusuf Khan, 1976.

Jansen, G. H. *Militant Islam: The Historic Whirlwind*. New York: Harper & Row, 1980.

Kahn, Margaret. *Children of the Jinn: In Search of the Kurds and Their Country.* New York: Seaview Books, 1980.

Katakura, Motoko. *Bedouin Village: A Study of a Saudi Arabian People in Transition.* Tokyo: University of Tokyo Press, 1977.

Khomeini, Ayatollah Ruhollah. *Islamic Government* (or *Ayatollah Khomeini's Mein Kampf*), trans. Joint Publications Research Service, Arlington, Va. New York: Manor Books, 1979.

———. *Islam and Revolution: Extracts from the Writings and Declarations of Imam Khomeini,* trans. Hamid Algar. Berkeley: Mizan Press (in press).

Khouri, Mounah A. *Poetry and the Making of Modern Egypt (1882– 1922),* Vol. I. Leiden: E. J. Brill, 1971.

Lewis, Bernard. *The Emergence of Modern Turkey,* 2nd ed. Oxford, England: Oxford University Press, 1969.

Mernissi, Fatima. *Beyond the Veil: Male-Female Dynamics in a Modern Muslim Society.* New York: John Wiley & Sons, 1975.

Mikhail, Mona N. *Images of Arab Women: Fact and Fiction.* Washington, D.C.: Three Continents Press, 1979.

Montagu, Lady Mary Wortley. *The Complete Letters of Lady Mary Wortley Montagu,* Vol. I. Oxford, England: Oxford University Press, Clarendon Press, 1965.

———. *Letters from Constantinople.* London: Methuen & Co., 1921.

Nakhleh, Emile A. *Bahrain.* Lexington, Mass.: Lexington Books, 1976.

Nazer, Isam R., ed. *Sex Education in Schools: Proceedings of an Expert Group Meeting, IPPF Middle East and North Africa Region, Dec., 1975, Beirut.* Carthage, Tunisia: International Planned Parenthood Federation MENA, 1976.

Nefzawi, Shaykh. *The Perfumed Garden for the Soul's Recreation,* trans. Sir Richard F. Burton. New York: Castle Books, 1964.

Nicholson, Reynold A. *Translations of Eastern Poetry and Prose.* Cambridge: Cambridge University Press, 1922.

Orga, Irfan. *Portrait of a Turkish Family.* New York: Macmillan, 1950.

Penzer, N. M. *The Harem: An Account of the Institution as It Existed in the Palace of the Turkish Sultans with a History of the Grand Seraglio from Its Foundation to the Present Time.* Philadelphia: J. B. Lippincott Company, 1966.

Polk, William R., and Richard L. Chambers, eds. *Beginnings of Modernization in the Middle East: The Nineteenth Century.* Chicago: University of Chicago Press, 1968.

Qaddafi, Muammar al-. *The Green Book,* Part III. Libya: Public Establishment for Publishing, Advertising and Distribution, n.d.

Qazzaz, Ayad al-. *Women in the Middle East and North Africa: An Annotated Bibliography,* Middle East Monographs No. 2. Austin, Texas: Center for Middle Eastern Studies, University of Texas, 1977.

Raffat, Donné. *The Caspian Circle.* Boston: Houghton Mifflin Company, 1978.

Richmond, Diana. *Antar and Abla, a Bedouin Romance.* London: Quartet Books, 1978.

Rodwell, J. M., trans. *The Koran.* London: Everyman Library, Kent, 1974.

Rumaihi, M. G. *Bahrain: Social and Political Change Since the First World War.* London: Bowker, 1976.

Saadawi, Nawal el-. *The Hidden Face of Eve: Women in the Arab World,* trans. Dr. Sherif Hetata. London: Zed Press, 1980.

Said, Edward W. *Orientalism.* New York: Pantheon Books, 1978.

Smith, Margaret. *Rabia the Mystic and Her Fellow Saints in Islam.* Amsterdam: Philo Press, 1928.

Stern, Gertrude H. *Marriage in Early Islam.* London: Royal Asiatic Society, 1939.

Suhrawardy, Allama Sir Abdullah Al-Mamun al-. *The Sayings of Muhammad.* New York: E. P. Dutton & Co., 1941.

Taskiran, Tezer. *Women in Turkey.* Istanbul: Redhouse Yayinevi, 1976.

Tawil, Raymonda Hawa. *My Home, My Prison.* New York: Holt, Rinehart & Winston, 1980.

Tinker, Irene, et al., eds. *Women and World Development.* New York: Overseas Development Council, 1976.

Tugay, Emine Foat. *Three Centuries: Family Chronicles of Turkey and Egypt.* Oxford, England: Oxford University Press, 1963.

Ullah, Najib. *Islamic Literature: An Introductory History with Selections.* New York: Pocket Books, Washington Square Press, 1963.

UNESCO. *Statistics of Educational Attainment and Illiteracy 1954–1974,* No. 22. Paris: UNESCO, 1977.

Watt, W. Montgomery. *Muhammad at Mecca.* Oxford, England: Oxford University Press, Clarendon Press, 1953.

———. *Muhammad at Medina.* Oxford, England: Oxford University Press, Clarendon Press, 1962.

World Health Organization. *Khartoum Conference Report.* Alexandria, Egypt: WHO Regional Office for the Eastern Mediterranean, 1979.

Yousseff, Nadia Haggag. *Women and Work in Developing Societies.* Berkeley: Institute of International Studies, University of California, 1974.

Yusuf Ali, A., trans. *The Holy Quran.* Washington, D.C.: Islamic Center, 1978.

Zeyneb Hanoum. *A Turkish Woman's European Impressions.* Philadelphia: J. B. Lippincott Co., 1933.

FOREIGN LANGUAGE BIBLIOGRAPHY

Afetinan, A. *Ataturk Hakkinda Hatiralar ve Belgeler.* Ankara: Turk Tarih Kurumu Basimevi, 1959.

―――. *Tarih Boyunca Turk Kadinin Hak ve Gorevleri,* Ataturk Serisi #10. Istanbul: Milli Egitim Basimevi, 1975.

Ahmet Mithat. *Bir Muharrire-i Osmaniyenin Neseti* [*The Birth of an Ottoman Woman Writer*]. Istanbul: Kirkambar Matbaasi, A.H. 1311 (A.D. 1893–94).

Amin, Qasim. *Al-Mara al-Jadida* [*The Modern Woman*]. Cairo: Matbaa al-Maarif, 1900.

―――. *Tahrir al-Mara* [*The Emancipation of Women*]. Cairo: Matbaa al-Maktaba al-Sharqiya, 1899.

Attilio, Gaudio. *La Révolution des femmes en Islam.* Paris: R. Julliard, 1957.

Baalabaki, Laila. *Ana Ahya.* Beirut: Dar Majallat Shir, 1958. Published in French as *Je vis.* Paris: Editions du Seuil, 1961.

Bittari, Zoubeida. *O Mes Sœurs musulmanes, pleurez!* Paris: Editions Gallimard, 1964.

Boudjedra, Rachid. *La Répudiation.* Paris: Les Lettres Nouvelles, Editions de Noël, 1969.

Cevdet, Fatma Aliyé. *Kitab Nisa al-Islam.* Istanbul: Matbaa al-Sharqiya, 1892.

Chami, Gladys. *Mille et un proverbes libanais.* Beirut: Les Librairies Antoine, 1968.

Chraibi, Driss. *La Civilisation, ma mère.* Paris: Editions de Noël, 1972.

―――. *Le Passé simple.* Paris: Editions de Noël, 1954.

Djebar, Assia. *Les Alouettes naïves.* Paris: R. Julliard, 1967.

―――. *Les Enfants du nouveau monde.* Paris: R. Julliard, 1962.

―――. *Les Impatients.* Paris: R. Julliard, 1958.

Ghazali, Muhammad ibn Muhammad al-. "Le Livre des bons usages en matière de mariage," *Vivication des sciences de la foi,* Bibliothèque de la Faculté de Droit d'Alger, XVII, trans. L. Bercher and G. H. Bousquet. Paris: Maisonneuve, 1953.

Goichon, A. M. *La Vie féminine au Mzab: étude de sociologie musulmane.* Paris: P. Geuthner, 1927.

Guellouz, Souad. *La Vie simple.* Tunis: Maison Tunisienne de l'Edition, 1975.

Güntekin, Resat Nuri. *Calikusu,* 11th ed. Istanbul: Nurgok Matbaasi, 1962.

Hafsia, Jelila. *Cendre à l'aube*. Tunis: Maison Tunisienne de l'Edition, 1975.

Halimi, Gisele. *La Cause des femmes*. Paris: Editions Grasset & Fasquelle, 1973.

Jelloun, Tahar ben. *Harrouda*. Paris: Editions de Noël, 1973.

Kamil, Raouf. *Le Limon rouge*. Tunis: Maison Tunisienne de l'Edition, 1975.

M'Rabet, Fadela. *La Femme algérienne*. Paris: Maspero, 1964.

———. *Les Algériennes*. Paris: Maspero, 1967.

Saadawi, Nawal el-. *Al-Mara wa al-Jins*. Beirut: Al-Muassassa al-Arabiyya lildirasaat wa al-Nashir, 1972.

———. *Al-Mara was-Sira al-Nafsi*. Beirut: Al-Muassassa al-Arabiyya lildirasaat wa al-Nashir, 1977.

Samman, Ghada al-. *Hubb*. Beirut: Dar al-Adab, 1973.

Tillion, Germaine. *Le Harem et les cousins*. Paris: Editions du Seuil, 1966.

Index